# FIGHTING
## FOR
## MANDELA

# FIGHTING FOR MANDELA

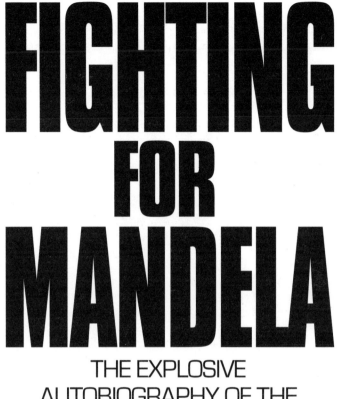

## THE EXPLOSIVE AUTOBIOGRAPHY OF THE WOMAN WHO HELPED TO DESTROY APARTHEID

### BY PRISCILLA JANA

metro

Published by Metro Publishing
an imprint of John Blake Publishing Ltd
3 Bramber Court, 2 Bramber Road,
London W14 9PB, England

www.johnblakepublishing.co.uk

www.facebook.com/Johnblakepub **f**
twitter.com/johnblakepub **t**

First published in hardback in 2016

ISBN: 978 1 78418 979 2

British Library Cataloguing-in-Publication Data:

A catalogue record for this book is available from the British Library.

Design by www.envydesign.co.uk

Printed in Great Britain by CPI Group (UK) Ltd

1 3 5 7 9 10 8 6 4 2

Papers used by John Blake Publishing are natural, recyclable products made
from wood grown in sustainable forests. The manufacturing processes
conform to the environmental regulations of the country of origin.

Every attempt has been made to contact the relevant copyright-holders,
but some were unobtainable. We would be grateful if the
appropriate people could contact us.

For the children of South Africa's struggle.
Especially for my beloved daughter Tina whose history
is tragic but who is working to help this country heal.
And for brave Solomon Mahlangu, hanged at the age
of twenty-two for having the courage to stand up to
oppression. I did everything I could to save him.
He is always in my thoughts.

# CONTENTS

# TELL MY PEOPLE THAT I LOVE THEM

....THEY MUST CONTINUE THE FIGHT. MY BLOOD WILL NOURISH THE TREE THAT BEARS THE FRUITS OF FREEDOM

These were the last words of Solomon Mahlangu, told to me in his death cell. At the age of twenty-two he was one of the bravest and most committed freedom fighters of the African National Congress.

The apartheid police had arrested him for a murder he did not commit. He was convicted, and sentenced to death by hanging. There were protests worldwide and petitions for clemency from the United Nations and the President of the United States.

On 5 April 1979, I learnt, as his lawyer, that all our efforts to save his life had failed. Solomon was to be hanged the next day. He was the first political prisoner to be executed for ten years.

White South Africans had cheered openly in court when he

was sentenced. They wanted to make an example of him, to dissuade other freedom fighters. Instead he became a noble martyr in a righteous cause.

I was allowed one last visit to him at 10 p.m. on the night before the hanging. I walked up towards the death cell block at Pretoria Central Maximum Security Prison. My heart was heavy. I had to tell him that all hope was lost.

Beyond the sound of keys clanking the security gates open and closed, I heard the low soul-stirring lament of hundreds of African prisoners. They were singing their liberation song 'Unzima Lomthwalo' – This Burden is Heavy. On the eve of an execution prisoners would sing all night, always freedom songs, hymns and prayers.

I was taken into a small room where there was a set of scales in one corner. They were to be used to weigh Solomon so that the hangman's noose could be adjusted efficiently.

Solomon walked in. I saw him – strong, composed and resigned. He held both my hands and looked into my eyes. 'It's over,' he said. I had come to admire this young man's courage and to care deeply about him. I had become close to his whole family. I lost my composure. I broke down in shuddering tears. It was Solomon who comforted me.

When our time was up, Solomon asked me to take a message to South Africans and to everyone who was fighting for freedom. He said: 'Tell my people that I love them. They must continue the fight. My blood will nourish the tree that will bear the fruits of freedom.'

I spent all night with his mother and the Ndebele tribal elders at his home, weeping and praying for him.

At 6 a.m. the next day we heard on the radio that Solomon had been hanged at dawn. We were later told by other inmates that he sang the ANC anthem 'Nkosi Sikelel' iAfrica' as he walked to the gallows. He was buried in a prison grave with no funeral allowed.

Today his last words are engraved on a memorial wall at an academy for young people, and on the hearts of every South African who fought against oppression.

After I travelled into Soweto to attend a commemoration ceremony for Solomon, just a few days later I was arrested along with three colleagues, including my husband, and we were detained for hours in the police cells, charged with entering Soweto without a permit. We were sentenced to fifty days in prison or a R50 fine, a large amount in those days. We all refused to pay the penalty and chose to go to jail on principle, but someone came forward to pay our fines. To this day I don't know who that was.

# CHAPTER ONE

# BORN TO FIGHT APARTHEID'S EVIL

I look back on a happy childhood full of love. Yet I realise now that the spectre of apartheid was looming over us all the time. By my fifth birthday in 1948 the concept of total racial segregation had become law in South Africa. It affected every aspect of my young life. Consciously and unconsciously I absorbed the daily acts of oppression which took away the dignity and God-given rights of every person who was not white.

I followed my father's lead and resolved not to stand by helplessly but to take part, and fight. I'm proud to say that, growing up, I gave myself over entirely to the battle against apartheid and was able to stand right beside the giants of South Africa's freedom struggle as their legal representative. I chose to study law for one reason only: to challenge the savagely unfair regime by exposing it through the courts of justice.

Nelson Mandela was my hero and became my client. His

wife Winnie was a close friend. Govan Mbeki, Walter Sisulu and many other South African stalwarts depended on me as their lawyer. At one time I represented every political prisoner on Robben Island. I adopted the baby daughter of black African activist Popo Molefe, sentenced to ten years in prison, when I saw that his wife Phinda could not cope. Now Tina is a beautiful twenty-nine-year-old with a good career and I'm happy I was able to give her an education and a loving home.

Many South Africans nurse personal regrets about their inability or unwillingness to act during those terrible times. In my older years, I can honestly say that I did everything possible to challenge the apartheid laws and I am proud of the success I had. Later I made a meaningful contribution to the new Constitution – the most liberal in the world – and to the creation of the legislations of the country's first democratic government.

This country is not wholly healed, and may never be, but I know in my heart that I did everything humanly possible to bring about unity and peace. I worked on hundreds of human rights cases in the courts and supported the grieving and terrified families of imprisoned clients. By night I joined some of South Africa's most courageous activists in an underground cell, plotting to bring down the government of the day.

Looking back, I see that I was born to do this.

My earliest memories are of my family being 'different' because we were Indian.

We lived in the Westville suburb of Durban city, in Natal, and all of our immediate neighbours were white. The richest residents lived across the road from us in swanky houses and we called them 'The Larneys', South African slang for posh people. We had a special status because we owned the general trading store and the Shell petrol pumps, and my grandparents lived with us and were quite grand.

But for as long as I can remember I was aware that we were Indian and not white. Everything we did was about being Indian – our lives as an extended family, our food, our shopping, our clothes and our school. I didn't even know any white people.

My grandfather had been a chartered accountant and he was proud of having lived in India in the days of the British Raj. I only ever saw him wearing a suit with a fob-watch and carrying a fancy walking stick. He was formal, and treasured his possessions of status, such as the set of crystal wine glasses kept in a rosewood display cabinet and only brought out for special guests, and his wind-up gramophone. Visitors to the house at 105 Devon Terrace marvelled at these things, I remember, and for a treat we would listen to Indian songs as my mother hummed along and drinks were sipped from the crystal glassware.

There was an order to our lives in the big rambling house with its huge garden where mangoes, pomegranates, guavas and lychees grew in the orchard. I played happily there as our Zulu gardener, John, tended the fruit trees. He lived on the property and during his time off he would play the banjo. It was the delight of my life, listening to him playing and singing. I used to follow him around, begging him to play. But one day John the gardener disappeared. It was a mystery, and an emotional blow to me as a small child.

Years later he returned to confess what had happened. In

traditional Indian fashion, my grandmother had buried some gold jewellery in the garden, in a metal container. It was supposed to be a way of keeping valuables safe. When she died no one knew where to find the gold. But it turned out John had dug it up while working in the garden. He left us and moved away, selling the jewellery. Some years later he had an accident and was now crippled. He believed it was karma – that he had done a bad thing and was now being punished.

My parents' forgiveness was a lesson to me. With the utmost humanity they forgave him, understanding that he was destitute. There was no anger, just understanding and compassion. I saw the fellow-feeling between them. Everyone who wasn't white was suffering.

It was through my father, a school-teacher, that I began to understand the politics of our daily lives. Unlike my grandfather he was anti-colonial and anti-imperialistic. He talked to us about apartheid. He was an unusual man for his time. He learnt to speak Zulu because he knew how important it was to have an identity: our identity, he said, was as South Africans.

My two brothers – Ramchunder, who we called Roy, was four-and-a-half years older than me and Dharamraj, who we called Raj, seven years younger – would sit quietly with me as our father explained to us how the South African government had designated us as inferior people. We could only visit a certain section of the beach along Durban's long and lovely coastline. We could only use designated buses and these were different to the buses used by whites, and others used only by blacks.

For us, as with all minority groups, it was a confusing time as we struggled to cling to our heritage while longing to achieve a sense of belonging in our daily lives. Through apartheid, we were at the same time forced to ignore our national identity as South Africans.

As a child, walking through the Botanical Park with my parents, I saw benches marked 'Whites Only'. Cinemas, restaurants and hotels were all for 'Whites Only'. Segregation was everywhere and with it went deprivation, the knowledge that we were considered inferior and therefore excluded. We shopped only in the Indian shopping areas and visited only Indian movie houses. We knew there were fancy shopping malls for whites. My father railed against this and there was growing tension at home.

He befriended a local Indian family who were considered to be of a lower caste and this enraged my grandfather with his traditional beliefs. He remonstrated angrily with my father, and I remember feeling mystified at this subtext to my life. We were ostracised as Indians in the wider community because of our colour, but now the ugly social stigma of the caste system was affecting our own family. The happiness of my childhood, the days in the orchard, climbing trees and building go-karts with my brothers, was to be dramatically interrupted.

Eventually things became so bad between my father and my grandfather that we had to move out. We went to live with my father's sister in Durban North, and through the chasm that had opened up in my family, and through my amazing Aunt Rukmin, I came to learn more valuable lessons about the need we all had to fight for equal status – for ourselves, for black Africans and for even our own people of lower caste.

My aunt was highly politicised. Her home was in the white people's area and she was totally accepted there. She was one of the first Indian women in South Africa to matriculate at school, and she excelled in sports. She had married into a wealthy family and was very stylish, owning a big house and employing a chauffeur. I idolised her. She and my father were my role models, but we were to move again.

My father was frowned on in the education system because he refused to accept the status quo and he was an unapologetic activist, describing the evil of apartheid openly to his students. His 'punishment' was to be sent away from Durban to distant Greytown, a dusty place in the middle of nowhere, dominated by its Afrikaner community and their Dutch Reformed Church, which taught bile and racial hatred. Its proud heritage was a local victory in the Boer War.

I thought it was a big adventure, travelling by train from Durban with my parents and my baby brother Raj. My older brother Roy had stayed with my grandparents. They couldn't bear to see him go and it was agreed he could continue his education there and remain part of their family.

But Greytown brought problems of its own. The racist white mayor seemed to target my father from the start, perhaps having been warned that he was a troublemaker. My father was accused of influencing pupils and discussing the injustices of apartheid with their parents.

Once again we were on the move. And this time, with my father given only hours to leave, we were forced to put our belongings on to a pick-up truck and drive out of town like gypsies. Earlier that evening, I had been playing outside with my friends and was called into the house where everything was suddenly in turmoil, complete chaos. My mother was crying, trying to put together all our clothes.

In the year in which we lived there I had enjoyed the rambling farmhouse, next to the school and set in a wattle field with sheep grazing freely around the house. It had been my first sight of sheep and I had come to love the rural environment; mine was a child's delight in the open fields with fruit trees everywhere. I had been used to tropical fruits such as mangoes and pomegranates and I was now enjoying the deciduous fruits like plums, apricots and peaches.

On the day we were ordered to move I was bewildered; the adults had no time to explain to me what was happening. My father's fellow teachers and the neighbours had congregated at our house, concerned and sympathetic.

I heard afterwards that the local community had petitioned the authorities to have my father reinstated, but with no success. All I knew was that we had until midnight to leave.

We drove off unceremoniously in the truck and were able to move into my uncle's house in Pietermaritzburg in the KwaZulu Province of South Africa, where I was sent to a state-aided Indian school. Later we found a flat to rent in Raisethorpe, a nearby town, and I moved up to Pietermaritzburg Girls' High School. All of us felt homesick for Durban and our home as an extended family.

My father began the lengthy process of protesting at the treatment he'd been given. There was a court date set for a tribunal to hear his complaints, then the education system decided to settle out of court. My father had won his case and was now appointed principal of a school in the centre of Pietermaritzburg city, a white stronghold.

My young life was fragmented, and at the base of all of it was our separation because of colour: apartheid had torn our family apart like it did so many others. At the age of nine or ten I began to put my increasingly radicalised thinking into an action of my own. I was my father's daughter.

In 1958 a national potato boycott by people protesting at

the way black workers were treated like slaves on farms took place. The workers were badly paid and suffering malnutrition. Decent people were refusing to buy potatoes and I wanted to join them. So I stood up in class and asked my fellow pupils to get their families to join in.

I was threatened with expulsion and my father was called to the school. He persuaded the headmistress, a firm but fair Englishwoman called Miss McArthur, to keep me as a pupil. I would love to have heard that conversation.

Two years later, when I had moved up to Durban Girls' High School, I caused another stir in the classroom. I publicly denounced the history we were being force-fed. Our textbooks were telling us of the Indian indentured labour, the poor workers sent over to South Africa by the British in India to shore up the labour force. In them, they were described as 'dirty, filthy, with bad manners and an inferior way of life'; the texts told us as historical fact that the white population, understandably, did not want to live near them.

Ironically, my father had moved me to this school so that I could study both maths and history, as that was not possible in the Pietermaritzburg school. Now I was being fed a version of history I could not accept.

I told the teacher: 'This is about us, we are Indians. We can't accept this description of our people. It's not true.' I knew something about this. My maternal grandmother had married an indentured labourer she met on the ship over from India.

There was big trouble for me in school. I was sent out of the class and accused of inciting others not to learn, told I was a bad influence. The teacher said this description of Indian indentured labour was part of factual history, whether we liked it or not.

I was sent home by the school principal, Miss Dori, and once again my father was called in. He told me later that he had a huge argument with the authorities. After a few days the school principal came to my house with my class teacher: they had come to apologise. It was a victory, and I had become something of a leader. My classmates began looking up to me and I had an assured place in class because I was doing very well in all subjects, despite my inclination to stir things up.

My father had other problems to deal with. Back in Durban my older brother Roy was in trouble at school for insulting a teacher. He was being spoilt and indulged by my grandparents at home and when he objected to something in class he threw an inkpot at the teacher. He was threatened with expulsion.

Once again my heroic father intervened and got my brother back into school. But Roy was an angry boy. He had become politicised in his own way and was very angry about the injustice of apartheid. He was showing it by becoming a rebel. Our family, like so many others, was suffering in a variety of different ways.

By the time I became a teenager my grandfather had died, leaving my grandmother alone in the house in Durban. We moved back into Westville, happy to be in our extended family, our natural life, again. There were aunties and uncles coming and going, and staying for weekends. And my father – by now the principal of a Durban school – would hold forth with his political views, his interest in the Cuban crisis, his sympathy for socialism, sometimes even communism.

I wanted to go out with my friends and my brothers felt the same. But my father was head of the family. We would sit dutifully at the dinner table, hours after the food had been eaten, and listen to him. He was an atheist, and a communist sympathiser, but mostly he was humane and he cared.

My mother wanted to celebrate our Hindu traditions. She was a very interesting woman, born to a mother of high-birth who had fled from her in-laws because they made her life hell in India. She was classy and beautiful. But on the ship on her way to a new life in South Africa she fell in love with a poor indentured labourer coming to work in the sugar-cane plantations.

My parents were a happy loving couple and there was mutual respect despite their different temperaments and needs. My mother was a strong woman and at the same time in awe of my father's intellect. In turn he respected her need for Hindu religious ceremonies, although he refused to take part. During Diwali he would retreat to his study for days.

It was my father who first made me aware of the charismatic freedom fighter Nelson Mandela. He was the leader who was galvanising black South Africans to claim their birthright, the right to vote and to take part in everything their country had to offer, and he was being tried for treason.

At this time I was preparing to go to university. My father had planned that I would study medicine in Edinburgh, Scotland. He was passionate about us all belonging to South Africa and being South African, but there was a long battle to win before girls like me would be able to study at top universities and achieve good careers. My only option would be a 'bush' university where students were segregated according to their race. The education and qualifications offered were considered inferior. Any family who could afford to would send their children abroad for higher education.

We were a middle-class family, not at all rich, but my father was determined that he would manage to support me at Edinburgh. All the arrangements were made. Then three weeks before I was due to leave, a family friend who taught with my father invited us to a party for his nephew, Ashok. I was a bit in love with this boy; he was dashing and good-looking. Now Ashok was asking me why on earth I was going to Edinburgh. He and his friends were going to India, our country of origin, for further education.

In the car on the way home I told my parents I wanted to go to India, too. My father said that all the arrangements had already been finalised. I threw such a huge tantrum with tears and protests that my parents agreed to reconsider.

My father had taken part in a welcome reception for the Indian prime minister's daughter Indira Gandhi when she had landed in Durban in 1942 on her way to England, and had corresponded with her regularly after that. So now he wrote to her by telegram and asked her to help.

My further education was thus arranged personally by India's future prime minister. I was to attend a stylish institution, the very best. It was Sophia College for Women in Breach Candy, in Bombay. I felt I was heading towards my roots and it felt good after my confusing early years in a country whose government all but rejected us. Over a long period I had become aware of my feelings of displacement. I believed I was totally Indian and wanted to be proud of that, but my father, who I admired, was adamant that we were South Africans.

In 1960, when Indians wanted to celebrate their centenary in South Africa, my father had been invited to join the national body who were organising it. But he opposed a celebration, saying there was no reason to celebrate the arrival of Indians in South Africa. They were treated so badly, looked down on and forced to work like slaves, he said, so it should be a commemoration, not a celebration.

I was grappling with all this when I arrived at Sophia College. It was September 1963 and the academic term had not yet started so few students were there. A girl I introduced myself to said: 'But how can you be Indian when you are South African? What are you really?' I began to ask myself: 'Who am I really?'

I already felt swamped by the proliferation of religious symbols around me; a totally new experience. There were Hindu temples, and now I was heading for a Catholic convent education. It was a psychological jolt, unnerving and confusing.

My arrival had been difficult. I came by boat and was totally overwhelmed when dozens of porters, known as 'coolies', clambered on board at the port, picking up my stuff and carrying it off. The nuns from Sophia College were waiting for me. They gave me a plate of cold meat to eat and I found afterwards to my horror that I had eaten beef and pork for the first time, something that, as a Hindu, I would never have done willingly.

Sunita Pradhan was the girl who first greeted me. She was not unkind, but she was puzzled as to my identity. I announced that I was Indian but she was adamant, saying: 'No you can't be Indian. Your hair is funny and your complexion is funny, you look different from us. What kind of Indian are you? What caste are you?'

It was true that I looked completely different from the local Indian girls. They all wore saris or salwar kameez, while I was in Western dress. Hindi was their mother tongue and they had a different accent to mine. I was the only one with short hair, and unlike them I had never prayed.

Later I discovered the Catholic mass and the nuns' beautiful singing and I began to enjoy my visits to the chapel. There was quiet and solace there; it was a place to help me recover from my homesickness.

By contrast, in the students' hostel there was always noise, hustle and bustle. All the dormitories were shared and the nuns were constantly checking on us, rustling their way up and down the corridors.

'Silent hours' took place every weekday afternoon but these were agony. We were not allowed to speak, so there was quiet, but the nuns were standing over us. The slightest whisper would echo and so we could not communicate at all. The two hours went by tortuously slowly; I hated that.

On special occasions there was a midnight mass, followed by hot chocolate and hot-cross buns for the congregation. I was looked on as positively pious when I insisted on attending those services.

But I still felt like an alien. I didn't understand the caste system, which seemed to be an obsession for the others. I was puzzled and disappointed. I felt rejection. I hadn't come to my roots after all. I wasn't going to fit in and be accepted here any more than I had been in South Africa. I was neither from the West nor the East. Once again I didn't belong.

And everywhere there was homage to the Hindu gods. I wrote to my father telling him: 'Thank God you are not here, you would go crazy. Everything is about religion.'

Yet it was illuminating to be in a free country with no restrictions. I could keep up with important news from South Africa by reading uncensored reports in the newspapers and listening to the radio, something I could never have done at home.

I came to realise that Sophia College was very upmarket, exclusive. The whole suburb of Breach Candy was a high-class enclave. There was even a British Club with a sign outside saying 'British Only'.

This enraged me and I got my school friends to join me in a protest. We wrote posters saying: 'British Go Home, Get Out of India', smuggling them out of the convent and standing with them outside the club. I was horrified that the Indian police came to disperse us, forcing us to leave.

I was more aware and more sensitive to insidious racial insults than my classmates. I was infuriated by signs at the racecourse which said: 'No Dogs or Indians Allowed'. It felt right then, and it feels right now, to have protested at this, albeit as an angry schoolgirl in her teens.

By then I had made some good friends, despite my feelings of displacement. And there was a flurry of excitement in my life when another 'different' sort of girl arrived to be my room-mate.

She was a princess, daughter of the Maharaja of Sandur, wearing a magnificent sari and with a fabulous hairdo; her staff carried her cases and bags of clothes. Her name was Vijaya Raje of Sandur and we became great friends. She actually looked up to me because I was so much more worldly-wise and bolder than her. She'd been so protected. She even brought her Ayah – her nanny – to college with her along with an aide-de-camp (ADC) who was ready at all times to drive her in the family Mercedes.

Vijay's parents approved of me and liked me. I watched how they broke any rules they cared to. For example, Coca-Cola was banned in India because of the anti-American sentiment in the country. But Vijay's parents were sending her cases of Coke and baskets of fruit. The activist in me wanted to reject these, but I couldn't help enjoying them. I grappled to get my head around that.

Vijay's lifestyle was so lavish that I was awestruck and amused by it, and she wanted to share it with me. She was tremendously elegant and had a huge cosmetic bag. It contained more than a hundred colours of nail varnish.

Her brother had been studying in Germany and now he was coming home. A huge family party had been arranged and I was invited. It was decided that the ADC would fetch me at 9 p.m. It was customary for everything to happen late in Bombay. I had taken great care with my appearance, choosing a pretty white minidress that my mother had made. It had bows and pin-tack decorations and tiny pearls sewn into it.

When we arrived at the party venue, a magnificent hall, I stepped out of the car and found myself surrounded by people in ballgowns, the men in suits with black bow ties, and an air of formality that made me want the ground to open up and swallow me. I had never remotely imagined that scale of lavishness and I felt completely under-dressed.

I was given my first alcoholic drink, a rum-and-coke. A woman nearby saw my discomfiture and made a sneering remark about South Africans not knowing about alcohol. Then I was rescued by a kindly gentleman who escorted me to a quiet corner and talked to me. He was Tiruth Mulchandani, a member of the family who owned Bush Radio, and he asked me about South Africa and my life there.

Later he welcomed me to his home for dinner and I was made to feel at home by his wife Sheila and the whole family.

I had to adjust to the idea of seeing so much wealth. I was bowled over by the idea of them having an elevator inside their house.

In the meantime, Princess Vijaya was becoming my close friend. We had fun shopping for saris and she taught me a lot. After my social disaster at the ball I started to wear saris and I wear them to this day.

Vijaya took me to her personal tailor. She taught me about the caste system, she taught me how to sit and talk like a sophisticated young Indian woman. I learnt that only low-caste people would wear bright colours and large bindis – the dots on the foreheads – and that we should wear muted colours and small discreet bindis. We should always speak softly and be selective about our friends.

My father was writing to me regularly. The Mother Superior would hand out our letters and there was one for me at least every other day. Through my father I learnt that Nelson Mandela had been caught while living underground, on the run, as a wanted man. The Rivonia Trial started in October 1963, soon after I arrived in India, and he described it in detail. He was ahead of many other Indians at that time: he had a strong vision of a free South Africa. My father told me how the regime was calling for the death sentence for Mandela. His anger was huge and I was greatly moved by the outpourings in his letters. On the day of Mandela's life sentence I felt my father's outrage.

I joined the South African Students' Association and I was able to keep them informed about Mandela and about apartheid politics. I knew by then that I was longing to be involved and play an active part in the struggle. Many Indians in South Africa were activists. In every significant trial there was an Indian defendant. Strangely, my father was always telling me not to get involved in politics. But he himself had sown the seeds in me. I was still at school but I was already politicised.

At the same time, Princess Vijaya and I were actually learning a lot from each other. I encouraged her to do things she had never dreamt of – staying out late, going to the cinema, breaking the college rules. Occasionally I would be caught and grounded. We weren't allowed to talk to boys, or even look at them. But I was already going out with a boy, having coffee with him and going to the movies. I liked him a lot. He was sophisticated and had studied in America; he was also older than me.

One day he invited me to his apartment and I had the chance to snoop around a bit. I found a letter from a girl who was clearly in love with him. I confronted him and then walked out, furious. His name was Prem and at the time I was heartbroken. In thirty-six years I didn't hear from him again. Then when I was Ambassador to the Netherlands he somehow traced me and came to visit with his wife. I could tell she didn't know we had had a relationship. Prem still calls me on my birthday.

After him I met Reg, whose family also lived in South Africa. He was attentive and I enjoyed that after feeling so rejected by Prem. We both came back to South Africa when term time ended and I found myself drawn into a drama which nearly severed my precious relationship with my father.

Reg brought his parents to meet mine and there was talk of marriage. My parents were absolutely against it because they wanted me to return to India and continue my studies. Reg's family were from Gujarat, they were business people. They were happy to see their son with me.

Soon after the awkward meeting with my parents, he sent me a ticket to fly to Johannesburg. My parents completely forbade me to go but I got there, and Reg had prepared for us to get married. His brothers and family friends came to the Register Office and we took our vows in front of a magistrate.

I returned home as if nothing had happened. My father was busy making preparations for me to return to Sophia College for the next term where I planned to prepare to study medicine as a career – my father's wish. But my cousin, who had a spice business in Johannesburg, went into Reg's brother's shop and while chatting discovered that we were married.

My father questioned me, and I denied it. But he already knew. He was the angriest I have ever seen him. He was not religious but The Truth was his god. Enraged, he put me on a plane to Johannesburg and told me to go to my husband.

All hell was breaking loose at my family home and my parents were both beyond furious. Then their Indian and family pride took over and they accepted the inevitable. They told me to come to Durban with Reg and that we would have a proper wedding together.

I will never forget walking into the house with Reg. We were man and wife, but he was not even allowed to stay. He had to go to his family members elsewhere in the city. The wedding was held at a big hall and my father acted throughout like someone at a funeral, as did my mother.

My place in the family had changed forever and now I was, according to tradition, to live with my in-laws. It was pleasant enough living with them in Vrededorp, a lively suburb of mixed races. Like District Six in Cape Town, this was an area where everyone knew each other. And I was living with an extended family again. But the place wasn't big enough for all of us, so Reg and I rented an apartment and I tried to apply for courses to study medicine again. Neither of us were going to return to India.

I knew I should study for my own sake and to make peace with my parents. Education meant everything to them and they would have sacrificed all they had for me to continue and become successful. But either the Ministry of the Interior was blocking me, as an Indian woman, or the university I applied to was blocking me. I could not get into medical school.

And then I realised that it was the law I really loved. That's what would give me the ability to become the activist I wanted to be; it would empower me to help others at a time when that was so badly needed in South Africa. I applied for a correspondence course with UNISA – the University of South Africa – and began to study at home.

It had been a year since the upset with my family, and my parents and I had by now been totally reconciled. I felt very glad of that when I received news that my father had suffered a heart attack. I travelled to Durban to be with my mother and once he had recovered my father came home from hospital and asked me to stay on a little longer to spend time with him.

He felt sure he was well enough to return to teaching, and my mother prepared a special supper for the whole family on the eve of my departure, and his return to work. By the next morning my father had died. It was the single most devastating thing to happen to me. My mother was totally crushed; she had lost her soulmate and the love of her life. My father was fifty-one, a principled, strong and decent man who had guided me unfailingly in everything I did.

In the days after his death it was one of his relatives who stepped in to get me back on my career path. My paternal grandmother's brother, who was a Professor of English on Salisbury Island, off the Durban coast, scoffed at my UNISA course and told me he would try to get me registered at the university college for Indians where he taught.

I was so happy to be allowed to attend full-time but the location of Salisbury Island was a problem. By then my mother was living alone in the big house in Westville. I moved in with her so that I would be close enough to attend university from her home every day. I had to leave at 6 a.m. to wait for a bus outside our house. At another bus stop I got off and walked to Pine Street in the dark to get another bus into the city. There I walked a long way under the subway to the ferry. The boat took me to the island, already exhausted by my travels.

I was the only female in my class. Some of my fellow students are judges today. Chiman Patel is Judge President of the Natal courts, and lawyer Ashwin Trickamjee is head of the Hindu Organisation.

But living apart from my husband and studying full-time was not acceptable to my in-laws. After my first year I was given an ultimatum, and I went back to Johannesburg to be a dutiful wife. Reg had been allocated a house in Lenasia, an Indian-only suburb where my in-laws lived opposite us. I hated it, a dusty little town where nothing happened. Houses had been thrown up any old how so that Indian people could be herded together, just as blacks and Coloureds were being segregated into areas away from the affluent whites. When we moved into our houses the roads outside were still being built.

Both of my brothers were politicised, influenced by my father. I remember my younger brother Raj staying with us for a while and one day, at our home in Woodpecker Street, the white foreman in charge of a gang of black workers came over to the garden fence to ask for water. It was a hot and humid day. One of the black workmen also asked for water and my brother headed into the house to fetch some.

I followed him in and saw he'd rinsed out a glass milk bottle and filled it with water, then took an elegant crystal glass from the cupboard and filled that too. I started accusing him of being a lackey of the white masters who had indoctrinated him to treat blacks as inferiors. But he waved me away and I saw that I was wrong – he gave the milk bottle to the white man and the crystal glass to the black man. I realised that, like me, he knew the importance of small defiant gestures.

My older brother Roy had a successful transport business and helped as many unemployed blacks as he could. He offered work to a young man who my mother had brought into our family years earlier when she found him living on the street near our home. His name was Maxwell Madikizela and he was distantly related in some way to Winnie Mandela's birth family. But he had run away from school and home and was destitute. My mother cared for him and gave him a room and some work in the garden. Later my brother not only gave him a job but adopted him as his son. Tragically, Roy died young from a heart attack and his business closed down. I reasoned with Maxwell that it was time to try and find his real family.

He had refused to tell us anything about himself for years. Now he and I drove down to Durban together and he directed me to his family's house. In a very emotional scene I saw his father greeting him, and I heard the whole family saying they had believed he was dead. This was symptomatic of the chaos of apartheid, the laws which prevented free movement of people who might otherwise have been able to find family members who had gone missing, and the deliberate cruelty of the authorities who would do nothing to help non-whites.

In Lenasia I had taken up my studies with UNISA again and in my stultifying surroundings I began to look for like-minded friends. My neighbour Hajira Momoniat, married to a doctor and the mother of three children, became close to me. She was highly intelligent and loved to read, but she could do nothing about a career because she was raising her children. Together we formed a reading group and called it Femina Circle 71. It was 1971 and I was twenty-eight years old.

We brought the wives of doctors, lawyers and business people together and we found that all of us were determined to give our lives more meaning. People called us a tea-party group with bourgeois ideas but I really believe our reading group brought light into our lives.

We invited Jonathan Paton, son of the celebrated author Alan Paton, to talk to us about literature. He was a lecturer at the University of Witwatersrand and enlightened us on modern novelists, including Norman Mailer. It was an exciting and eye-opening time for us.

And we had Don Mattera, a budding poet in Johannesburg, come to read his revolutionary works to us. Fatima Meer, a highly-respected Indian activist and writer, came to inspire and galvanise us. We hosted evenings of Indian classical dancing and invited people to join cultural events of fashion, music and dance.

We were fortunate to be invited to the home of Des and Dawn Lindberg, who had a private theatre in their home in Houghton, an affluent Johannesburg suburb. We enjoyed previews of many shows and plays and on one occasion we were introduced to the British actor Leonard Whiting who had starred in Zeffirelli's great movie of 1968, *Romeo and Juliet*. I had this slightly outrageous idea that we could stage a version of *Romeo and Juliet* with him – a white actor – and a black Juliet. He loved the idea and we began to organise it together.

I was becoming involved with the Black Consciousness Movement around that time and they suggested to me that budding artist Nomsisi Kraai would be perfect as Juliet. We forged ahead with our plans, holding rehearsals and arranging a grand show in the Vishnu Hall in Lenasia. Nothing eventful ever happened there and suddenly there was this exciting prospect. The hall was full when the curtain was raised.

I took to the stage to welcome our guests, my heart pounding. Then an uneasy commotion began to stir in the audience. My friend Hajira told me the security police had arrived. Within minutes there was confusion as people left in a hurry. Anticipating trouble we quickly found an escape route for Leonard and Nomsisi through the back door.

The police swamped the stage. Colonel Heysteck walked towards me and said the gathering was illegal and I was under arrest. They ordered the crowd to disperse and took me with them to the dreaded police headquarters at John Vorster Square.

This was the pattern of our lives: arrests, detentions, the breaking-up of meetings, intimidation and assault.

I was clear in my mind that I had done nothing illegal, but I was scared. This was my first arrest. I was taken to an office where a huge contingent of senior police officers awaited me and I spent the entire night there answering a barrage of questions about the agenda of Femina Circle 71. Our little book club, born out of the desperation of intellectual boredom, was now a matter of national security, it seemed.

The police screamed at me, banging their fists on the table and demanding to know our real agenda.

I told them the truth: we were a group of women in Lenasia, finding ourselves completely stifled and wanting to do something meaningful. We had decided to brighten up our lives, and raise money to help poor children in Soweto, by putting on a show.

But I was there all night and when they returned me to my home in the morning it was with a grim threat – that I would be under police vigilance, monitored and watched. They had chosen to make an example of me, knowing of my growing interest in the Black Consciousness Movement (BCM), the anti-white initiative headed by Steve Biko. He was the inspirational leader already marked out by police as a threat to the government. They also, of course, would have known that I was studying law and would surely one day use my degree to support the oppressed black population.

I had first become aware of BCM while at Salisbury Island, studying. Activists there admired Biko for his confrontational stance, forming a movement that was not necessarily going to be a political party but a strategy by which non-whites could find, appreciate and share all that was good about their own culture.

He preached of walking tall, of being proud of our identity, of being black or being Indian or mixed-race. His philosophy appealed to me. We should not aspire to be white but organise ourselves as a formidable and separate group of South Africans.

I admired the intelligentsia who were joining BCM. A close friend, Dr Joe Veriava, was a member and I would occasionally attend meetings with him. Biko himself was inspirational.

For me, the turning point was a BCM conference in a church

hall at Hammanskraal, north of Pretoria, one Saturday morning. The hall was packed when I took my seat. The audience was mostly made up of Africans with some Indians among them. Biko was the speaker. He didn't claim to be a great orator. He was more like a wise teacher, encouraging us to learn. He was openly anti-white, saying we blacks could organise our struggle ourselves, we didn't need them. This should be a blacks-only organisation.

I listened to his definitions and was amazed. I realised you didn't have to be African to call yourself black. All of us there in that hall were oppressed and suffering. There was no need to fumble with our identities. Indians like me could be totally part of this. Until now I had been aware of the vacuum in me, not belonging to black or white, just being 'different'. Now I could be part of a group. I had found solidarity and I felt uplifted. The BCM and Steve Biko were an exciting new initiative at a time when the ANC leadership was in prison, impotent, and I anyway had never felt they welcomed me as an Indian. Now it was hitting me like a thunderbolt. At last I knew where I really belonged. I was twenty-eight years old and ready for something.

Back at home I told my husband Reg and he listened and was supportive. From then on I hosted meetings at my house. Biko himself came once but he was not there to assert his leadership: he did not believe in hierarchy. His was an intellectual and thoughtful organisation and I was proud to be a member.

Those bad times in South Africa were being denounced all over the world and it felt right to be actively involved in the battle for human rights. But there were some apartheid laws which it was not possible to fight.

The Group Areas Act – implemented in three parts – had designated residential areas according to racial type. The apartheid government, obsessed with separating citizens on a racial basis, announced its intention to be 'achieving a greater future for Afrikaans people'. Indian, coloured and black people were ruthlessly restricted to living and trading in designated areas.

Whole communities were seeing their homes physically crushed and their belongings thrown on to the streets. There was no way to resist the bulldozers and the forced removals to allocated areas. More than three million South Africans lost their homes to the State's bulldozers. We never thought it would happen to us. Our family had lived peaceably in Westcliffe for generations and our eight-roomed house was well-kept and solid.

Even when my mother received a notice of eviction we didn't really believe it would mean gangs of ruthless men and a bulldozer ploughing through the building. But she telephoned me in tears and said the date had been set for the following Monday.

For all of us there were distant echoes of the disaster which had actually killed my uncle Raghu six years earlier, while I was studying in India. His home had been an architectural landmark in Blinkbonnie Road, Mayville, an upmarket suburb of Durban. It looked like a castle inside and out, with crenellated turrets, tennis courts and grounds laid out with fish ponds.

Uncle Raghu had been forced to watch from his son's home a kilometre away as his magnificent house was attacked by bulldozers. He had made his wealth from a furniture factory, a successful entrepreneur who worked hard for everything he had. On the day of his home's demolition he suffered a major heart attack and died.

Now I was anxious about the effect having her own home demolished would have on my poor mother. My husband and I drove to Durban to find my brothers, uncles and aunts already at the house. We spent the weekend there together, not wanting to believe the eviction would really happen.

One of my uncles was an estate agent. He arrived on the Monday morning, bringing us breakfast and taking charge. My mother had been weeping all weekend. She faced losing her home and all her belongings. None of us had packed a thing, we were in a state of shock. My Uncle Ram acted like the head of the family, thinking straight. He was an organiser, General-Secretary of the Natal Indian Congress and there to do what he could for us.

He told us to get our valuables, everything and anything we treasured, and to put them in the outhouse in the garden. We could maybe collect them later. I went into my childhood bedroom and sobbed.

Our dining-room table, which seated twenty people, was made of rosewood and constructed where it stood; it could not be moved out of the house as it was too big. Someone carried out the rosewood display cabinet and my brother still has it. Everything else, photographs and jewellery, all the kitchen equipment we had used over the years to cook together and to entertain, that was all crushed as the bulldozers moved in.

A small crowd of neighbours had gathered outside when dozens of white workers arrived. The machinery made a terrible menacing noise as it was driven into the walls of our home again and again. My mother was hysterical and there was nothing but dust and noise and crying. That is my recollection of that terrible day.

Later, remembering all the things we had left behind, we thought about the special photograph we had of my great-grandfather with Mahatma Gandhi, a family treasure. Gandhi had come to the launch of a reformist Hindu group called the Arya Samaj Movement, which my great-grandfather helped to found. We loved that picture of them and had had it beautifully framed. It had pride of place on the wall in our living-room. Now it was lost somewhere in the rubble.

Westville had been designated for whites only and we were the first family to be forced out. My uncle put us in his car and took us to his home in Asherville, not far away. He had an empty property which he was able to move us into. But there was no furniture, no comforts. It was like destitution for us, utter misery. After two weeks my mother rented an apartment in a new block. She was in such shock and distress at that time that she could hardly speak.

To this day the sound of the bulldozers rings in my head. It is a lasting devastation, to lose your home. Since then I have acted in court for many people, sometimes whole communities, who have been forcibly removed. They have asked me: 'Who are these men who pulled down our houses, where are they today? How do they feel now when they look back? They cannot say they were just obeying orders, they must be ashamed.'

But I don't believe that. I think they probably feel no remorse. I have seen the many attempts by South Africa's Truth and Reconciliation Commission (TRC) to elicit some sign of contrition, compassion or remorse from people who did terrible things during apartheid. I believe many of them still feel nothing.

My mother seemed to die along with my father when his time came. When the house went, with all our family memories entombed in it, it was the end for her. She lost all zest for life. She had loved her garden and orchard. Now she was in a flat with no garden. Everything had been taken from her because she was not white.

I saw what happened to her and it strengthened my resolve to fight this cruelty. As a lawyer I would not just be representing people treated badly: I would feel it all alongside them.

# CHAPTER TWO

# ON THE PATH
# TO ACTIVISM

It was 1974 and time to sit the final exams for my all important law degree. But unfortunately, in the early summer months in South Africa, it was also the season for picking mangoes.

In the Indian family tradition, often a suffocating experience in which something like mass catering is demanded of a daughter-in-law like myself, there was no option but to take part in a prepping and pickling operation that would last for days.

I wanted to revise for my exams. I needed hours of solitude to immerse myself in my law books. Instead, I was in the kitchen with my mother-in-law, tackling ten bags of green mangoes. I had to wash, deseed and chop them up on the big worktable. It took hours. I had to semi-dry the fruit while roasting fenugreek and salt. Then the whole mix was pounded and crushed with a pestle and mortar.

There were seven brothers in my husband's family, all living nearby, and my job was to provide mango pickles for all of them. I cried the whole time I was pounding and crushing. I wanted a divorce. I wanted my husband Reg to stand up for me. Already in the run-up to my exams I had had to help with the weddings of two of my brothers-in-law.

When Monday morning came I was worried sick. I knew that my work and studies deserved an 'A' but now I would be fortunate if I passed at all. I made my way to the showgrounds opposite Wits University where we sat the exams under watchful eyes. I felt despondent and resentful. What bad luck that law exams and mangoes came to fruition at exactly the same time of year.

It would be a month before our results were known and by then I could not bring myself to go to the UNISA buildings in Pretoria where they would be posted. I called a friend and begged her to look at the noticeboard for me.

She called to say that I had passed. I had qualified and I could start to practise law. I just needed to find a firm that would accept me to do my articles.

Through my good friend Dr Joe Veriava, today a senior academic at Wits University, I had heard there might be an opening with Ismail Ayob. He had a good reputation in the community. Ayob interviewed me in his first-floor office in Commissioner House, a business block in Commissioner Street in downtown Johannesburg. It was not at all fancy, just utility furniture, but I knew it was the hub of vital legal services to a struggling population always in and out of the courts.

He took me on and it put me at the heart of activities I longed to be part of. I was poorly paid and I would leave home early just to get a parking place somewhere near his office, with none of my travel or other expenses paid. Nevertheless, it was a stepping stone to the career I wanted.

Ayob was very keen to never fall foul of the police. He had to carry off a balancing act, representing the poor and downtrodden in a white-biased court, and at the same time avoid banning orders and detention. He also had a sick daughter who spent a period each year in America for treatment and he needed to remain free for her sake.

He wanted a life without problems and harassment, so he dumped a lot of difficult political cases on to me. During his trips abroad I would have full power of attorney. I had been pushed in at the deep end.

One of the troublesome files now on my desk was that of Winnie Mandela, the bold, charismatic and sometimes recklessly courageous wife of the ANC's imprisoned leader Nelson Mandela. She had been a heroine of mine for as long as I could remember. I had actually met her once on an occasion still etched in my mind.

Fatima Meer, a renowned Indian academic and activist, had been staying at my house and had said she needed to meet Winnie for a clandestine chat. They were great friends. Both of them had been banned and detained, at one time in prison together. So I tagged along, tremendously excited, as we discreetly popped into a clothing store in West Street, Johannesburg, and made our way into the back of the shop. Winnie – in my eyes the epitome of a beautiful black woman – was stylishly dressed, wearing a turban hat. Her face was wreathed in smiles as she hugged Fatima, then it was my turn. I was absolutely in awe of her. I told her about life in Lenasia and my law studies. I think we bonded then, and I was to see a great deal more of her in the future.

Winnie was telling Fatima of her recent visit to Robben Island, and relaying messages to the ANC leadership. Winnie was a banned person under the Terrorism Act and was not allowed to be in the company of more than one person at a time, or to take part in any political activity. Her life was severely restricted but nothing could dampen her determination, her anger against the system. Fatima, an acclaimed writer, was working on Mandela's memoirs and produced the finished book, *Higher Than Hope*, some years later as Mandela neared the end of his time in prison.

In Ismail Ayob's office I was now going through Winnie's file. Ayob had told me: 'This is a difficult one. You can handle all her matters from now on.' He prized Winnie as a client, and was well paid through the benevolent Swedish organisation which funded her legal actions, but he found her difficult and demanding in person and was glad to pass her over to me.

However, there were other pressing files that needed action. One of my first court matters was to defend a young man called Michael Tsagae, head of South Africa's Revolutionary Youth Council (RYC). He had been one of the organisers of the mass rally of students in Soweto in June 1976 when police opened fire and killed hundreds of young people. He and other leaders had advised on a rally instead of stay-away strikes from schools teaching in the Afrikaans language.

By this stage, Michael was being targeted. His RYC, affiliated to the Black Consciousness Movement, was closely monitored by the security services. Finally they had arrested him and accused him of assaulting a police officer. False evidence was given that he had kicked the officer during a demonstration.

I managed to get him acquitted and my colleagues and I told him after the case: 'This is it for you now. They are going to get you one way or another. You need to run for your life before they find another reason to arrest you. You need to leave the country.'

Michael was only fifteen or sixteen but he took our advice and I helped him to leave South Africa to train at an ANC military camp in Botswana. Immediately after court, I bundled him into my car and took him to a street corner where a young comrade was waiting to pick him up. He was determined to keep up his work with the country's youth, by now radicalised and angry. Young men like Michael knew the fight was going to be a lifelong affair, not just a one-time run-in with the authorities.

This was a time when the police killings in Soweto had turned the tide for South Africa. There was worldwide outrage at the murder of schoolchildren, and the youth was galvanised. I had witnessed some of the chaos of that terrible day myself when I received a call from a woman client, calling from a public phone box. She said she had seen her son being dragged to a police vehicle, she had heard a shot and was sure he was dead. I had no idea of the scale of the uprising, so I got in my Mazda car and headed to Soweto to see her. She had sounded hysterical and desperate.

I encountered police roadblocks and headed for the back roads, but it was impossible to enter the area. I got out of my car to protest that I was a lawyer and should have safe passage, and that was when I was tear-gassed. I could not breathe, it was a terrifying experience. Someone splashed some water on me and I recovered enough to drive back home. I couldn't get to my client.

The next day I agreed to go to the mortuary with her to search for her son. We went to one hospital after another, with so many other families searching for loved ones. At Baragwanath Hospital there were hundreds of people, sobbing and wailing. I let the mother go and look for her child: I could not face the rows of bodies concealed under shrouds. She came out hysterical, she had found her son's body, and I couldn't do anything to help her.

I didn't realise that the Soweto uprising and its bloody aftermath would prove a turning point for the country. Many other student riots sprang up. At one stage I went to the Attorney-General's office to insist on bail for a minor. He told me that in the dangerous, fearful mood now sweeping the country he might give bail to an ANC guerrilla fighter but never to an activist youth.

Since the mid-1960s, resistance in South Africa had been minimal. The ANC and other anti-apartheid organisations had been crushed by the imprisonment and exile of their leaders and the curtailment of local activity by banning orders. Now there was real anger accompanied by the fire and energy and recklessness of youth, who had nothing to lose. Their lives were hellish and their prospects of careers under the apartheid government were few. Many had already lost family members to the struggle for freedom. In the absence of any other realistic possibility they were prepared to take up arms.

I was now beginning to visit a number of clients held in prison. The Soweto Students' Representative Council was very active and its members were constantly in and out of court and prison. Almost all of these young people became my clients.

My days started at 6.30 a.m. for any hope of a parking space near the office. As I walked through the corridor, glancing at the reception and the waiting room, I would pass a long, patient queue of desperate people. Many were being kicked out of their homes because of rental debt, or had been arrested under the iniquitous pass laws. Some needed help to find a family member who had disappeared, picked up somewhere by police and now detained or dead. Some of these family members never made it out of detention and there would not even be a decent burial.

I saw the dread and anxiety on their faces. The reception staff would send cases into my office. There were days when it was horrendous just to listen to their stories. And there were dozens of people; I just couldn't see them all in one day. Black people were facing the wrath of the law for every little thing. In a normal society ordinary people wouldn't need a lawyer. But every black household needed a lawyer in those days.

Ayob had links to sympathetic organisations, mostly foreign, who would sponsor cases and pay the bills. But you simply couldn't do justice to this number of cases. I found myself rushing things. I would stay late in the office and then take files home to try and finish them.

I had known it would be something like that, working as a human rights lawyer in an oppressed country. After all, my natural compassion for people in distress was part of the reason I had chosen this work. But I hadn't realised how heartsore it would make me day after day.

I tried to soothe mothers frantically worried about their sons and daughters who had been arrested. Or who had quietly left home to get over the border into Swaziland or Mozambique for military training with the ANC. I dealt with civil cases too – the families who could not make their hire-purchase payments and who had received a summons. I would try to negotiate staged payments so that their furniture or kitchen equipment would not be repossessed. I was in court every single day. Many families had been left destitute without a breadwinner when the men were arrested, just picked up off the street having been targeted as troublemakers. They could not afford food for their children and had no way of finding payments for their furniture.

In my first year as a practising lawyer I was learning about the real horror of apartheid. As a student I knew it was evil and wrong, as an Indian I had been forced to live in an allocated area and could only use certain buses or visit certain beaches. What I was seeing in Ayob's office was different. Here were people in trouble whose entire lives were embroiled with the police. Children had disappeared, family members were killed and there were mass forced removals. It was a shock to my system; I had not imagined things could be this bad.

I took it to heart and allowed it to devastate me. Every day I was meeting people who were going through the worst kind of atrocities and I was going home to my own little space but could not possibly enjoy it. It made me think what our lives were really about. This oppression was in people's homes and on their streets; it was really happening and I let myself become overwhelmed by it for a while. I realised the need to be strong but all this was affecting me so much. One day Ayob came into my office and found me crying my heart out. He tried to console me and we talked about staying strong in order to help others. I could be of no use to them otherwise.

At this time I realised I could not even dream of having a family and children of my own, things that a normal newly married couple would be planning.

I found that particular cases would prey on my mind. I

became very upset over the problems consuming trade union activist Rita Ndzanga, an incredibly brave woman. She was secretary of the Railway Workers' Union. She had been banned for running an underground ANC cell and both she and her husband were detained for six months under the Terrorism Act.

Rita was imprisoned in Pretoria Central Prison along with Winnie Mandela and others. She had no change of clothes for the entire six months of her detention, and she was seriously assaulted in prison.

She was banned again as soon as she was released, then detained a second time. Her husband was killed during his detention and Rita was released on the day after his funeral. She continued to recruit members to her ANC cell.

Later, she served three terms as a member of parliament.

When I represented Rita, Kehla Shubane was her co-accused and I found them shivering in court, brought up from the cells wearing T-shirts and light clothes in the middle of a severe winter. They had nothing warm to put on. I went home and found two of my husband's jackets to give to Kehla in prison. When Reg was looking for them soon after, I had to tell him they were now on Robben Island where Kehla was doing five years.

I was seeing clients faint with hunger, actually starving. I bought food for them and gave them my own clothes. Unlike their family members and friends, as a lawyer I could enter prisons without a search.

These were difficult, horrible times and we didn't know if we would survive them. But I will never forget the mood of the people. It was the real 'ubuntu' – the famous South African expression for strong comradeship and togetherness. Morale was high and so was morality. People were pulling together, with the struggle as the main agenda. If a family had extra slices of bread they would share them with neighbours. Everyone was in it together.

I can honestly say that is what I miss today. It is what mass action produces in people, a common purpose and common decency and kindness. It was what kept us going against crushing odds.

My office had become the hub of the whole youth uprising. Schoolchildren were leaving the country to join Umkhonto we Sizwe (MK), the ANC's military wing, so they could return to carry out acts of sabotage. The security police were arresting suspects in regular dawn raids, kicking doors down and randomly picking up citizens in the streets. The ANC's network of underground cells was increasing.

I was getting a name for myself as a lawyer who would go all out for her clients. I fought for them in court, I comforted their families at home. If the breadwinner was imprisoned I would organise help as much as I could, and all the time I knew it was the right thing to do, just as using every possible angle of the law to fight cases and win acquittals was the right thing to do.

This was giving me confidence in the work I took on. So when the exceptional case of Solomon Mahlangu landed on my desk, and in my view needed exceptionally bold handling, I just got on with it knowing I was actually risking my position with Ismail Ayob. If things became difficult, I decided, I was ready to strike out on my own. And that is exactly what happened.

The murder file I was handed became one of the biggest landmark cases in the appalling history of apartheid-era judiciary. It shocked the world.

By June 1977, a year after the Soweto uprising, a virtual onslaught against anti-apartheid activists was taking place and a general heightening of oppressive measures such as arrests, detentions without trial, prosecutions and torture. There was tremendous uncertainty about the ANC's military wing and its plans for a nationwide backlash.

On the afternoon of 13 June, that uncertainty developed into national hysteria and the fear that there could be random killings of white people.

Two young men had returned to Johannesburg after training with MK in Angola. During a search of their belongings as they were climbing into a taxi to travel to Soweto, police had found an AK-47 assault rifle.

The two men – Mondy Johannes Motloung and Solomon Mahlangu – fled the taxi rank and disappeared into the crowd. They were shot at by a police officer and Mahlangu was hit in the ankle but the pair kept running, turning into Goch Street. Mahlangu ran into a busy warehouse and hid behind packing cases. Motloung, panicked, entered the warehouse and fired shots. Two white workers were killed.

Police surrounded the area and Mahlangu came out from his hiding place with his arms raised.

A huge crowd had gathered and I was in that crowd. I had been drafting pleadings and reading records in my office nearby when I'd heard the police sirens and seen people scattering. The entire city centre was alight with confusion and fear of imminent danger.

Once the two men were arrested there were cries of 'the ANC has come to kill us'. Evening newspaper headlines announced 'Terrorists kill white people'.

The families of Motloung and Mahlangu came to Ismail

Ayob's office to ask for help. I immediately informed the police that we represented them, but the following morning they were taken to court without legal representation. We had not been told there was to be a hearing. This was increasingly the case. I had no option but to seek out my new clients in Pretoria Central Prison.

Mahlangu's case has since become a cause célèbre in the history of many gross injustices in South Africa.

Motloung, who did the shootings, had been beaten so severely by police and prison officers that he sustained serious brain damage. My first sight of him was shocking. His face was completely deformed and there was a huge injury on his head. In the cell with him Solomon Mahlangu told me he had been given electric shocks to his genitals and that his head was covered with a wet sack while he was beaten.

He was an exceptional young man. When his mother broke down in tears at the sight of him, he asked her: 'Why are you crying in front of these dogs? I don't care what they do to me. If they spill my blood it may give birth to others like me.'

He and Motloung were detained incommunicado for nearly a year. During this time they were severely tortured. They had no access to family, friends, lawyers or doctors.

When we finally got to the Supreme Court for trial, Motloung was declared unfit to stand trial and referred to a psychiatric unit. I visited him often over the years until his death in October 2006. He was never aware of Mahlangu's fate and the huge international interest in their case.

Before his trial the media had already found Solomon Mahlangu guilty. He faced extreme hostility in the court from police and prison officers, court officials, the prosecution team and the judge himself.

We had searched for months to find a senior counsel prepared to take the case working with me as attorney. Only Clifford Mailer, a junior counsel, had the courage to join me in court. Like me, he was utterly traumatised by the circumstances of Solomon's trial, and remains so to this day. He argued that the doctrine of common purpose was being totally distorted and misused. He fought against the appointment of the notorious Judge Theron and his two assessors, the whole team having a reputation for toughness, cruelty and outright racism. He sought to have the judge recused, but failed.

Mailer has described to me how lonely he felt throughout the trial in the absence of a silk to lead. He said: 'To my dying day I will be disgusted that no senior counsel came in. It was the most distressing case of my career. There was mob hysteria, with whites choosing to believe that terrorists were on the loose in Johannesburg city centre.

'It was clear that Solomon had had no intention to kill. The circumstances were clear. I had questioned him closely and all the evidence pointed to his truth. He was an exceptional young man; I had never met anyone like him. He was utterly dedicated, quiet, respectful and courteous towards us, understanding that we were doing our job as well as we could in the face of ferocious opposition.

'His conviction for murder was a travesty.'

Senior Counsel Ismail Mahomed was able to join Mailer to put mitigation to the court before sentence was announced. But both lawyers were subjected to open abuse by the general public in the gallery and the judge. There were threats to throw us out of court and to report us to the authorities. The judge occasionally stormed out of court. He interfered with the cross-examination of our witnesses and would unduly assist the State's witnesses.

We had no consulting room; we could talk to Solomon only in his police cell surrounded by officers who were listening in.

Advocate Mahomed produced a formidable argument. He was fighting against the notion that Solomon was guilty of murder because of the law of Common Purpose. This law argues that all parties together committing a crime should face the same consequences, regardless of whether they carried out the same acts or knew of each other's intent.

There should have been a maximum five years' imprisonment for Mahlangu if he was found guilty. But the media and the public wanted more and the State was asking for the death penalty.

Mahomed gave a powerful and moving account of Solomon's young life in an attempt to save him. He had, he said, been brought up in abject poverty by his domestic-worker mother, abandoned by his father. He had sold apples and other goods on the streets to help support his family. He had been picked up by police on the streets many times and arrested and beaten. He was bright and sensitive, an intelligent youth who was conscious of the disparity and discrimination he and fellow black people were suffering. Mahomed said he was a living example of apartheid's devastating policies and this had ignited in him a burning desire to do something to overturn them.

When Soweto students revolted against Afrikaans as their tuition language, Solomon's consciousness had been sharpened. He joined the liberation movement. He was known as gentle and caring, compassionate and respectful. He preferred a non-confrontational approach and wanted nothing more than to be able to study. But he had to help achieve freedom before he could achieve education. He spent six months training with MK, a crash course in sabotage.

He had been sent back to South Africa through Swaziland to await further instructions for a mission. The rules were that no civilians should be killed in any sabotage operations. Solomon was to attack hard targets only.

Mahomed presented his mitigation with passion and sincerity. There had been no intention on Mahlangu's part to kill, and he had taken no part in his comrade's actions. But this had no effect whatever on Judge Theron. There was to be no mercy or compassion for Solomon Mahlangu. He was labelled a terrorist and a murderer.

I saw to my horror that there was actual joy in the public gallery. Heavily-armed security police took Solomon's mother and brothers out of court and there was an upbeat, jovial mood among the public, by now anticipating the ultimate sentence.

Judge Theron found him guilty of Common Purpose formed in the ANC training camp. He held that the purpose was to kill white people in sabotage operations and that Solomon must have foreseen that.

The iniquitous and controversial Common Purpose doctrine was used ruthlessly during apartheid to the detriment of true justice. Introduced as part of the Riotous Assemblies Act, it was used to criminalise protest action. If a murder or other offence was committed by one person in a crowd, everyone in the crowd could be convicted and sentenced as they shared a 'common purpose'.

Some years after the blatantly unfair use of this doctrine in Solomon Mahlangu's case there was a similar outcry when twenty-six people were convicted of murder during a protest. Police had broken up a township rally and a crowd had gathered outside the house of one police officer. He fired shots at them, and was then attacked by the entire mob and died as a result.

Everyone attending the protest was sentenced to death and the case rumbled on for several years while courageous attorneys appealed the sentence, finally achieving justice in 1989.

For Solomon there was to be no such justice: he was to be hanged. I heard gasps of delight from a white crowd baying for blood.

He held his head high, turned around and raised his fist. Taking a lead from Mandela at his own trial, he shouted: 'Amandla!' Power to the people.

I made an instant decision to raise my fist in solidarity and shout the response: 'Awetu' – which means 'To Us'. In doing so I was going against my legal duties and my status in court, but it was irresistible. I would do the same thing today.

For that breach of lawyerly conduct I was made to suffer. Judge Theron laid a complaint of unprofessional conduct against me to the Law Society. Its members, part of the secretive pro-apartheid conspiracy of brothers known as the Broederbond, tried to have me struck off.

I saw then that there was no justice. I saw that the entire system was designed to perpetuate apartheid. In all the human rights cases I was taking to court I was to achieve rare successes. In South Africa there were no fair trials for black people. There was no independent judiciary and no impartial officials of justice. A fair trial was a myth.

The apartheid state wanted the world to believe that all of

its people were afforded a fair and just trial. But the judges were chosen from the minority white ranks and generally they were allies of the system. Judges for cases such as the Mahlangu trial were especially selected to frustrate a fair defence and, as with his trial, the maximum sentence was delivered. There was a case where an accused man was found guilty of scribbling 'Viva Mandela' on his coffee mug. He was given four years' imprisonment for furthering the aims of a banned organisation.

In the moments after Solomon had been sentenced and pushed roughly down the steps to the cells I searched for his mother who had been removed from the court earlier – a sure sign that he was about to receive the ultimate penalty. I found her sitting on the pavement outside, absorbed in grief. 'Solomon did not kill anyone,' she was saying over and over. 'Why is this happening to him?'

I had no answers. Back at my office I drafted applications to appeal. Twice I was denied leave to appeal. Solomon would hang.

As a last resort I wrote letters to the United Nations Security Council, to sympathetic governments and international civil societies, pleading with them to intervene for clemency. I used my employer Ismail Ayob's letter-heading. He was irate, furious even. He threatened to summarily dismiss me from my article-ship and demanded that I make a choice between being a political activist or a lawyer.

I rejected this with the contempt it deserved. Decency and humanity told me there was no choice. My priority was to behave as a human being and to use my position as a lawyer to further justice. I owed this to my client Solomon and I owed it to the black people of South Africa and the principles of justice. Lawyers were a necessary part of the struggle. I had no regrets whatsoever. I was probably going to lose my job and did not regret that either.

It was proving difficult to be a human rights lawyer. I was constantly targeted by the security forces and my home and office were raided continuously.

Meanwhile, the international campaign for clemency for Solomon was gaining momentum. Virtually every country in the world and every head of State petitioned the South African government to spare Solomon's life.

We collected millions of signatures, and I was regularly visiting Solomon in the Pretoria death cells. He frequently witnessed the hanging of fellow inmates and was trying to give other prisoners courage. He taught them about the liberation struggle and its songs and anthems.

Not one of our own country's leaders had played a role seeking a reprieve for him, and now the date for his hanging had been set: 6 April 1979.

As a last resort, two days earlier, I had approached Archbishop Desmond Tutu with my friend Joe Veriava. We pleaded with him to take our petition to the government in Cape Town as a last desperate resort. He seemed reluctant, so Joe and I spent the entire night in a car outside his house, ready to make sure that he caught the first flight to Cape Town.

Tutu took the petition for us, but it made no difference.

Solomon's mother had spent some time with her son on his last day. I had been allowed an appointment with him at 10 p.m., and we all knew by now that the end was inevitable.

My heart sank as I entered the room allocated to us at Fort Prison. The hangman's scale was in a corner. I was shaking with trepidation and I could not speak. Solomon by contrast was strong and composed. He saw his role was to comfort and console me. He told me his last message to an unkind world: 'Tell my people that I love them. Tell them to continue the fight. My blood will nurture the tree that bears the fruits of freedom.'

As I left, the low mournful singing of liberation songs was still echoing around the death cell block.

I went to his mother's house and sat with her and the elders on the floor to talk and pray, according to their Ndebele custom. We cried and hoped and waited.

At 6 a.m. we heard the news on the radio. Solomon had been hanged.

A great wailing sound went up outside, it seemed to shake the foundations of the house. Thousands of youths and schoolchildren had gathered outside. They were singing anthems and their plan was to march to the prison to claim Solomon's body to bury him like a hero. But the ever-watchful police had also gathered. They were preparing to use tear gas, so I walked outside and addressed the youths. I said, this is not what Solomon would want. It would be suicidal and he would not want them killed like the schoolchildren in Soweto.

The police could not restrain themselves. They threw the tear gas and dispersed the crowd.

There were fears of a mass uprising if Solomon's body was released, so he was buried without ceremony in a pauper's grave by prison officers.

I knew the security police were monitoring me, but I could not fail to attend the commemoration ceremony for Solomon. I entered Soweto without a permit and they enjoyed arresting me. I was convicted and sentenced to pay a R50 fine – a large sum of money then – or serve fifty days in prison.

Arrested with me were community doctor Dr Abubaker Asvat, Joe Veriava and my husband Reg. We were taken to Johannesburg Prison and I was separated from the men.

It was my first taste of prison and the experience has stayed with me ever since. If I had expected to be treated with sympathy, and perhaps comradeship, by other female inmates I was completely wrong.

Every newcomer, I learnt, was to be looked on with suspicion and hostility. There was no interest whatsoever in my 'crime'. I was led into a cell containing about ten other women, all black, who huddled in a corner and stared openly at me. I was unknown, I was unwelcome, and I was Indian – 'different'.

When food was delivered it came in a plastic dustbin. It was mealy pap, a tasteless porridge made from mealies. It looked revolting and I didn't touch it.

I was expecting this wretched cell, and its inmates who refused to talk to me, to be my home for fifty long days. But about four hours later a warder came to unlock the cage door. An anonymous stranger had paid our fines, unasked, and I was free to go.

It had been a mercifully brief glimpse of prison life, but now I knew the reality of the detention that many of my clients were experiencing, often without a release date and often without trial.

It was fear of the harshness of prison, and the political impotence that came with it, which hung over all of the country's activism. I had nothing but admiration for the hundreds of thousands of South Africans who were risking this punishment every day of their lives. I was proud to be contributing my own individual courage in the best way I could. The role of a human rights lawyer in South Africa at that time was a continual contest against the inhuman laws of the land.

My short-lived prison experience was horrific, but there was something even more terrifying about the thuggery of the security police and their state-approved random acts of violence. One night in the early hours, my husband and I were woken by the sound of broken glass and an explosion. A firebomb, crudely made by stuffing a petrol-soaked rag into a bottle and setting it alight, had been thrown through our bedroom window.

The curtains caught fire and Reg rushed downstairs to get buckets of water in an attempt to douse the flames. I was screaming, and the whole commotion woke our neighbours who of course came running to help.

The State's determination to defeat people like me, and to send us running out of the country, knew literally no bounds.

The next day I was visited by a black American lawyer called Millard Arnold, President of the Lawyers' Committee for Civil Rights. He was on a fact-finding trip and wanted to talk to the Mahlangu family.

He was absolutely horrified to learn that my house had been petrol-bombed and when we arrived at Mrs Mahlangu's house the police were waiting for us, threatening us with arrest. I recall him actually being reduced to tears and to us that seemed so strange; we were much more likely to be moved to anger and fury, not tears.

Many years later, at the Truth and Reconciliation Commission (TRC) hearings, Solomon's mother Martha described how she carried with her the pain of losing her son every day. 'He wanted to become a school teacher,' she said.

'He was very conscientious and humble. He was unshaken in his beliefs. Now in my old age I miss him even more.'

In 1993, Solomon's body was reinterred at Mamelodi Cemetery where a plaque states his last words, spoken to me in his death cell. A commemorative wall at the college also bears his last words. A statue of him was unveiled in 2005 in Mamelodi and a stamp bearing his image was launched by the South African Post Office to mark the thirtieth anniversary of his execution in April 2009.

The Solomon Mahlangu Freedom College was established in 1977 in the city of Morogoro, Tanzania, and flourishes to this day.

Oliver Tambo himself, the greatly revered President of the ANC in exile, described Solomon as '…towering like a colossus, unbroken and unbreakable. In his death this spirit towers over us'.

In March 2014, I was asked to give the speech at his mother's funeral. Thousands of mourners packed the public stadium in Mamelodi.

I talked of how she had cherished her youngest son and was heartbroken when he left home to join the liberation struggle. He left her a note saying: 'Do not look for me'.

I told the crowd: 'Mama, your son is our son. A true son of Africa. You gave him to us so that we could all be free. You endured so much pain, so much suffering and hardship.

'We thank you for your sublime sacrifice. Solomon's death is not in vain.'

Many, many students have now attended the Solomon Mahlangu Freedom College and I am proud to say that my own niece Mala and my nephew Pritiraj have spent time teaching there.

My own career reached an important milestone due to his case. I was ready to leave Ismail Ayob's office and strike out more boldly on my own.

# CHAPTER THREE

# MY FRIEND WINNIE MANDELA – MOTHER OF THE NATION

Winnie Mandela had become a close friend. Since that initial meeting in a clothing store our paths had crossed many times in the intense and tightly knit world of Joburg activism.

Winnie remained indomitable at a time when the ANC itself was going through a dormant, almost impotent, phase in the mid-seventies. While I was taking a conventional route towards the goals of freedom and unity, battling human rights cases in and out of the courts, Winnie by contrast had gone far beyond convention.

With a crushing prison sentence behind her – seventeen months of hell and torture in solitary confinement at Pretoria Central Prison – she re-emerged undaunted as the people's hero and immediately, and provocatively, formed the Black Women's Federation and the Black Parents' Association. These were closely allied to the Black Consciousness Movement, the pro-black initiative which drew us together.

I often went to her home in Vilakazi Street, Soweto, with BCM stalwarts Aubrey Mokoena, Kenneth Rachidi and others to take part in stealthy planning meetings and to organise subversive activities such as boycotts and protest marches.

In fact I was not allowed in Soweto without a permit but I took my chances, ducking down in the back seat of Aubrey's car, a scarf covering my head. It was worth it to hear Winnie's fiery oratory, to see and feel her resolve and her determination. She was ferocious in her belief in the struggle. These were among the worst days of apartheid, the ANC was currently non-existent, yet Winnie had faith.

I sometimes thought she was in dreamland and my reality was that we were nowhere near defeating apartheid.

But her enthusiasm was infectious, she gave us hope to carry on. There were several declarations of States of Emergency and security police were constantly monitoring her movements, but nothing deterred her. She was on course to succeed.

She defiantly kept open house at Vilakazi Street. There was always a cup of tea on offer there. It was a poor household, typical of the township, just a square brick-built house where you walked through the front door and straight into the sitting-room. Even so, it was impeccably clean. Winnie had a strong instinct for orderliness, perhaps an antidote to the utter chaos of her public life. I would say she was elegantly poor, a beautiful woman who dressed in style and was extremely articulate.

At public meetings she would speak passionately for an hour without notes. She outshone other great veterans of the struggle like Albertina Sisulu and Lilian Ngoyi, both good speakers. The moment she walked into City Hall, or even addressed a crowd in the street, people went mad to hear her, and Winnie loved that. She was not just Nelson Mandela's wife: she was Mother of the Nation in her own right.

Collectiveness and democracy was the mantra at the time, but that was not Winnie's way. She was authoritarian and undisciplined with it; a charismatic woman and public speaker with total belief in herself and her message.

Later, in the mid-eighties, she could have been a natural leader of the newly formed United Democratic Front when it brought together a powerful coalition of civic society, church leaders, students and workers. But they did not ask her to even join. She was too independent, too much for them to handle, impossible for them to control. It was both her weakness and her strength.

In the immediate aftermath of the Soweto school students' uprising of 1976 Winnie was targeted and suspected of incitement. She helped to mobilise a group which went to the Protea police station to plead for a halt to the shootings of students, giving them further reason to step up their witch-hunt.

Winnie had already been banned innumerable times, and imprisoned, but she had bounced back and was at the height of her powers at the time we formed our friendship. There was comradeship and a shared belief at its base, but also a womanly mutual admiration. I saw the caring, humane side of Winnie. She had trained as a social worker, and she was to all intents and purposes a single mother. She had the energy to operate at street level and at the same time dominate the big picture.

She was causing a severe headache to the security police, and even the ANC in exile could not tame her. She recognised only her husband as leader, not Oliver Tambo and the leadership running the organisation from Zambia.

Winnie would talk to me about going to Robben Island to see Nelson. 'Our leader', she always called him, never 'My husband'.

She was indomitable, but she needed the support of comrades and friends like me. I was happy to provide it. She would hug me and tell me that I was her lawyer, and her friend, her sister.

By now I was handling her legal matters as well as I could and it was a demanding role.

I wanted her to meet my husband and our neighbours, so I invited her to lunch to our home in Lenasia. I had asked her if she and her family liked curry, our national dish, and she had said she did. The only thing they didn't eat was prawns. I had made special side dishes of prawns for other guests, but Winnie and her family descended on them and ate them instead of the curry. Even in the matter of a lunch it was impossible to predict her or to keep any control. Winnie would overwhelm any plans.

We had a mutual friend, a neighbour of mine who was a travel agent. He regularly made arrangements for Winnie's daughters Zindzi and Zenani to get to and from their boarding school in Swaziland. Winnie had contrived to send them there for a decent education and to give them some stability away from the incessant raids on her Soweto home. Donations from sympathisers overseas made that possible.

The travel agent and other neighbours were always happy to see Winnie, even when she turned up out of the blue with a retinue of family and friends. Sometimes my husband Reg would be drawn into the last-minute logistics of the girls' travels, taking them to the airport or organising a journey by road. Like everyone else, he could not refuse Winnie; he adored her. She had a flirty charm with men which they found irresistible. He would give her advice, groceries, anything she wanted. One day she came to our house, unannounced as usual, when Reg had just bought two Rottweiler dogs for extra security. Winnie loved them. She announced that she needed them more than we did and by the time she left she had our dogs in the back of her car.

The truth is that I felt enormous compassion for the way she was living, and enormous admiration for her courage. We had a house with nice furniture and plenty of food, a car and a decent income. Winnie was living on handouts. Her husband, who she adored, was Public Enemy Number One and in prison for life, and she was at her wits' end trying to bring order into her daughters' lives. No stable financial assistance was available to her and the State enjoyed seeing her living in poverty and distress. Occasionally envelopes arrived from abroad, often from Britain, with gifts of money for Winnie. They came to Ayob's office and we handed her quantities of cash from all over the world, glad to be putting food on Winnie's table or paying her electricity bills.

She worried constantly about the girls' school fees and the expense of clothes for them, and her taxi fares, and the help that she readily doled out to needy neighbours and street children in Soweto. At times when the cash ran out, there were friends like me and my husband to turn to.

Winnie had a queenly presence in public. She wore full-length elegant kaftans and a turban and was always well-groomed even when we knew she had come because she was in dire need of our help. A crowd would gather when it was known she was in my street, walking through my front door without any sort of invitation. I could be at home working, or cooking, or entertaining guests with supper. No matter, a car would draw up outside in the darkness and Winnie would step out. She walked into the room and everyone was knocked out by her presence among us. There were hugs all round and we were once again totally disarmed: we were going to give her whatever she needed.

She had a huge street-following and could pack a hall or a stadium at a minute's notice, but she was living day-to-day at the mercy of the ruthless security police. They rightly suspected that Winnie was an enemy of the State. She was proud of it and tested it to the limit.

I was glad to be her friend, to be respected for the part I was playing in the struggle we shared. But she was more hard-line than me. She pushed her legal boundaries to the very limit and my priority was to just to try and keep her stable and within the law. I could only imagine the brutality of those months she suffered in solitary, being spat on and derided by the prison warders, and subjected to days of relentless interrogation. I saw my role as desperately trying to keep her out of prison in future.

Her great gift was that she believed the apartheid state was not sustainable, it would end. She believed heart and soul that the ANC would overcome not through negotiation but by the sheer force of righteousness. In the wake of the Soweto uprising there was beginning to be a new energy in the country and Winnie encouraged it as heartily as she could. The youth were angry and restive. They wanted to go to MK training camps to learn about sabotage.

Winnie set up a huge recruiting network. Her trusty recruit-ment officer was an activist called Norman Monyepoti. Between them groups of young boys just out of school were lined up to be sent to Mozambique or Botswana or Swaziland to the MK camps. It was a difficult and dangerous system, smuggling boys across the border. But Winnie had her networks. She needed help with documents and fares for them, and the ANC willingly provided that.

Droves of youngsters were being recruited, fired up by Soweto. I worked up a structure by which their names would be sent to Oliver Tambo in Lusaka, along with details of their arrival, so that MK operatives on the ground could organise collecting them.

We worked in tandem, with me advising caution at all times. An early victim of this recruitment programme was Norman Monyepoti. He was gunned down outside his home by security police, a callous warning shot to Winnie, me and everyone involved in the new ANC surge which had followed the Soweto schoolchildren's uprising.

Winnie had been delighted when I joined Ismail Ayob's law practice. Ayob himself was no activist and he resisted Winnie and her lack of discipline and, just as he thought that having me take over her files would make things easier, so did Winnie. I was taking care of her, she was the heart of the ANC on the streets and she was inspiring the youth.

This recruitment drive she was helping to run needed money and now I became very involved in facilitating the movement of funds arriving from all over the world. I had my own network of couriers. I remember the first was a white guy with long blond hair. He was from somewhere in Scandinavia. He presented himself at my office as a client, and gave me a small package. He said it was a gift from a friend.

It looked for all the world to me like an unopened bar of Lux soap. But when I took it home and had a proper look I found a message scribbled on paper, folded up and inserted into the middle of the soap. It told me where I should go to collect a parcel and hand it on to my fellow activist Beyers Naudé.

I called at an anonymous-looking house with my scribbled message and was given a bag of money. There were hundreds of English pounds inside. My friend Joe Veriava had in the meantime been told to collect a similar package from a house in Yeoville, a Johannesburg suburb.

We entrusted all these funds to my legal assistant Ilona Kleinschmidt Tip and she passed them to Beyers, an extraordinary man who had been ordained in the Dutch Reformed Church but who had abandoned their racist agenda and joined us in the struggle. He had the means to get the money where it was needed – funding the transport, food and clothing for recruits slipping over the border.

I was receiving a lot of messages in this way, always from white men, always strangers and never the same. They posed as tourists, dressed casually, and just popped into my office to hand me a message and leave immediately afterwards.

I was at the same time often representing Winnie at court. She would be accused of breaching her banning order, of holding meetings to incite terrorism, of being a communist. It was deliberate harassment. But it did nothing to deter her.

Then something happened which was so stupendously harsh that it stopped her in her tracks. Citing the Suppression of Communism Act, police raided her house in the early hours of the morning, threw her clothes and a few sticks of furniture on to the open back of a pick-up truck, and told her they were taking her out of town, to a place where she could cause no more trouble.

Winnie Mandela had been banished, one of the first such actions to be undertaken by the apartheid government. She was bundled onto the back of the truck along with Zindzi, aged just fifteen, and driven out to the desolate wastes of the Orange Free State, an Afrikaner-dominated province of pre-democratic South Africa.

Her home for the next eight years was to be a three-room hut on the outskirts of an Afrikaans town. It was number 802 Phathakahle Section in Majwemasweu. Police had warned her neighbours not to talk to her or help her in any way. Made of cement bricks, with a cement floor, the matchbox house had no electricity, running water, stove or indoor toilet. The roof was made of corrugated iron and there was no ceiling. Winnie was to be under constant police surveillance.

I heard news of her banishment on the radio while still at home that morning and felt devastated. I was convinced this could not be lawful and that we could challenge it. Ayob too was very concerned. He was close to both Winnie and Nelson Mandela. He feared this was a new and ominous episode in their relationship with the State. He wanted me to visit Winnie immediately. She had been sent into isolation but there was still provision for her to see her lawyer at all times.

I flew to Bloemfontein with advocate Clifford Mailer, now senior counsel, who had appeared in many human rights cases with me since we first worked together to try to save Solomon Mahlangu. We took groceries with us, fruit and vegetables and some essentials. We hired a car and drove into the miserable township. As we travelled through the Free State we were dumbstruck by the starkness of the countryside. To me it seemed like how I imagined Siberia to be – barren and cold and hostile. It took hours to get to Brandfort, that one-horse town where she was destined to live in the adjoining black township. All along the way we saw security police parked up, watchful.

When we drew up outside number 802 we saw it was half a hut. The tiniest matchbox house imaginable, with literally nothing in it but a few sticks of furniture and a mattress. I started sobbing; it was unbearable. Clifford was so uncomfortable, he didn't know what to do or say. He retreated to the car so that Winnie could not be accused of breaking the terms of her banning order by having both of us in her home. Winnie was a banned person and could only be in the company of one person at a time other than a lawyer or a doctor. We knew the police were parked less than two hundred yards away, waiting and watching.

Inside there were Winnie and Zindzi, in such a state of shock they could hardly speak. They just sat while I told them we would do everything we could.

The town of Brandfort was an Afrikaans stronghold. The congested area, designated for blacks only, on the outskirts, where Winnie was forced to live, was a place of extreme poverty. This place, right in the centre of South Africa, epitomised apartheid.

Black people were living under severe conditions, virtually enslaved to the whites. The only work available to them was for white farmers or white businesses; they were totally dependent on them for any sort of livelihood. In fact they were totally dependent on them for their entire existence. They lived in fear of their white bosses.

Before Winnie arrived, the township dwellers were warned not to associate with her or Zindzi, not to speak to them or socialise with them in any way. 'This woman is a dangerous communist', they were told. Even if they had wanted to, there was in any case a language problem. Winnie was Xhosa, and these people spoke Sothu. They were terrified of the powerful State system and kept their distance from the new arrivals.

The name of the place, Phathakahle, translates as 'Handle with Care', an irony that compares with the black township in Cape Town called Khayelitsha, which means, 'Our New Home' – a wretched settlement where hundreds of thousands of people were sent to live after forced removals under the Group Areas Act.

As a human rights lawyer I had already witnessed and experienced some of the worst atrocities in apartheid South Africa, and to me Winnie Mandela's persecution was among the most severe. As we left I felt overwhelmed with sympathy. A weaker person reduced to those living conditions could easily contemplate suicide. Leaving her there with Zindzi I was terribly traumatised. Clifford and I talked of ways we could possibly overturn the banishment, and ways in which we could possibly bring her some relief.

We talked intently and somehow missed our turn-off to the airport. When we back-tracked and finally got there we had missed our flight to Johannesburg. This was a big problem. Indians were not allowed to stay overnight in the Free State without a permit.

There were no mobile phones in those days and we had no credit cards, or friends living anywhere close. We had a hire car and about R7 – a tiny sum – between us. We decided to drive to Kimberley, the next big town where there was an airport. It was the middle of winter, intensely cold and the car's heating system was not working.

Late at night we spotted a bar open and felt enormously

relieved. But the proprietors and patrons there were rude and abusive to us. We were not allowed in. Once in Kimberley we found a hotel foyer to sit in. We managed to make contact with a neighbour of mine, Mahomed Momoniat – husband of my close friend Hajira – who was attending a conference in town. He generously paid for hotel rooms for us and we stayed overnight. In Johannesburg the next day we were met by irate family members who had been anxious and unable to find us.

Back in my office I looked at ways to attack the banishment order. A few days later when I visited Winnie again I had to break it to her that I could not find a way out for her in law. I took her a portable battery-operated TV so that she could at least know something of the outside world.

She was devastated by her situation. She didn't cry but she was grief-stricken for herself and for Zindzi. She was beyond crying. Her surroundings were absolutely bare, with not a blade of grass anywhere. The neighbours seemed terrified of her and had not spoken a word to her or even exchanged a look.

I began to visit her regularly, bringing Joe Veriava with me. He was a doctor and therefore allowed inside the house. My husband Reg would come with us, but had to wait outside in the car. Ismail Ayob could have come with us in his capacity as a lawyer but frankly he would have almost died if he had seen that place. He believed in avoiding any sort of trouble with police and he would have panicked at the first glimpse of Winnie's life in Brandfort.

My legal assistant and good friend Ilona drove out there one day with another sympathiser Jackie Bosman. They had brought a little paraffin fridge with them and a cooking stove, and although they knew the crippling restrictions surrounding any visit to Winnie and kept to the rules, the consequences of their acts of kindness were disastrous for them.

Ilona told me how she had spotted a security police officer hiding in bushes near Winnie's home as she approached the door, and how Jackie had stayed at some distance, both of them mindful of the need to stay within the conditions of the banning order. They managed to speak to Winnie for about half an hour, telling her of all the support she had back in Johannesburg and asking her whether there was anything she needed.

Within days of their return they were both served with notices under the Criminal Procedures Act to make statements about the visit. 'We refused,' Ilona told me. 'The last thing we wanted to do was make things worse for Winnie by giving the impression she had breached her banning order.'

Ilona, with a four-year-old daughter at home, was imprisoned for three months. Jackie, who had driven her to Brandfort, got four months.

'It was a terrible, cruel experience,' Ilona told me. 'We were both in isolation in Pretoria Central Prison, treated like common criminals. We weren't allowed to have books, not even the Bible, and no contact with other prisoners. I missed my little girl's fifth birthday.'

Opposition MP Helen Suzman used her influence to get a slight relaxation of the rules. Ilona and Jackie were then allowed to spend an hour each day in each other's company. Ilona said that looking back they were at least fortunate to know the length of their sentences. Many other activists, detained without trial, could be thrown into jail for months or years without knowing if it would ever end.

Helen Joseph, a fearless activist, was also kind enough to

try and lighten Winnie's harsh life with a visit. She arrived in Brandfort with a friend, Barbara Waite, a devout churchgoer and sympathiser who drove them both out there in her car. Like Ilona and Jackie, they knew the rules and did not contravene them. But they were also ordered to court to report on Winnie. Helen was imprisoned for ten days and Barbara for four months.

I represented all four women at their court hearings – two of them, Jackie and Barbara, had no connection with politics or activism. It was with a heavy heart that I listened to the punishments handed down. I found a technicality on which to base an appeal. It took a year to fight through the system but we won. The day after she was released from prison Helen was issued with a new summons. That was the pattern of an activist's life.

In this way the government's unemotional relentlessness set out to beat us all down, to wear us out. It had the opposite effect. Winnie was never to be crushed by them and nor were we. Her banning order was being so closely monitored that she was once arrested in a shopping centre, where of course there were many people. Despite not speaking to any of them she was accused of another breach.

She used a public payphone to inform us that she had to be in court the next day in Bloemfontein. I attended with George Bizos, who had represented Nelson Mandela at the Rivonia Trial, and Clifford Mailer. We picked Winnie up from her house, with police cars parked nearby, and several plainclothes' officers came in without invitation while we were there. She told us that they parked near the house all the time in full view in a process of intimidation.

I had wondered if Winnie could survive this intolerable

combination of isolation and harassment. But she was as strong as ever. In court she appeared every day in wonderful outfits, always in the ANC colours of green, black and gold.

The prosecutor demanded: 'Mrs Mandela can you tell the court why on every day you appear here you come dressed in the colours of the banned ANC?'

I was sitting next to George Bizos and became extremely agitated. There were no rules stipulating dress colours. I told George to object but in his usual cool and calm way he signalled me to be quiet.

He knew Winnie would be able to handle the question. He was right.

Winnie grasped the railing of the witness box and leant forward. She looked the prosecutor in the eye and told him loudly and firmly: 'Mr Prosecutor, of the limited rights that I have in my country I believe I still have the right to choose my own wardrobe.'

He sat down with no further questions. These small victories were important, and they demonstrated to me that Winnie was far from losing her fighting spirit.

But she was physically ailing. She suffered from hypertension and her sojourn in Brandfort was bringing her down. She had endured ill health throughout her time in prison and now she was falling ill again. Not one doctor in the Free State was prepared to treat her.

I was visiting most weekends and often bringing Dr Veriava with me but she needed someone nearby. Winnie herself found a white doctor in Welkom, a Dr Hattingh, who agreed to see her. He began to make regular weekly visits and take care of her medical needs. I think he actually became very fond of her.

One day after a consultation at her home, Dr Hattingh was

driving back to Welkom and had a fatal crash unexplained to this day. His car had gone off the highway into a ditch and Dr Hattingh was found dead at the side of the road. Police declared it was an accident.

He had previously told Winnie that he was being harassed by the security police who tried to dissuade him from treating her. But he had persisted and had become a family friend. His sister Suzanna, who was herself studying medicine and later qualified as a doctor, was always absolutely convinced that her brother's death was suspicious. She and I became good friends and she bravely joined the anti-apartheid struggle, becoming totally committed. Nelson and Winnie Mandela invited her to be godmother to one of their grandchildren.

The death of her friend Dr Hattingh was a heartbreaking setback for Winnie, but her resilience to all the heartbreaking setbacks in her life was astonishing, even to me who knew her so well.

She had started a little garden in the front plot at her hut, growing spinach and carrots from seed. One day I saw that this had encouraged her neighbours. One by one they were growing vegetables of their own.

And there was communication. Winnie's charm – and her plight – was beginning to touch local people despite their initial wariness. Her skills as a social worker were clear. Through donations that we brought to her, the English pounds and other cash from all over the world still arriving at our office, she bought food and stored provisions in her shed, often handing them out to poor local children.

A neighbour who lived two doors away, Nora Nomafu, described years later how police had called on all of them before Winnie and Zindzi arrived. 'We were not even allowed to speak to her,' she said. 'We had to tell our children not to go near this communist woman. She was very dangerous. So when she called out to the children they ran away screaming. One day I felt so sorry for her that I asked my little son to help her fetch water and we began to make a connection.

'I saw her becoming ill and her lawyer somehow got permission for me to help her and we began talking about many things.'

Winnie also started a little nursery for local children, and a clinic where the well-known activist Dr Abubaker Asvat would come from Johannesburg to help local people. Later the clinic was burned down by security police and Nora was amazed to find Winnie undefeated, stronger than ever. 'Winnie was not even angry,' she said. 'She would just say, "I know these dogs. Be careful, they can kill you any time".'

She admired the way Winnie would never show her terrible suffering, her loneliness without the husband she loved. 'She would say she needed us to be strong so as to face the Boers. Madiba was forgiveness and reconciliation. Winnie was strength. She liked to provoke the Boers.'

Looking back, other residents remember her as a kind woman who started the medical clinic and a small book-lending library in her yard. And they remember Winnie's pride and defiance, walking into local shops through the whites-only entrance, which they would never dare to do.

One of Brandfort's white residents, Charmaine Alberts, whose husband was a photographer, told of how she believes Winnie kept the ANC alive from her hut in the township. 'That was Winnie's doing,' she said. 'Not Nelson Mandela.' She was open in her admiration.

In recent years, with the publication of Nelson's letters to his wife in those terrible days, we have read of his advice to her to make a virtue of isolation. During her time in prison he had written to her.

> You may find that the cell is an ideal place to learn to know yourself, to search realistically and regularly the processes of your own mind and feelings... The cell gives you the opportunity to look daily into your entire conduct to overcome the bad and develop whatever is good in you.
>
> Never forget that a saint is a sinner who keeps on trying.

Winnie took comfort from all of her husband's letters but she was the first to say that, unlike him, she would never mellow towards their persecutors as he did. Her fiery righteous anger was, to my mind, what saw her through the deprivations she was forced to suffer.

I had known Winnie as a vibrant woman who drew others to her. She loved the company of others, and she also knew that men admired her very much. She enjoyed their admiration and she enjoyed being flattered, and pampered.

There were activist women in the anti-apartheid movement who were clearly jealous of her, and were condemning of her. I saw that they knew of men visiting her in the house in Vilakazi Street before her banishment, and that many newspapers were saying outright that she had lovers.

It was not my place to condemn or to judge her. My friends and I would never do that, although it was sometimes hard to condone because Mandela was of course our great hero and we believed he deserved her loyalty.

All the men we knew of were married. I felt strongly that

if Mandela had not been imprisoned, this chaos would never have happened. Her love for him was deep and intense. But he was not there, and Winnie was a big-hearted woman with needs. My feeling today is that Mandela understood that. It is known that cruel prison warders deliberately taunted him with rumours of Winnie's love life while he was on Robben Island. He could do nothing except appear to be strong.

At that time Winnie was the biggest news item in South Africa. She was either being arrested or sent to prison, or banished, or having fights and being detained, or having love affairs. The townships were rife with rumours. I wished she was more discreet; I feared that Mandela must know and I hated that notion. But I had no right to put that to Winnie, and I never discussed it with her. I could see that beyond her daily life and needs there was unshakeable respect, love and loyalty for her husband and for the movement. At the same time she was someone who needed affection and she welcomed kindness wherever it came from. None of that, I believe, touched the depths of her feeling for Mandela, the real love of her life.

One day in Brandfort, Zindzi called me from a public phone box to say that her mother was very ill. She was worried about her drinking and her health. Winnie had a serious heart condition and had taken to her bed. Zindzi was tearful and pleading.

I went there the next day with Joe Veriava. He brought medication and had a long talk to her, sitting at her bedside. Winnie had pneumonia and a high fever. But she was planning to fly to Cape Town the next day so she could catch the ferry to Robben Island. She had permission for a visit to her husband. Joe and I told her she really shouldn't travel, but she was adamant. She had never missed a visit and she was not going to miss one now.

'He will be waiting for me. I can't let him down,' she said.

It was as simple as that.

Their relationship was playing out like a huge tragedy, both of them sacrificing personal happiness for the sake of the fight for freedom. Him, imprisoned for life, her doing the best she could to promote the movement they believed in all the way to success, however long that took and however much agony it caused them.

I had taken a stance of non-condemnation at Mandela choosing the political movement over his wife and family, and over Winnie leading some kind of personal life without him. I had a great deal of sympathy for both of them.

On one of the many occasions when Winnie was arrested, before her banishment to Brandfort, she had had a Preventive Detention Order slapped on her and was sent back to Pretoria Prison, this time with activists Fatima Meer, Bertha Smith, Sally Motlana and a number of others from the Black Women's Federation.

I was acting for all of them after their families called me. There was no prosecution, just detention until the authorities saw fit to release them. I went to prison many times to see them, to encourage them and bring them messages. They were doing well under the circumstances but some had lost their jobs and were in despair about their families' finances.

For my visits to Winnie I took many messages and gifts. Male friends of hers were sending letters, chocolates and fruit. I had to open the letters and share them with her, then take them away with me. It was difficult. She needed this love and support. She enjoyed the boxes of yellow cling peaches and she read the outpourings of love. I am certain this helped her through the hardest times, and I was there to be her lawyer and her friend, not to judge.

During her time in Brandfort I also carried messages and gifts. These small gestures were helping her get through. I was certain that her husband would have approved of anything that sustained her through these dark days.

Years later new shocking evidence of the way Winnie's life was dogged during those lonely years came to light.

During the Truth and Reconciliation Commission hearings that followed the dawn of democracy in South Africa, a former Free State security police officer applied for amnesty for the way in which he had taken part in the State's campaign against her. He admitted bugging the miserable hut she lived in and also took part in the petrol-bombing of the clinic she set up next to it.

Nelson Mphithizeli Ngo, aged thirty-two, said his job was to gather evidence that could be used to bring further charges against Winnie. The security police were convinced she was housing young activists there. She certainly had visits from students, continuing to recruit them into MK and helping them to leave the country to join the training camps. Some of the youths were themselves arrested and tortured. Trevor Sikhota later recalled spending hours at Winnie's house. He said: 'Despite police harassment we visited Mama for political discussions at her house. We knew that after each and every visit that same evening we would be arrested and interrogated.'

I had seen that Winnie's daughter Zindzi was suffering, and this teenage girl had done nothing against the law. She could not see friends or socialise or enjoy any freedom of movement without being followed and monitored. Previously she had studied at school in Swaziland, safely across the border, with her older sister Zenani. But now Zenani had become engaged to the Swazi Prince Musi and they were to be married.

Zindzi felt abandoned and alone. When her mother was sent to Brandfort she felt her best move was to join her. She was very unhappy and disoriented there but could not leave her mother alone. They were virtually imprisoned together.

Zindzi was clever and outgoing, and beautiful. All the local boys were longing to spend time with her but it was impossible. Anyone visiting the house would be interrogated afterwards or even detained. Zindzi, so naturally charismatic and charming, had to suppress her real self. She felt like a pariah. Young people of her own age were literally scared to come near her. She became isolated, with no job or studies, just a stressful daily life.

A boyfriend from Johannesburg did come to stay, but he was harassed terribly by the security police and eventually taken away for questioning.

I was worried that Zindzi's life had become meaningless, and she was by then still only seventeen years old. I felt sure we could challenge her situation successfully through the courts.

But just as Clifford Mailer and I were preparing court papers, with reluctant agreement from George Bizos, we realised there was a problem. Winnie could not sign the court application as Zindzi's parent because she had no legal standing. Under the Bantu Administration Act a black woman was deemed to be a minor. There was only one person authorised to bring the application for Zindzi – her father Nelson Mandela.

Ayob suggested we should apply for permission to consult with him on Robben Island, but he was pessimistic about the outcome. I thought it was at least worth trying, so I called the head of prisons, a Brigadier van den Berg and told him I needed to consult Mandela urgently on a court matter.

He left me waiting on the phone for an eternity then came back with the permission I wanted. I was completely bowled over, anxious, excited and absolutely beside myself. Aside from the very real need to help Zindzi, this visit would be the realisation of my great dream, to actually meet Nelson Mandela. I had followed the Rivonia Trial avidly and every utterance he had ever made remained with me. He was my philosopher, my guide and mentor, my inspiration and my leader.

Nelson Mandela personified the reason I joined the ANC.

I felt overawed that as an inexperienced junior lawyer I was about to meet one of the world's greatest icons, a renowned leader, a phenomenal lawyer and a freedom fighter without equal.

The ferry trip to Robben Island was going to be challenging and the entire project unsettled and unnerved me. But none of that mattered once I was on my way.

# CHAPTER FOUR

# MEETING NELSON MANDELA

The gloomy hut at Jetty One where we waited for the ferry to Robben Island gave me my first taste of the hostility that Mandela must have suffered every day.

I had walked through the desolate shipyard in Cape Town's waterfront with Clifford Mailer and now we took our place with a dozen or more warders who had nothing but contempt for those who represented the prisoners. They were Afrikaners trained to impose the harshest possible regime on a band of men they regarded as traitors and terrorists. They were rude, sneering and refused to make way for us during embarkation.

They had certainly never had an Indian woman among them before, complete with sari and a dot on her forehead. They stared openly.

The sea was choppy and the whole trip felt dangerous. But all that mattered was what lay ahead of us, the most important meeting of my life.

On the island there was a short walk from the harbour to the basic little building where we would have our consultation. I could do nothing about my heart pounding. I was actually trembling, and couldn't seem to regain my composure.

The young warder who showed us in had asked me about the dot on my forehead, the bindi. I measured his contempt with my own and told him as a Hindu I had to meditate at dawn every day and then screw this device into my head. He stared at me wide-eyed.

Then Mandela was shown in. A tall impressive man whose dignity outweighed the degrading prison uniform he wore. We shook hands and introduced ourselves, then he hugged me warmly.

I forgot my professionalism in a second and blurted out: 'I wish you could feel my heart!' immediately feeling embarrassed. He smiled that Mandela smile. In his thirteen years on Robben Island this would have been the first physical contact he had had with a woman. Visits with Winnie were no-contact occasions where they were separated by a pane of glass and spoke only on a phone link, listened into by the warders.

What is more I think he enjoyed the obvious warmth I was showing him, and we also had important matters to discuss. Every visit for him was a lifeline to the outside world where he might bring some political influence to bear. He valued every minute, desperate for news about the movement and also about his comrades, friends and family.

I had to tell him that Zindzi needed our help and his signature. This was of course news to him and he was concerned about Winnie and how she was managing in Brandfort. There was no good reason to describe to him the utter misery of the life Winnie and Zindzi were leading, but the court papers in front of him were spelling it out anyway. He signed the application.

But he wanted to know a lot more. He asked me to convey messages to Oliver Tambo, the ANC leader in exile in Zambia. He wanted Tambo to know that he and the other Rivonia trialists were being held together and were able to support each other and that they were surviving Robben Island. He wanted him to know that their passion for the movement was stronger than ever and that Tambo and the others should keep up the momentum internationally.

'Tell him there must be an upsurge in outside pressure, in sanctions and protests,' he said.

Our consultation was by law deemed to be private, free from bugging. But I thought that was probably a myth and, sure enough, when I transgressed the rules by reaching into my briefcase and producing a gift of chocolates for Mandela the young warder stormed in and forbade it. Something about this crassness and pettiness totally enraged me. I unleashed my wrath on that warder, actually screaming at him.

Here was one of the greatest men of all time, reduced to the wretchedness of prison life by a regime motivated by nothing but hatred, and I was not allowed to show a tiny gesture of kindness. It absolutely incensed me.

But Mandela himself was bigger than that. He said it was unimportant, that warders had their whims and fancies, and to let him confiscate the chocolates; we had more important issues to discuss.

That was a lesson to me, a lesson in leadership.

I was absolutely taken aback when he told me he was not only reading Afrikaans literature but studying the language. I said this would horrify the youth back in Soweto where they were literally sacrificing their lives to protest against Afrikaans being taught in their schools. Many of them had already been brutally killed.

Mandela listened to me and did not argue. When I finished talking, he calmly and rationally explained the need to know, understand and learn the language and the culture. He said it was important to analyse the psyche and strategies of the enemy through their own language. How else to prepare for a counter-attack?

I deferred to this and found myself impressed by his insight and vision. I was learning a great deal.

We spent almost three hours together. I sat beside Mandela with Clifford across the table from him. As I showed him the documents about Zindzi he was able to make notes, and I realised he was writing key words and names for me to address without alerting the warder. He wrote down the names of comrades and asked me many political questions. Some of the people he enquired about were completely unknown to me. He was hungry for news and wanted to know about the ongoing trials for students who took part in the Soweto uprising.

I told him there was chaos and the youth were angry and joining the freedom fight in their droves. For all his dignity and status, Mandela was desperate for any snippet of news, any examples of hope in the progress he longed to see. His life was draining away in this godforsaken place and he needed to know that the battle was still being fought, that the sacrifices he and like-minded comrades had made were worthwhile.

It was hard to describe to him the changes taking place in the townships. The studied pace of the revolution that he knew, and the calm with which he was trying to lead it from Robben Island, was a world away from the craziness now going on elsewhere. Everything had changed since the Soweto uprising; the country was re-energised, angry. I hoped that what I was telling Mandela was gladdening his heart, lightening the load he had been carrying for so many years, and that he would have renewed hope now that the youth was solidly behind our movement for change.

When I came away from Robben Island I felt an all-consuming rage that Mandela, this great man with all his political potential, this natural leader and Xhosa chief, had had the indignity and cruelty of prison life imposed on him. And I was more certain than ever that my work as a lawyer and my commitment to the struggle were inseparable.

I was articled to a lawyer who had been trying to force me to separate these two issues ever since I had used his letterhead to appeal worldwide for clemency for Solomon Mahlangu. But Ismail Ayob was wrong, and after meeting Mandela I knew I would be able to find the strength to follow my own beliefs and try to make a difference, even though Ayob would surely dismiss me from my articles. A sort of hell was currently being unleashed in the country and I wanted to be among people who had the courage to confront it.

Through Mandela, many other political prisoners on the island now became aware they could enlist my support. Dozens of them had never had legal representation. They began to write to me for help with troubles they were having with the Prisons Department. They were being punished for insubordination, or they wanted permission to study; they needed funds and some of them needed help to contact their families. I became their lawyer, friend, confidante and social worker. My meeting with Mandela had opened up a whole new dimension in my work for the movement.

Over time, I came to represent members of every political party on Robben Island – the ANC, PAC (Pan African Congress), AZAPO (the Azanian People's Organisation), BCM (Black Consciousness Movement), SACP (South African Communist Party), SWAPO (South-West Africa People's Organisation) and many others. A long line of prisoners would make appointments to see me, and at one stage I had to give them just five minutes each as they filed in and out of the consulting room on the island.

Among the politics the prisoners also brought up intensely personal matters, which I could not resist. For example, a prisoner with Mandela in B Section, the maximum security wing, had not been in touch with his family for more than ten years. His name was Justice Mpanza. All he had was a scribbled address on a scrap of paper.

It made sense to us just to go to Kwazulu Natal (KZN) in the distant east of South Africa and knock on the door. But this family, like so many others, had been forced out of their home by the Group Areas Act. The neighbourhood was derelict. No one nearby had heard of them.

But Mpanza was desperate. He had a son, he told us, who he hadn't seen since he was a baby. Mpanza had joined the ANC and gone to training camps, living underground and unable to make contact with his family. He didn't even know if they were alive. He desperately wanted to know about his son.

We had left messages with a number of people in KZN and to our astonishment, one day a young man dressed in rough clothes, with a shy awkward demeanour, came into my office in Johannesburg. He had travelled straight from the bush and had hitched a lift to the train. He told me that he knew his father was on Robben Island and he was anxious to see him. I found him somewhere to stay with the Council of Churches, and we set about applying for a visit to the island.

It is impossible to describe the joy and tears that came with that journey. I had gone earlier to tell his father that he would be coming. Now they were reunited, father and son. Despite the untold cruelty of being obliged to sit apart, separated by a pane of glass, they gradually got to know each other during regular visits.

I was gratified by these successes, but my office was becoming inundated with similar tracing requests and more. We had to find girlfriends and babies, friends and family members. We had to track down some dry-cleaning that one of our clients had had to abandon when he was arrested on the Swaziland border. Another prisoner had his belongings searched by the police and now his favourite cap had disappeared. We found the dry-cleaning, and the cap.

Aside from this, Ismail Ayob was increasingly demonstrating that he did not have the stomach for hardcore political activity. I see now a certain irony in this, given that he knew only of my very public behaviour. Knowledge of what was really going on might have had him running for the hills. My profile had been considerably heightened by my closeness to Nelson Mandela and the comrades on Robben Island.

One day I received a cryptic message from a courier who came to the office on foot. I was to go to a wooded area of Booysens, park my car at a certain spot, proceed twenty steps forward, ten steps to the left, fifteen steps to the north and so on until I found Cedric Mayson waiting for me. He was on a motorbike.

He wanted to recruit me into an underground cell under

the command of Thabo Mbeki who was in exile. Our mandate would be to investigate, research and report on security installations in South Africa and report back to sabotage teams.

Cedric was a former Methodist minister. He was in a powerful position to carry out anti-apartheid activities in the name of Christianity and spread the word to others worldwide. Together with another of the movement's leading lights, Beyers Naudé, who had turned his back on the racist Dutch Reformed Church and the Broederbond, he had formed the Christian Institute of South Africa in 1963. A religious God-fearing organisation dedicated to bringing down the apartheid government with all necessary force, it was invaluable to the ANC.

This meant they gave their wholehearted support to the armed wing, MK. They were inviting me to join in secret operations to smuggle blueprint plans of government installations to the ANC leaders in Lusaka. Trained operatives would then be drafted from the MK camps in Angola, Mozambique, Botswana and Swaziland and we would help to get them over the border.

The MK soldiers' mission was to bomb hard targets, to carry out sabotage that would cause chaos in the community, and make the country ungovernable. Our network would help to smuggle those who carried out these acts back to safety.

My own mindset was that I would do anything necessary to bring down the apartheid government. I agreed to join the underground cell with an unusual mix of people: Cedric and Beyers; Enoch Duma, a well-travelled journalist; Vuyisile Mdleleni, a prominent youth leader; Jackie Selebi, a dedicated activist; and Auret van Heerden, a white student.

Our meetings were held at a church hall at St Peter's Seminary in Rosettenville, Johannesburg. Times and dates were shrouded in secrecy. I would be informed by a coded message sent to my office to be there at a certain time, usually at short notice.

Each of us arrived in borrowed vehicles, never using our own cars, and no one in our families or workplaces knew where we were. Lookouts were posted close to the building and occasionally an alarm would be raised: strangers were approaching. We would pause in our perusal of lists of names and places, our sharing of floor plans of government installations, and our arrangements to provide transport, clothes and shelter for operatives soon to arrive.

Once we actually tore up and ate our notes. Another time we disposed of hours of hard work by shredding it and flushing it down the toilet. On another occasion we burnt all the papers in our possession.

Because of my easy access to Robben Island, I was uniquely useful to the group. I would return to the mainland with coded messages from the ANC High Command, consult with my fellow members of the cell, and compose reports for Oliver Tambo. There were undercover reconnoitre expeditions to plan, messages to channel back and forth to the leadership, and always the social support of families.

Meeting Vuyi Mdleleni recently – now the director of a mining corporation – he reminded me of the grass-roots nature of some of our work together. There was a comrade who assembled second-hand car parts into useable transport for MK operatives, and these needed to be disposed of when there was an arrest or a police raid. If there wasn't time to dispose of them to comrades close to the border, those vehicles inevitably ended up at my husband's business premises, where he hid them and later got rid of them.

Sometimes there were changes of clothes in the boot of the vehicle, sometimes food for the brave young guys slipping across the border. On one occasion I had a consignment of hundreds of illicit ANC pamphlets which I was driving around with, intending to deliver to Beyers or other comrades. These pamphlets were called 'Sechaba', produced in Lusaka as part of the ANC's strategy and dissemination of information.

Once I carried a stash of AK-47 rifles. I was acting for a client, Kingsley Sithole, charged with treason, and received an urgent message from a family friend of his to retrieve a bag full of weapons from an address in Soweto where he had hidden them. They had to be moved before the security police tracked them down.

I managed to sneak into Soweto with a messenger from my office and we went to the address I was given. We found a black canvas bag underneath a car outside the house. There were at least half-a-dozen AKs in it. He'd told me to dump them in marshy ground but all we could do was to put the bag in the boot of my car as I needed to rush back to my office on a legal matter. I didn't have time to dump the rifles anywhere, I had to get to court. I was totally stressed, turning it over in my mind during the forty-minute journey to Springs. The bag was bulky and dangerous, the AK-47 – the weapon of choice for all MK operatives – itself was a dread word.

My messenger went along with whatever I decided moment by moment, although he was at least as stressed as I was. On our return from court several hours later, I arranged for a comrade from the Congress of South African Students (COSAS) to collect the bag and its deadly contents. By then

I'd had the guns with me at my office and subsequently at my home. Finally the comrade came to my house at night and we did a rapid transfer from my car boot to his, inside the garage.

Life at that time was founded on risk and you had to take the risk even though you knew what the consequences could be. We didn't shy away from it; there were risks every day.

Vuyi described how he always had a bag ready for when the police called. He'd have a tracksuit in it, and trainer shoes without laces, all ready for the knock on the door which would lead inevitably to prison. The process had become so routine for him that he knew to remove the laces, as they were considered a suicide risk and would be confiscated on admission to prison.

'I never worked out how you could commit suicide using a pair of laces,' he said. 'The police said we might hang ourselves with them but that seemed unlikely. Besides, every one of us was in a fighting mood and I don't know of anyone who wanted to kill himself.'

He recalled how nothing mattered in those days except trying to keep one step ahead of the enemy. 'There was a sort of fever in the townships in the late seventies,' he said. 'There was only one subject of conversation: the struggle. Every boy wanted to fight to get dignity for black people. Our only vehicle for a while was the Black Consciousness Movement, which taught us to be black and proud, to have self-realisation. Allegiance to the ANC came later.

'We were living side by side with death or persecution. That's all there was.'

He described vividly what spurred him on to fight, to take up arms, to do anything necessary to cast off enslavement: 'I remember being in our house and my father's boss called to talk to him about some work issue. He had a job in a steel-casting factory. In those days all the older men wore hats, even in the house.

'My father actually took his hat off just to speak to his white foreman on the phone. That really got to me, it made me angry to see how far we had been beaten down.'

He and I remembered also the way black people would have to go to the window of a fish-and-chip shop, never inside. They couldn't enter, they would have to eat their food outside whatever the weather. 'We were treated like vermin in our own country,' he said. 'Young guys like me were not going to take that any more.'

His radicalisation was completed after listening to a heroic figure called Abram Tiro who had been a law student when he was expelled from a university in the north for being involved in political activities. He came to Vuyi's school in Soweto as a supply teacher and set about radicalising the youth in the classrooms. 'Many of us needed little persuasion, our hearts were already in it,' said Vuyi. 'He just helped to fire us up, to show us the way.'

Tiro was blown up by a parcel bomb sent by the apartheid security police in 1974.

At that period Vuyi and I were both realising that our devotion to the Black Consciousness Movement was leading us logically to the might of the ANC, and that we should embrace this. Steve Biko's BCM was a philosophy that helped us to walk tall and we would remain loyal to it always, but the ANC had mastered the politics. My membership of our underground cell further persuaded me that this was the future. Only the ANC could provide the firepower to achieve our goals.

The notion of violence, causing explosions, blowing up powerful institutions, did not come naturally to me. But I found myself wholeheartedly behind it. Mandela himself, a peace-loving man, had been driven to it as a last resort. He formed the MK, the military wing of the ANC, only when the political party itself had been banned and outlawed.

I too longed to do substantial harm to the apartheid regime.

And I was very well-placed. Vuyi described my usefulness: 'We all had letters written, sometimes just scribbled on a piece of paper, for our families to take to you in case we were picked up by police,' he said. 'We needed to know that you would take on our cases and fight the detention or banning order or imprisonment we were facing. We needed to see you there when we appeared in court.'

Locked in an office drawer, gathered over the years, I had piles of these letters, just scraps of paper some of them, authorising me to represent comrades.

Chaotic as it was in some ways, there was a structure to the underground cell's activities. With Cedric and Beyers I would receive reports from further down the line and I could send instructions from above – from Lusaka – to others in either direction along that line. It was a hive of constant activity, as funds came into our hands for disbursement to MK operatives on the move, and transport and people needed co-ordinating. We supervised dangerous recces, then helped to draw up plans and send them off to the leadership.

There were no mobile phones in those days and it would have been dangerous to use landlines. So I drew on help from staff and friends, even family members, to carry messages and documents to Harare in Zimbabwe, to London and Lusaka. My brother Raj once took documents to Thabo Mbeki in

Zimbabwe, and later I sent my own professional staff, junior lawyers like Hanif Vally, to Lusaka to consult with the ANC Executive for important directives. Hanif later became one of the main cross-examiners at the Truth and Reconciliation Commission set up to investigate the true depths of apartheid.

All the documents we handled were coded. Once I sent my friend Espree Pather to Lusaka to deliver some paperwork to Oliver Tambo. In addition to the secret documents, we had given her pipe tobacco and a bottle of good malt whisky for Tambo. Espree set off from the airport smartly-dressed in a sari and wearing a nice bindi dot, looking like a tourist. All the papers were sealed and she had no idea what they contained. But she had memorised the code – for example, Alpha meant John, Beta meant Ismail, and so on. There would be names and places and structures.

These were precious documents which had come to me via a brave Wits University student called Ben Greyling. With an associate who had been conscripted into the South African Defence Force, he had managed to steal blueprints of the security regime's plans to send hit squads to ANC training camps in neighbouring states. There were to be cross-border raids and assassinations.

Both men were later tried and convicted under the Suppression of Communism Act, that all-embracing piece of legislation designed to stamp on any form of anti-government activity.

Espree's role was vital. She had spent hours in my house memorising the secret codes. She seemed calm. But it turned out that when she arrived in Lusaka, a gang of big burly MK men boarded her plane on the runway, brandishing weapons, and she went numb with fear. They were intending to protect and guide her to Thabo Mbeki, but nevertheless, when she saw them she was terrified. They took her to a hotel and five minutes later Thabo arrived to bundle her off to his house.

She had thought this would be simple. But instead it was heavy-duty, a situation she'd never been in before. I had sent her because she looked so respectable and law-abiding. Now that worked against her, and she went to pieces. I found out on her return that Thabo had become frustrated. Espree couldn't remember the code, she just went blank. Thabo was annoyed and told her the all-important documents meant nothing if there was no code with which to crack them. Nevertheless, she stayed a few days, enjoying her time with the ANC leadership and even cooking for them. But she was no activist and not sufficiently worldly-wise to carry out an undercover mission.

The abortive trip to Lusaka taught me to always send someone more confident in future. We had no training in such things, and just learnt as we went along that we needed a formidable team. For example, *Rand Daily Mail* reporter Gabu Tugwana, now a spokesman for Johannesburg City Council, was perfectly level-headed and also motivated, a comrade. He and several others were willing to carry messages to the leadership in Lusaka, and were properly trained to take on covert missions.

During this time special forces went into Lesotho, Zambia and Mozambique where they gunned down dozens of our guerrilla comrades in a raid intended to undermine us.

These were difficult times. We were continually on our guard against infiltrators, and there were many. On one occasion, I managed to smuggle a bundle of crucial documents out to Lusaka where Oliver Tambo kept them in a vault. But they disappeared and we heard later that informers had been able to infiltrate even at that level.

Closer to home, I had succeeded in sending a detailed report on the layout and accessibility of the Durban law courts: they were to be bombed in a major operation. My good friends and comrades Victoria and Griffiths Mxenge, both human rights lawyers – both later cruelly assassinated – had given me the documents personally when we had supper together in Durban. I had taken the documents home in an envelope and hidden them under a pretty gold filigree box I kept in my bedroom.

The next day, in a rush to get to a court hearing in Johannesburg, I realised I had left the envelope behind. I received an anguished phone call from my neighbour Hajira's husband, Dr Mahomed Momoniat. Someone had clearly informed on me. The police were raiding the house with my mother hysterical inside. By the time I spoke to her on the phone they had ripped open every mattress and cushion and even opened every can in the kitchen store-cupboard. She told me they had eventually left but had warned her they would return with dogs. I told her to lock the doors and open them to no one.

Soon afterwards, the police were back, using loudspeakers to say they were about to break down the door. I told her she must give in and let them into the house. By the time I got home there was complete chaos. Pictures had been pulled off the walls and the frames broken open, furniture was smashed and the stuffing from cushions and pillows was all over the floor.

I found a way carefully through the destruction and reached my bedroom. By some miracle the filigree box was intact and the precious envelope was still underneath it.

I sent the documents successfully to Lusaka. As a result, several Durban court buildings were badly damaged in explosions, with no casualties.

Two MK operatives were charged with sabotage and when I represented them in court we were all three astonished and horrified to see the prosecution produce a handwritten note from one of them announcing 'mission accomplished'. Edgar Mhlobo, who had been vehemently denying the charges against him, fainted dead away in the witness box. His co-accused, Ben Martins – who many years later became Minister of Minerals and Energy, then Minister of Correctional Services – clung to the railings of the dock until his knuckles were white.

There had been infiltration at a high level, far more serious than the informers we knew about on the country's borders with neighbouring states. We knew many MK members were getting arrested on the borders and assumed local people were informing in exchange for money.

Infiltration in Lusaka itself was of much greater concern. And these government stooges were audacious. One day we had held a big commemoration celebration for the Soweto uprising, in the Johannesburg Indian Social Workers' Association Hall, and a large number of people came back to my house afterwards. We realised there was a man moving about comfortably from group to group but that nobody actually knew who had invited him. Joe Veriava cornered him. He was of Indian origin, but an informer, and Joe landed some punches on him. The next day, he went to Dr Asvat's clinic in Soweto and beat him up in retaliation. It was becoming the law of the jungle.

My boss Ismail Ayob knew little of these activities, and even less about my membership of an underground cell dedicated to sabotage. But he was becoming increasingly uneasy about the continual police presence in his office and the anonymous phone calls threatening raids or arrests.

When Steve Biko, a giant of the revolution, to the outrage of all decent-thinking people worldwide was brutally killed in 1977 during police detention, I addressed a huge angry meeting in Lenasia. At the Regina Mundi Church in Soweto, cornerstone of the liberation movement, I prayed and wept with the crowd in mourning and exhorted them to continue Biko's work. I was becoming too much of a public figure for Ayob's liking

At the same time, the ANC leadership, in South Africa and in exile in Lusaka, was constantly in touch with me from the time I first visited Mandela. Prominent revolutionaries like Dr Yusuf Dadoo and Joe Modise would regularly send messages to my office via a courier.

We set up a routine using public phone boxes, sending the numbers through and making a date and time for calls.

I was getting a lot of calls at home too. My friend's little boy answered my phone once and called out: 'Auntie Priscilla, there's a man called Oliver who wants to speak to you.' It was Oliver Tambo asking about comrades in trouble in the townships, asking me to get details or find an MK operative who had gone missing.

Among the heavy tasks there were quirky problems too. Mandela had sent a message asking me to visit him on Robben Island to discuss an urgent matter. It seemed that Winnie, like the loose cannon she was, had rather recklessly sold film-making rights to more than one person. Two major black Hollywood stars were claiming they had the sole rights to the story of her marriage and comradeship with Mandela and both had already paid a substantial sum as an advance.

Mandela found this embarrassing in the extreme. Lawyers were threatening to sue and it was imperative that no court case went ahead, demeaning the ANC and putting Winnie in a bad light.

I studied the contracts and told him firmly that I could not defend Winnie in this matter. It was indefensible. I sent a courier to Lusaka with the documents, passing the headache on to Oliver Tambo. He found a way to cancel both contracts and may even have refunded the complainants.

All these clandestine activities were making Ayob nervous. He wanted a trouble-free life and that was not possible with me around. He used my 'insubordinate' behaviour over Solomon Mahlangu's death sentence to bring our working relationship to an end. I had continued to feel aggrieved by his lack of support during the Mahlangu case, and now I walked out with pleasure, spelling out to him my intention to combine the law with activism for the rest of my career.

I felt strongly that I had seen the landmark Mahlangu case through to its end, appearing in court every day of the trial. But Ayob had never turned up, not even on the day of sentencing, and I held this against him. He had let me down and the whole international campaign had rested on my shoulders.

But now I had no job. Back home in Lenasia I talked to friends and someone suggested talking to Shun Chetty, a leading light in the Black Consciousness Movement who was dealing with many trials emanating from the Soweto riots.

One evening around this time, I answered a knock on the door and found Ayob's brother Omar waiting to see me. He was a kind and gentle man, sending apologies from Ayob and asking me to return to work at his office. But I was adamant, I had to say no.

Later Mandela himself, a man I found hard to refuse, tried to instruct me to return to Ayob. I told him that would never happen. Instead, in 1978, I took up the offer from Shun Chetty to be his professional assistant and immediately knew it was the right decision. Ilona Kleinschmidt Tip, his secretary, became my lifelong friend.

Now I was working for a man who wouldn't mind me using his letterheads. He was a radical with a huge BCM caseload. He was happy to give me free rein, preparing the defence for many members of the Soweto Students' Representative Council.

Chetty had been Steve Biko's personal lawyer. I felt I had found my rightful place, close to the heart of the action.

His office was in a busy shopping complex, the Oriental Plaza, an Indian hub. The office itself was vibrant, busy from morning to night with activists and student groups. People just walked in, looking for advice or setting up planning meetings. The BCM had spawned several groups and they all met here.

We had union meetings and student meetings and took on seemingly unwinnable cases. In 1978 there was a strong need to commemorate the brave youth who took part in the 1976 Soweto uprising. They wanted church services and a rally. Chetty's office was the natural focal point for everyone to gather and discuss these plans. We found venues and speakers for them, ours was the law firm activists naturally turned to.

The first commemoration service for Soweto was in Lenasia at the Civic Theatre where I gave the opening speech with Sadeque Veriava, brother of my friend Joe. They were both BCM members and close to Biko. I was suddenly meeting all my heroes – Jairus Kgokong, Kenneth Rachidi, Tom Mantata,

Nat Serache and many others. And they were beginning to look to me for advice. In the past I had had a good launch into the world of the Mandelas and their close comrades. But this was the real thrust, the place where I belonged.

One of the greatest heroines of our times, the fantastic Lilian Ngoyi, arrived one day to see me. She was a legend, a brave woman from a modest background who nevertheless brought 20,000 women together for one of the biggest public events in South Africa's history, in 1956, leading them to march on the Union Buildings, the seat of government in Pretoria, to protest at the pass laws.

She was a leading figure in the ANC's Women's League and a great orator. She had undergone two long periods in solitary confinement in prison, and was banned several times. In her day, she had addressed enthralled crowds in Europe as well as South Africa. She had a crowd of supporters in Trafalgar Square in central London listening to her every word.

But the restrictions of those banning orders, one after the other, had curtailed her activities and rendered her virtually penniless. I was shocked beyond belief to see her – this woman we had idolised and sung songs about – looking like a pauper. She was old and drab, dressed in shabby clothes with no demeanour or dignity. She needed my help with a family issue and I did everything I could to support her. She died a year later, never to see the glorious results of her life's work.

Those were hard days, continually knocking us backwards.

My activities with the ANC cell had been forced to come to an abrupt end with the arrest of Auret van Heerden, one of our white members, and we feared that his detention, which was very likely to involve coercion and torture, might break him down and expose us.

His detention led to panic among other comrades throughout the country and many began to leave. I received instructions that I should also leave for my own safety, but I stubbornly refused. For me fleeing was not an option. I could not live in exile, where it would be impossible to work as a lawyer, and while my own country was burning.

My good comrades Jackie Selebi and Enoch Duma had gone over the border, trying without success to persuade me to go with them. They could continue to be used effectively by the ANC to further its cause, but my place was in South Africa, taking the dreaded ferry journey regularly to Robben Island and working in the courts and townships to support people in trouble and need. I had spent years working up a unique network that connected the High Command in prison to the freedom fighters on the street and all the way to the leadership in Lusaka. Fleeing for my own safety, to my mind, would be desertion. It was out of the question.

Now there was no longer a cell with direction from Thabo Mbeki by remote control – we had been forced to abandon that – but all the outlets I needed were still in place and I was still receiving direction from him in exile. Couriers could still drop into my office with coded messages, Mandela and the senior ANC leaders were still available on Robben Island, and I had my own ways of collecting important operational documents and getting them to Lusaka.

Through Shun Chetty I was also meeting prominent members of the BCM and I still felt great loyalty to the organisation which had first fired up my activism. I spent a fruitful and satisfying year at his law practice.

Then, early one morning, I received a phone call telling me he was in Botswana, having fled there overnight with his wife in the face of certain arrest and imprisonment. I was numb with shock, dazed and aghast at this news. I got up and showered and decided to see him face to face. My mother was staying with me, so I told her we were driving to Botswana together.

It became big news that Shun Chetty had fled, but I was the first to know. He told me the Law Society – the sell-out band of race-prejudiced lawyers who ran our professional body – had demanded to look at his books. They wanted to see a list of his clients, they wanted to examine the accounts. They planned trouble for him.

Chetty was politically brave and he was a smart man, but he knew his books were not well kept. He knew the Law Society minions would unearth sloppy records and that he could be struck off. Their real agenda would be to remove him from the political scene, possibly into a prison cell, and he knew that too.

Chetty told me on the phone that he felt bad for me. The Law Society was confiscating all his files and his practice would be shut down. He was sorry, he would make arrangements to pay us all.

During the exhausting trip to Gaborone, I considered my future. I realised all this could one day happen to me if I persisted with my career. I could tell that Chetty was never coming back, so I had to make some decisions. I tried to explain all this to my bewildered mother. She was worried for me but had no way of really understanding the situation I was in, or why.

We drove for many hours, arriving at the Holiday Inn feeling extremely stressed. Chetty and his wife were waiting for us in the foyer. He looked very upset; he was apologetic and full of concern for us and his clients.

He gave me detailed instructions about dealing with outstanding cases, and we had lunch together. It was a sombre affair; Chetty was irritatingly sheepish and defensive whereas I was in a complete flap. I had no idea what I was going to do.

My mother and I didn't stay. We left and drove all the way back home. I had just wanted to get away from all the explaining and apologies. I felt strongly that Chetty should have kept his books in order, knowing it could become a weak point and a target for the Law Society. Instead, I well knew he had led a full social life to the detriment of his practice.

He remained in exile and was of course struck off as a lawyer after examination of his chaotic book-keeping. But he successfully landed a job in Geneva with the United Nations Human Rights Commission, only returning to South Africa more than twenty years later when we had achieved democracy. In 1999, Chetty applied for reinstatement as a lawyer and with others I tried to help. But Chetty died in 2000. He was eventually reinstated posthumously in 2006.

When he fled South Africa it had felt like a personal blow. I had felt abandoned, lost, with no plan for the future.

The day after our understated lunch in Gaborone, I was contacted at home by the Law Society, who summonsed me to appear before them. I went to their office and told them where Chetty was; everyone knew by then anyway. The newspapers were full of it.

Then I claimed attorney-client privilege and said I would tell them no more. I accompanied them to our office and had the miserable task of clearing away his personal things, photographs, diaries and journals.

I went home and talked to my husband about the future. I had no money or capital but I had plenty of fighting spirit and a great deal of learned knowledge as well as the unique inspiration of many visits to Robben Island. I called our secretary Ilona and asked if she would continue to work with me. She agreed, and with the support of my husband Reg and our friends, I decided it was worth launching my own practice. Looking back, that was daring in the extreme. I was already known as an activist, and now I was making myself even more visible to the security police by becoming the first black woman to start her own law firm.

So I found an office in Abbey House, a block in Commissioner Street, Johannesburg, close to where I had started my career. People donated furniture and equipment. My brother's friend Bridge gave me a beautiful big desk and two very fancy swivel chairs.

I registered the business: Priscilla Jana and Associates. I had to get a fidelity fund – a statutary requirement which insured clients against their loss – and I had an impressive sign painted. It was pale beige with bold black writing. I had arrived. And to prove it, my first client was the handsome young son of Walter and Albertina Sisulu, beloved stalwarts of the anti-apartheid movement.

Ilona had told me he was in the waiting room and wanted to consult me. My heart skipped a beat when he walked in. Zwelakhe was incredibly smartly dressed, dapper even, in a three-piece suit. He had the polished manners of a highly educated and well-travelled man. He had just returned from America after completing his Nieman Fellowship Studies at Harvard, a rare honour for a black South African.

Zwelakhe greeted me in his deep husky voice and sat down in one of my impressive swivel chairs. He wanted me to represent his mother, who was being prosecuted for contravening her banning order. It was going to be an honour, a privilege.

But as Zwelakhe talked he gradually leaned back in the chair. Suddenly, as the chair gave way, he did a complete backwards somersault and landed on the floor. The entire office staff rushed in on hearing the commotion and I am ashamed to say that I was convulsed with helpless laughter. Zwelakhe was not amused; he was furious.

But we got through that somehow and he took me on as the Sisulu family lawyer. I never lost one of their cases.

Albertina herself – universally known as MaSisulu – was the embodiment of *ubuntu*, that very African notion of togetherness that means literally 'I am because of you'. She was utterly devoted to her husband, Walter, the leading light and éminence grise of the ANC who was serving a life sentence on Robben Island, and a caring loving mother to their children.

MaSisulu gave herself completely and utterly to relieve the distress and poverty of others and was self-effacing and humble. House arrests and banning orders were repeatedly served against her and she was prosecuted and imprisoned for furthering the aims of the ANC and for treason. It was extraordinary how this motherly, unassuming and softly spoken woman could also be so assertive and ferocious in her dedication to the movement.

I felt honoured to be asked to represent her and her family. But there was hardly time to work on that before a huge case landed on my desk. The Black Municipal Workers Union had called a strike over pay and conditions. Uncollected rubbish had piled up all over Johannesburg and was rotting.

The workers were mainly migrants who lived in the single-men's hostels in Johannesburg. Their leader was the charismatic

Joe Mavi. Barely literate himself, he could nevertheless pull in thousands of people for an impromptu protest in the streets.

The government responded by trucking the workers back to their homelands. They said the men were only allowed into Johannesburg for work; they had chosen to stop work and now they must go home.

It was a chaotic time. I decided to launch an urgent application to stop the removal of workers in the High Court. We had to take statements from individuals and we were writing their affidavits under lamp-posts as the men were being piled into trucks in the dark. Many of them also turned up at my office, hungry and homeless. There were so many that I ended up with every bit of furniture broken. My husband brought in emergency supplies of bread and peanut butter. He couldn't think of any other way to feed hundreds of people.

We finally got our court documents in order around 11 p.m. The court registrar had to find the duty judge, Nestadt. He turned up at the High Court very grumpy, having pulled on his robes in the middle of the night. It took him just five minutes to dismiss our application.

Clifford Mailer and I had been sitting it out for hours in the corridor with no food or drink. We had expected to lose, and we lost.

The strike continued, as did the chaos in my office.

We had many other cases to deal with. After 1976 in Soweto, there were student uprisings in every city and township. We were running around dealing with students arrested for burning buses, attacking police vehicles with stones, and a lot of public order offences.

We had many setbacks, losing cases and never receiving fees.

Eventually, church organisations started sending us money. These groups, under the umbrella of the South African Council of Churches, were a great source of support and comfort to many penniless activists in those times. In Cape Town they ran a boarding-house which gave refuge to hundreds of family members of the political prisoners on Robben Island. It was a place of shelter and true charity, bringing desperate people together at a time when they needed a safe haven, somewhere to stay overnight on their way to and from the island.

By now my office was carrying the majority of the country's political cases. My friend and secretary Ilona Kleinschmidt Tip recalls those days as chaotic but full of good heart. She reminded me recently that our office was 'a haven and a home, a family' for those in need.

Her former husband, Horst Kleinschmidt, a formidable ANC member who ran the International Defence and Aid Fund (IDAF) in London – the front organisation for funding the legal defence needed by activists – told me that the ANC wanted to support us. We were carrying the country's activism. There was not a political leader we didn't represent in exile or in South Africa.

I had brought in many activist lawyers, good people like Caroline Heaton-Nicholls, Hanif Vally, Ike Grant, Salim Ahmed, Salim Ibrahim, Riaz Saloojee, Graham Dyson, Dilip Morar, Chris Watters, Richard Spoor, Julie Mahomed and others. There was a young Chinese woman called Joyce Nam, but her mother removed her from my practice, saying we were terrorists. It was invigorating to have backing, together with the freedom to go full steam ahead with a legal practice challenging the government, the enemy, at every step.

They were adrenalin-fuelled days when we never ran out of energy. We were a fighting force with all the intellectual weapons we needed. But it could be exhausting. We couldn't resist any challenge. When an Indian family, the Naidoos, were thrown out of their home under the Group Areas Act in the Mayfair suburb of Johannesburg, designated for whites-only, Joe Veriava and I slept on the pavements with them in solidarity. We only left when the local priest pleaded with us for the safety of others.

At the same time, I was being constantly harassed by the security police. They would phone at least once weekly and tell me to report to their headquarters, the notorious high-rise block in John Vorster Square where so many were detained, tortured and beaten to death in those days.

They wanted to know why I was at a particular place, or rally, or meeting and who had been there with me. I was always very stroppy with them, telling them I had the right to be there. They would keep me waiting for long periods without a cup of tea or any water. They tried to intimidate me by saying there were ways and means they could use to get information out of me.

It was intended to undermine me, but on the contrary, it spurred me on. Sometimes they came to my house, demanding a list of comrades' names. I got to know some of them. There was a tall mixed-race officer called Lt. Sonn and a big burly man called Col. Heysteck. Another one was blond-haired and blue-eyed, a sort of devil, Lt. van Niekerk. Occasionally they just walked uninvited into my office. They had the right to raid the place and search it from top to bottom.

One day a member of my staff disappeared during a raid and I found him afterwards clinging to the drainpipes outside, out of sight. If he had fallen from the second floor he would have suffered serious injury. He was Penuell Maduna, later to be appointed Minister of Minerals and Energy, then Minister of Home Affairs, and later Minister of Justice in our new South Africa.

We laugh about it now but he first arrived at Abbey House in a pinstripe suit, carrying a briefcase. He had no law degree and had been part of the famous Zululand trial accused of public violence for boycotting university along with many others. They were acquitted, and Maduna was set on a career in law.

He said he wanted a job. But I couldn't article him as he did not have the necessary academic qualifications. I could only take him on as an unqualified clerk. He was a big confident man, burly and fearless. I would ask him to monitor a case in court then hear afterwards to my horror that he had borrowed a lawyer's gown and conducted a defence. He was so keen that he would often be in the office before me in the morning. He would call me at home to warn me, 'The dogs are here', meaning a police raid.

It did not deter me that I was constantly harassed, far from it. I had experienced trouble for many years and knew I was probably a target for some sort of punishment.

I had travelled to Lesotho at the request of Dr Yusuf Dadoo, founder member of the South African Communist Party and a powerful leader whose passion was to link the country's Indian population and its struggle to the African majority for the sake of a united front. He had been forced into exile and now contacted me to press me to join the ANC underground cell he was running. I was now swamped with legal cases and felt I was already running my own network and could not commit to another cell. But I agreed to travel to Lesotho to help a heroic lawyer and teacher, Phyllis Naidoo, who had been seriously injured by a letter-bomb.

She had been running a formidable operation as an MK leader, using her law practice in Durban in a similar way to my activities in Johannesburg. She had many former Robben Island detainees as her office messengers, including Jacob Zuma – later to become South Africa's president. I was able to visit her in hospital and bring her some comfort and encouragement, but I continued to refuse to join another underground cell.

However, I did continue to carry out public demonstrations of my fierce opposition to the government and all who supported it. When Chief Buthelezi, head of the Inkatha Freedom Party, gave a talk in Lenasia, I caused a riot in the meeting by accusing him of being a government stooge and demanding his resignation. He was part of a structure in KZN which had official support and he was a sell-out. I had a lot of support for my stance but increasingly it was my name that ended up at the top of the wanted list.

At another event held by sell-outs from the South African Indian Council, where the key speaker was Dr J. N. Reddy, I broke up the meeting by throwing eggs and tomatoes. Like many Indian people I saw the council as a stooge for the government. The newspapers next day named me as a rabble-rouser and a hooligan. I was getting a reputation.

When advocate Ismail Mahomed, who had become my mentor over the years, approached police to compile a defence for me against harassment and threats of detention, they handed him the weighty file they had built up against me. He was livid with me, ranting and raving about the risks

I had taken over the years. He'd had no idea of the depth of my involvement in the struggle.

There was an inevitable conclusion to this sort of notoriety. I had seen it happen to Winnie, to MaSisulu, to many clients and some dear friends.

The government had invented the perfect antidote to the solidarity of our mass movement: the banning order. The end of life as you know it. All public and personal activity other than a robotic form of existence was forbidden. A prison sentence loomed over you at every moment.

Steve Biko told me once that a banning order was like being in a prison where you are your own jailer. I was about to find out what that felt like.

# CHAPTER FIVE

# SILENCED BY THE GOVERNMENT

It was a chilly Monday evening in late August 1979 when my husband opened the door to a smiling member of the security police.

Officer Dietleef was a familiar figure to us. He seemed to be especially assigned to harass me, smirking openly whenever I saw him on the corner of the street or sitting outside my house in an unmarked car, watching and waiting.

Now he was looking positively happy. He insisted on seeing me privately, away from neighbours and friends who were visiting. I showed him into the dining room as my heart sank. This was no routine visit to take me in for questioning. This was something I had dreaded for years.

In his hand Dietleef held a small booklet and he was reading me a charge under the Suppression of Communism Act that stated I was deemed a threat to the safety and security of the State. He handed me a banning order for five years and it felt like a death sentence. The death of all my anti-apartheid activities, perhaps the death of my law practice, only recently opened.

I was so stunned and angry that I could not speak. I knew the restrictions very well. From that moment on I could be in the company of only one person at a time, aside from a doctor or a lawyer. I could take no part in any political activities and I could not leave the Johannesburg municipal area. I was to be under curfew in my house from 6 p.m. each day until 6 a.m. the next day. Every Friday I would have to attend the police headquarters at John Vorster Square and sign a book to record my compliance with the banning order.

For five years my life would be on hold. In that instant, I felt my busy social and political life had come to an end. I thought about my ageing mother living in Durban. How would I ever get to see her and care for her?

I knew what a banning order could do, and what it was intended to do. It broke people down, even strong people, and it cancelled out the one aspect of the struggle that kept us going – togetherness. Even Mandela in his cold prison cell on Robben Island had the comfort of comrades around him. He had life-saving solidarity and *ubuntu*.

My situation was by contrast a prison cell without bars. The Act gave security police the right to observe and monitor my movements, bug my phone, and question my friends and acquaintances. They enjoyed banning orders. They believed it would drive activists into exile, and as long as they left white-dominated South Africa that was a good result.

I would be allowed to continue working as a lawyer but be restricted to cases in the Johannesburg Court. For security reasons, most cases of detention, alleged sabotage, breaches of banning order and the like were heard in courts outside main cities. So I would not be able to represent my clients properly or even consult with them to prepare their cases while they were held in prisons in remote areas.

As I signed Dietleef's paperwork acknowledging the order, I could hear the commotion elsewhere in the house. My husband had warned our guests not to come to me. From that moment we could not talk as a group.

Joe Veriava was there and called the press. I could hear comrades and friends arriving to commiserate. I could not talk to them. I was unable to see visitors, friends, family, well-wishers or neighbours. There would be no socialising, no speeches, no public statements, no press comments, no meetings or rallies. I have known people to collapse and weep under this pressure, but that wasn't me. I was quietly furious, livid. And extremely anxious about my mother.

The pernicious system of slapping a banning order on anyone, without any provable reason, was a perverse stroke of genius on the part of the apartheid government. They could abruptly change the life of literally anyone they believed to be a nuisance. Any junior in the security system could report someone, rightly or wrongly, and that person would be banned. It was a kind of tyranny and it always lasted for five years, sometimes to be instantly extended for a further five.

My anger was intense, I was burning inside. But I had learnt to show no emotion to the security police. I suppressed it all until our friends had left, then my husband and I spent a sleepless night trying to console each other and work out how to get through it. Reg never blamed me. He knew and understood the need to fight for justice had driven me through the years. We had both known it would come to this, although I don't think we realised how painful it would be.

From the moment of my banning, the security clampdown by plain-clothes police was blatant. There would be three, sometimes ten, sometimes twenty police patrolling the neighbourhood. If they suspected I had company they had the right to enter the house by force if necessary, and arrest me on suspicion of contravening the order, or search the entire place as disruptively as they could.

My law practice, with my brand new sign, Priscilla Jana and Associates, had been open for only a couple of weeks. I thought of all the urgent cases I would have to put on hold, the burden I would be placing on my assistants and fellow lawyers.

There was nothing for it but to comply, but the police made it as difficult as possible. At John Vorster Square for my weekly signing-in I would be kept waiting endlessly. The police tried to humiliate me, pointing at me and jeering and calling me a terrorist, a communist, a 'coolie meisie' – Afrikaans slang for 'Indian girl', intended to belittle me – any insult they felt like.

Years later at South Africa's Truth and Reconciliation Commission, many highly-placed police from the 1970s and 80s pleaded for amnesty and were obliged to detail their activities towards 'suspects' like me. One of them, Supt. Eric Goosen, admitted he had harassed Beyers Naudé and Cedric Mayson, fellow members of my ANC cell, during their banning orders. He described how up to ten vehicles, all swapping places, would follow them and their families wherever they went. Three men would follow them into any building they entered. The police had the legal right to demand information about every meeting or conversation they had. By night, Goosen and his team, he said, regularly threw bricks through Beyers's and Cedric's vehicles outside their homes. It was deliberate intimidation, they said, against enemies of the State.

The officers revealed that there was a security branch 'safe house' in a street behind Johannesburg's Eastgate shopping centre. There would be fifteen to twenty security operatives staying in the house, running a fleet of vehicles. Their job was surveillance and intimidation; they said it was 'standard practice' to harass and terrify suspects with threatening phone calls and acts of vandalism.

Another former security branch officer, Paul Erasmus, told the Commission enthusiastically about the methods they used against people like me. In his sixteen years as an intelligence operative he oversaw the system by which all post arriving into South Africa was monitored, twenty-four hours a day, from Johannesburg's Jeppe Street head office. At least one employee in every one of the country's post offices was installed there as a spy, reporting to Jeppe Street.

Mail was opened and examined at random, or on specific request if it was addressed to a suspicious person like me. He told the Commission: 'Our main purpose was to harass people until they left the country. We considered them dangerous, the enemy within.

'My job was to damage their lines of communication and interfere with their subversive activities. We wanted to slow down what they were aiming to achieve, the overthrow of the country and our way of life, and replace it with a communistic or socialistic way of life. So I organised teams to throw bricks through windows, make death threats in phone calls, and splash paint remover on their cars.'

Warming up to his subject, Erasmus told the TRC: 'It was actually great fun at the time. We would carry out an act at night and read about it in the next day's newspapers. We bugged phones and heard targeted people telling each other what we'd done.'

He said that Beyers Naudé, today acknowledged as one of the great heroes of the movement, was seen by them as 'an absolute traitor to Afrikanerdom'.

Erasmus asked the TRC to set aside his malicious injury to property, theft of belongings during raids on suspects' houses, attempted murder by setting fire to vehicles outside homes, and harassing people with death threats by phone. He said he personally attacked Beyers's car with a firebomb on several occasions and admitted that it could have spread to the house and endangered the lives of anyone inside.

His plea in mitigation? 'I was a young man in those days,' he said. 'I was enjoying it, having some fun.'

He said people like me were considered 'dangerous, worthless scum' and boasted of throwing paving stones through cars and calling in the middle of the night with anonymous threats. Erasmus said he had stolen books, clocks and many plants and flowers from suspects' homes and gardens, transferring them to his own home. He stole a quantity of T-shirts with political slogans and used them to polish his car.

He claimed that many members of his team were carrying out similar activities all over the country.

Questioned about the notorious tenth floor in John Vorster Square, he admitted systematic torture took place, using electrical wiring to produce severe shocks without leaving marks while the victim had a wet sack over his head.

Sleep deprivation was routine, with police officers on shifts to keep prisoners awake.

Erasmus revealed that the tenth floor contained the so-called

Truth Room – a soundproof strongroom with steel doors and multiple bolts. By the time a prisoner was in there he would not know if it was day or night, and when he screamed he would not be heard.

Chillingly, these men perceived their actions as an honourable mission. They had the backing of their unit commander and approval all the way up the chain to the Minister of Police. In 2000, it was grim to listen to these appalling admissions. But in truth I had known at the time, as every activist lawyer knew, that this government-sanctioned behaviour was taking place.

From the moment I was handed my banning order, I admit to having been defiant. When a group of MK cadres were arrested after a shoot-out in a bank in Pretoria soon after my ban, I hardly gave a damn about the consequences of representing them in court. The case became known as the Silverton trial (referring to the suburb where it took place), my first major hearing since opening my own practice.

I applied for an exemption from my banning order so that I could represent the MK soldiers outside of the Johannesburg area to which I was confined, but despite senior counsel Jules Browdie giving the magistrate a personal assurance that he would accompany me to court and back every day and be responsible for my whereabouts during the trial, it was refused.

So I just got in my car and drove to the Supreme Court in Pretoria anyway. There, horrified to see me arrive, was Clifford Mailer, my trusted friend and a courageous advocate. We'd worked on many cases together since we originally met over the Solomon Mahlangu trial and hanging, but now he was furious, yelling and screaming at me to turn back. He said

I would be arrested and that would jeopardise the entire trial. I saw the sense in this and agreed to head home, thankfully without arrest.

He told me later that each and every one of the accused told the judge they wanted me to represent them. They knew I was banned but they believed I would find a way to help them. This confidence and trust in me was energising, the first real boost since I had been banned. It gave me renewed courage and determination to go on with the fight despite almost impossible circumstances.

They were all found guilty and given the death sentence. On appeal, their sentences were commuted to life imprisonment and after many years – once my banning order expired – I actually got to meet them on Robben Island. When we finally came face to face, it was an empowering moment.

A truly painful aspect of my situation, though, was that my mother was ailing. My family members were finding it excruciating that our normal interaction was on hold, and now there was a real emergency with her health. I could not bear to think of her needing me while so far away, so I got into my car and drove to Durban. I picked up my close friend Espree on the way and we went together.

I was pretty sure I could not get away with this. There could be arrest, detention, prosecution and imprisonment. But we were able to spend the evening together, enjoying dinner with my mother before she had an early night. It was very special to see her again.

Then came the thunderous banging on the door. We knew it must be the police and froze. More than twenty cars were parked outside in the dark.

We decided not to answer the door, a foolish move when

I look back. The police switched off the electricity supply, plunged us into darkness and began a countdown from one to ten, warning us they were going to break down the door. My brother Raj let them in, there was no other option. Police searchlights blinded us as they barged in, dozens of them.

It was quite a show for the neighbours as we were all arrested and marched out of the building. I felt bad for all of us, including myself, and I knew the police would enjoy this, a blatant breach of my order.

We were driven to Durban police station and a long and tedious interrogation continued until the early hours of the morning. We were all held separately and I was told I would be going to Johannesburg while my brother and mother would be held in Durban. Espree was busy contacting lawyers by phone for us.

I had come to see my sick mother, genuinely worried for her and the heart and chest problems affecting her, and now I had put her in this situation. I travelled in the back of the police car with a security branch officer either side of me. I kept asking about my mother. They said she would be OK. They were enjoying my anxiety.

We reached John Vorster Square and I was put into an interrogation room. Why had I gone to Durban? I was asked. What was my real intention? Who was I planning to meet? What messages from comrades was I intending to convey?

I refused to make a statement, so later that morning, inevitably, I was taken to court and charged with breaching the banning order. But then I heard that my mother was still at Durban police station. She was telling them that they could put her in jail or do what they liked, she would not answer questions or make a statement.

I had made a phone call to attorney Gaby Pillay asking him to represent my mother and get her safely home. But he called me to say: 'Priscilla I know you are very stubborn but by God your mother is impossible. She will not co-operate with me. She refuses to even sign an innocuous statement, she is completely defiant. Tell me what to do with her.'

And I was proud of my mother, of course, but I could not let the authorities use her against me and I knew that was their plan. I had seen this happen many times to my clients. They were emotionally blackmailed to admit to offences so that their mothers, fathers, brothers or sisters would not have to suffer.

I had no choice, I pleaded guilty. Clifford appeared for me, and I was given a suspended sentence.

I had seen much worse happen. My clients' relatives – even their grandparents – would be subpoenaed to give evidence against them and they would cave in during cross-examination. The agony on their faces when confronted with their grandmother, terrified and only able to whisper to the court that yes, she knew the youth had left the country and that he came back with weapons, was something terrible to see. If relatives, even grandmothers, refused to testify there would be an automatic five-year prison sentence for them.

At that time, the judiciary was making my working life as well as my personal life difficult. My cases would be put to the bottom of the pile so that I often waited a whole day in court then had to come back again and again just for a postponement. Court officers were openly hostile, obstructive and rude.

One day I was trying to consult with a client, Norman Ngwenya, accused of treason. As usual there was no consulting room for us to use, not even an empty cell. While the court was adjourned I had to sit with him in the courtroom where police officers followed us to a bench at the back and listened in. I was trying to talk to his father and a police officer near us was noisily eating a pear, and spitting.

I called him a pig and told him to go away, using colourful language. As a result I was charged with crimen injuria – the illegal use of obscene or offensive language intended to insult someone – and convicted. During that hearing, Norman's father was forced to give evidence against me. Norman himself was mortified and deeply upset and disappointed in his own father. But I knew he had had no choice.

In any case, I took the case to appeal and won. The judge decided that the word 'pig' was not serious enough to constitute crimen injuria. But the damage done to Norman's relationship with his father by this perceived betrayal was permanent. That, of course, was the intention.

Families could be torn apart by these methods, and I did not want that to happen to me. I saw it as extremely important to try and keep my own family together, so when my niece Narini invited me to her wedding in Durban, I was desperate to attend. Her father, my elder brother, had sadly died early in her life and together with my mother I had helped raise her from birth. She was totally dependent on me and I loved her and felt responsible for her. As her *bua*, her paternal aunt, it was my duty to represent her father at the wedding.

My application for an exemption was once again refused. But somehow Clifford, without my knowledge, approached MP Helen Suzman, who then appealed to the Minister of Justice Kobie Coetsee. She persuaded him, and permission was granted.

I was not a fan of Helen Suzman and did not agree with

her politics. I felt her Progressive Party was too liberal and too white. The prevailing situation in our country needed radicalism and instead Suzman and her party had joined the government, claiming they could fight it from within. I had clashed with her many times in public and now I felt somewhat embarrassed by her intervention. Before I was banned we had gone head-to-head during a BBC interview and it was unlikely I would have agreed with Clifford to approach her on my behalf. But he knew better than to even ask me, and I will anyhow always appreciate her generous mediation.

My memories of the actual wedding, however, are of a day fraught with emotional upset. I was not allowed to go anywhere except to the venue of the ceremony. Anyone who knows about Hindu weddings will know what huge family affairs these are, involving the women particularly in a great number of social visits and a great deal of preparation. But I could not take part. I was not allowed to socialise or be in the presence of more than one person at a time, an impossible restriction. There were to be more than 600 guests.

My husband drove me to Durban and at my mother's house I was bundled into a room where I could greet one person at a time. Each morning and evening of my brief visit I had to go to the local police station to sign in.

I was in floods of tears as I sat on the stage with other senior family members, representing my dear brother on this special day for his daughter. My husband's brother Jason Jina addressed the guests and pleaded with them not to speak to me. I could not take part in any of the key parts of the ceremony, giving away the bride, exchanging garlands or the lighting of the sacred fire.

Of course, I will always be glad I was physically there for

Narini but on the day itself I was overwhelmed with sadness, and felt such outrage at my lack of freedom.

I was receiving many invitations during this time to speak in public about the impact of security legislation. Each time I applied for permission or needed a passport to travel, it was declined.

I was invited to speak at a United Nations Security Council conference on the legal status of apartheid. It was to be in Lagos, Nigeria, so I would need a passport. Every opportunity to spell out the reality of life under the apartheid regime was important. But I was not allowed to accept the invitation.

However, the most distressing aspect of these pernicious banning orders was that they disrupted family and home life at every level. My own husband, so generous, supportive and caring over the years, was finding it hard to accept the day-by-day restrictions. I could no longer go with him to dinner parties or any social event. He started to invite a colleague or a friend instead. Reg was changing. He still treated me with courtesy and we had a friendship, but I was increasingly absorbed in work without any time or space for our relationship.

When a woman friend began calling the house at odd hours I realised Reg was having an affair. Then the affair became several affairs. Our marriage was sinking under an intolerable strain. He continued to be at my side when emergencies cropped up. He never failed to pitch in when extraordinary events unfolded – his great fall-back was to supply food and hospitality, just as he had during the municipal workers' strike.

One day in 1980 I came home from my office to find dozens of children in the house, with Reg feeding them vast supplies of bread and peanut butter, and juice. A great activist, a woman called Irene Motsoaledi, had collected up the children of clients who had been arrested en masse in mining towns in her area in the East Rand. She had saved them from arrest and beatings and had nowhere to take them but to me. We had children sleeping in every room, in the passageways of the house, even on the bathroom floor and in the bath.

Reg stood by me during these crises, but now our marriage was cracking up. I issued a summons for divorce against him, but he really didn't want that. He wrote an affidavit saying that he was sorry for causing me heartache and gave me an undertaking to be faithful.

I believed then, as I do now, that the banning order had ruined my life and my marriage. Those years were the worst in my memory. I was forbidden to exercise my fundamental human rights, my freedom of speech, freedom of expression, freedom of association and of movement. I consider the psychological effects to be more severe than imprisonment. I felt lonely and isolated and helpless.

Any small gesture that relieved this was of enormous value, and there were some.

For example, one day I let a junior lawyer on my staff, Grant, use my car but warned him not to drive into Soweto because my insurance refused to cover that area. But he had a legal matter to attend to there, and drove in. At 6 a.m. the next day he called me at home, mortified to tell me that he had been hijacked and the car had gone.

I was furious. There would be no compensation and I could not afford a replacement. But while we talked on the phone

Grant heard a knock at his door. He came back on to tell me the hijackers had brought the car back. They had found my name on some files in the back seat and realised I was a comrade.

It was a great moment. Reaffirmation of my rightful place in the liberation movement – plus, I still had a car.

But I couldn't take part in political activities, my mother was very ill and Reg and I, like so many other couples, had seen our marriage fall apart under the strain.

The security police had free rein to call at the house any time of day or night. They would force their way in and demand to see where I was, even if I was actually in bed. They had the right to come into my bedroom to question whether I was in nightclothes or had been involved in outside activities and had slipped into bed fully-dressed when I heard them at the door.

My next-door neighbour and close friend, Hajira Momoniat, remembers the constant police presence. A good, decent person whose doctor husband ran his clinic from their house, she was bringing up two sons in those chaotic times. Her activist brother had fled the country fearing arrest, and her husband had been questioned many times.

Recalling those days recently with me, she remembers police cars parked everywhere in nearby streets: 'What I remember most is that feeling that we were all in it together,' she said. 'It was us against the system. It had to be, there was no choice if you were not white.'

Her son Ismail was a brave boy who became involved with protest activities at school. Later he became a founder member of the UDF and was arrested three times. I represented him in court, and Hajira's attitude then, as it is now, is one of pride in him.

'When they took him to Johannesburg Prison we weren't allowed to see him,' she said. 'All we could do was to take food and hope that it was given to him. We brought food for other prisoners too, in the hope that it would get through.

'For years I could not drive past Johannesburg Prison without crying. We wanted to move away from the area, find somewhere safer to live. But the system made that impossible.'

Hajira came under special scrutiny for being my neighbour and friend and as a consequence suffered extreme anxiety for the safety of her husband and children. She had been the first person I called when my house was fire-bombed during the Solomon Mahlangu trial and now she was interrogated about my activities (other Lenasia residents were actually asked to spy on me).

Hajira's house and mine were both under attack. One night police thugs threw Molotov cocktails – glass bottles with petrol-soaked rags inside, lit with a match just before they were thrown – into her husband's surgery, and simultaneously through my window. We all heard the crash of glass and ran into the street in our nightclothes. The bombs had failed to ignite and lay in the gutter. After that we never had a peaceful night's sleep. The police had added sheer terror to the relentless intimidation techniques and the threatening phone calls.

At one time my mother was staying with me. She answered the door in the early hours of the morning and found police standing there in heavy rain. A normally kind and hospitable person, she nevertheless slammed the door in their faces. She had developed a deep hostility towards the system and was distressed by what was happening to me.

When we drove to a grocery store together we would see police cars openly following us. They would wait outside the shop and then follow us all the way back home, parking nearby in plain sight. It was deliberate intimidation, and over a period of several years it worked.

There was not one day when I didn't get a threatening call. A sinister voice would say: 'I'm just warning you. We've placed a bomb in your house.' Sometimes they would claim they had placed a bomb in my office. I would have to go to the police, the very people I knew were behind this torture, to ask them to search the place.

In the meantime, my law practice was constantly being raided. I was a particular target, being the first black woman to set up a legal practice. Once I was banned I had to rely on associates like Ilona Kleinschmidt Tip and Nana Williams, who were my anchors and my support.

Ilona, who was also my most valued confidante, had to take the arduous trips to Robben Island in my place to deal with our huge caseload there. She and Nana kept my law practice alive. But they were both often taken away for interrogation along with my team of junior lawyers. There would be continuous raids during which the police would rummage through files and confiscate documents, leaving others in chaos on the floor.

The intention of course was to demoralise them and to undermine me. And I began to realise there was something more sinister going on: they were actually trying to build a case against me that would land me in court for treason. I could be sentenced to life imprisonment, or sentenced to death. Either way, they would have removed me from the scene.

Already it was clear they had put together a huge file on me. Now they went for the jugular – they targeted my close friend Joe Veriava and contrived to hold him in indefinite detention until he disclosed all my underground activities and exposed my ANC contacts.

They arrested him after he had addressed parents and students at a school in Lenasia where we feared there could be a repeat of the Soweto massacre by police. Students were planning a boycott and we supported that. But Joe was keen to bring their parents into the plan for safety's sake. As he left the school, three police cars were waiting and he was told he was under arrest.

For four whole months he was beaten and abused under interrogation, a period which grieves us both to this day. He never gave the security police one single piece of information about me. I can hardly imagine the mental and physical pain he suffered, and the iron courage he showed in the face of that pressure.

We have found it hard to talk about this over the years. But recently he opened up a little more.

He recalled how he knew straight away that the police were desperate to know about his links to me. And Joe knew a great deal. He had helped to disburse money sent to my office by couriers, and taken it to Beyers Naudé and others for undercover ANC operations.

He was a totally altruistic man who was a senior doctor at the government-owned Coronation Hospital and a colleague to Dr Abubakar Asvat who ran clinics for the poor in several townships. Joe was also a lecturer in health matters at Wits University. He was open about his affiliation to the Black Consciousness Movement and had accompanied me to meetings in St Peter's Seminary where I discussed sabotage plans with Cedric Mayson, Jackie Selebi and others; he knew how the key networks of the anti-apartheid movement operated.

It was a classic manoeuvre on the part of the police to emotionally blackmail activists like me by taking in my friends and associates. The pressure on us both was enormous. For him, there was actual torture, and worse when he was told during his detention that his father had become ill with anxiety and died while Joe was still incarcerated. It was heartbreaking for me not to be able to attend his funeral, since my banning order forbade it.

Today Joe is chairperson of the Council for Medical Schemes, a senior academic at Wits and a key member of the Steve Biko Centre for Bioethics. He refuses to dwell on the physical assaults he suffered. But recalling the events of those days in a lengthy conversation we had in preparation for this book he told me:

I had spent a day under questioning some years previously so I knew what to expect. I said to the arresting officers that I realised they were planning their usual methods of persuasion.

From the first day, they stripped me naked and went as far as they could to force me to give information without actually rendering me unconscious. I had known for a long time that this day might come and I had tried to prepare for it. But nothing prepares you for the sleep deprivation, the batteries of questions and the threats, and the loneliness of solitary confinement.

I spent time in both John Vorster Square and at Protea Prison. I got to know my interrogator quite well, the big and burly Col. Heysteck. He warned me I would be left to rot in my cell unless I talked. Each day I tried to plan how I would get through the next interrogation. My only answers to them were that I admitted I was an activist. I did not give in to any pressure.

In that situation you ask yourself – do I really believe in what I am doing, or have I just joined a big noisy mass movement and got carried away with the momentum, the public hysteria?

And I asked myself also, do people commit suicide in jail because they are emotionally beaten and exhausted, or have they let themselves be driven that far down? I feel the injustice of my situation and want to fight. Would suicide be a way of fighting, of defeating them?

A big influence on me at that time was a young political prisoner held in a cell close to me. I never even knew his name but I heard him singing every day. I only saw him when he passed my cell on his way to the bathroom. Once he passed me some cigarette roll-up papers and some tobacco. I tried to smoke it but almost burnt my face. That didn't matter, it was the kindness that mattered. I discovered he had been there six months, refusing to give State evidence against a comrade. He inspired me, and we both survived.

I knew what they wanted most out of me, enough incriminating information to bring Priscilla in and charge her. I couldn't be responsible for that. If I had given them information I could not have lived with myself. Then, I would have to commit suicide.

I was insulted and derided by my interrogators. They told each other, 'This guy doesn't seem to feel pain, he must be a drug addict', and they threatened electric-shock attacks.

I kept thinking to myself that I'm a doctor. They won't really harm me. They used to beg me to give them information. They used to say please, please talk to us, then you can go.

I found myself trying to plan my next session of interrogation. I became obsessed with that, and how to deal with the assaults. They warned me that this investigation was making no progress and that now they could hold me indefinitely, incommunicado, and that I was doing this to myself.

Up till then I knew there were restrictions on how long they could hold a detainee, but once they had moved to another section of the Criminal Procedures Act I could be there indefinitely.

I was worried about my father. I heard through the prison grapevine that he was taking my detention very badly. He was already suffering pneumonia and renal failure at the time of my arrest, and now I heard he was in hospital. Much later, my mother told me he did not believe I would survive in detention. Instead it was him who did not survive.

One of the worst emotional experiences of my life was to go, under guard, to Coronation Hospital, my own workplace, to see my ailing father. I was accompanied by two plainclothes' security police and as I walked through the ward I saw distressed fellow doctors and nurses in tears. They were not allowed to talk to me, they were just openly horrified at what they saw. Their senior colleague, beaten down and restrained by the cruel government that ruled us all, helplessly approaching his father's deathbed.

The hospital doctors said they thought it would be best to transfer my father to Johannesburg Hospital.

They were finding it too traumatic to have him there as a patient. But soon after he was transferred I was informed by the prison authorities that he had died and that I could only attend his funeral under strict supervision.

It was an evening funeral, attended by hundreds of people. I was sad that Priscilla could not be there. She was a banned person and she told me afterwards she had been warned she would be arrested if she attended.

But it was the love and support of all those mourners that comforted me for the rest of my stay in detention. It helped so much to know that people cared about my father, about me and about the movement.

Priscilla had done everything she could to get me released, and to make my detention more bearable. She got me a TV, which I could share with other prisoners once I was in a communal cell. I remember us watching tennis ace John McEnroe playing in the Wimbledon finals. And she sent me money for food. Prisoners were allowed to spend R20 a month of their own money and with that I could buy biscuits and other luxuries to share with my cellmates. Priscilla never stopped petitioning behind the scenes to get me out.

But one thing was puzzling me throughout my detention. Priscilla's husband Reg had shouted a message up to the cells – by standing in the public street at the back of the police headquarters – and it had been passed on to me by comrades. He said, 'The big black bird has flown' and I had no idea what that meant until after my release.

I was given a release date, and it proved to be a trick, but I was finally allowed out on 10 August, a date I will

*above left*: Tina as she was when Priscilla first saw her. Her biological mother Phinda sent her this treasured picture.

*above right*: Priscilla's father Hansrani at his graduation ceremony, a precious photograph as it is the only one the family has.

*below left*: Tina's second birthday. Priscilla with Tina's biological mother Phinda, at the Tina family home in Lenasia, Johannesburg.

*below right*: On International Women's Day in Dublin where Priscilla watches with pride as Tina delivers her own forceful speech, dressed in classic African style. Seated next to Priscilla is Dublin's Lady Mayoress.

*Left*: Close friends and fellow activists: Dr Joe Veriava with Winnie Mandela and Priscilla in Priscilla's garden in Lenasia in the 1970s.

*Right*: Nelson Mandela, the day after his release, back at his home in Diepkloof, Johannesburg, after twenty-seven years in prison.

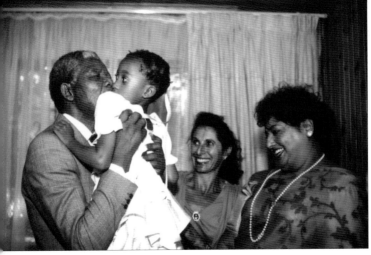

*Left*: Nelson Mandela hugs Tina, with Priscilla and her legal assistant and friend Ilona Kleinschmidt Tip.

*Left*: Priscilla with Nelson Mandela at a party in her garden in Mayfair, Johannesburg, to celebrate his release from prison, with the new South African flag behind them. Also present were Priscilla's second husband Regan and Ilona.

*Right*: With singer Bono, her neighbour, and government officials at her residence in Dublin where she was hosting a dinner for Archbishop Tutu.

*Left*: Priscilla with ANC stalwart Jacob Zuma, later to become President of South Africa, and the Chinese Ambassador to the Netherlands, at her official residence in 2003.

*Left*: A family photo with (*from left to right*) Priscilla's niece Mala, brother Raj, mother Hansraj, Mala daughter Surekha, Priscilla and her husband Reg, and Tina, at her home in Lenasia 1988.

*Right*: Priscilla and Reg dancing at a wedding in India, 1965.

*Left*: Tina's graduation ceremony at Trinity College, Dublin. Priscilla and Tina's cousin Shivesh stand proudly beside her.

never forget. I learnt that the 'big black bird' was Jackie Selebi. Priscilla wanted me to know that he had fled the country so that if I had to give any information it would be safe to talk about him, as he was already in exile.

Our cryptic messages often worked in coded phone calls and in scrappy handwritten notes, but that one had eluded me.

Joe is still today one of my dearest friends and it's hard to express my gratitude for the depth of loyalty he showed me. We have even managed to laugh at some of the extraordinary episodes we experienced in those days.

On one occasion, I was in consultation in my office with a client, Imbali Seheri, when more than twenty police entered without warning, intending to arrest him. They disrupted the office for half an hour then left without him. I had obstructed them as much as I could with loud protests, but once they left I really didn't know where Seheri had gone.

Seconds later, he emerged from under Nana's skirt where he had been hiding as she continued to sit at her desk, typing, throughout the confusion.

We laughed of course, but I have seen people permanently damaged by the banning orders. I believe the harassment, banishment, detention and banning orders against Winnie Mandela, in many ways the strongest of all of us, changed and soured her over the years.

The eighties were the worst years for State oppression. There were States of Emergency, banishments, banning orders, prosecutions and detentions. I became very pessimistic. I knew this was the South African government's last-ditch onslaught against us, intended to beat us down and keep us down.

A little later, in 1985, when a *Washington Post* journalist recalled that time as a period when the government softened, I exploded, telling her that was rubbish, that it was a public relations ploy by which they had tried to woo the rest of the world. Like so many others, she had been fooled by the entirely cynical strategy of creating Bantustans, so-called homelands, for black people, giving them a meaningless form of 'independence' while stripping them of their South African citizenship. The apartheid government claimed this as an act of generosity towards blacks, describing it as a softening of their previous stand. We knew that it was totally perverse, a means of marginalising the country's majority population still further.

Ironically, one of the most important cases of my entire career landed on my desk during 1982, and served to throw a spotlight on the iniquitous homeland system.

I was asked by parents of an MK operative jailed in the homeland of Bophuthatswana if I could possibly get him transferred to a jail in South Africa as the journeys to visit him were too strenuous. He was Maphuti Marwane, a name now in the annals of the country's famous law cases.

Marwane had trained in an MK camp in Angola and had been slipping back into South Africa, heavily armed, through the Botswana border. He was caught in Bophuthatswana and detained in isolation for a period before he was eventually tried, convicted and sentenced to fifteen years for treason under the Terrorism Act of South Africa. He had been severely beaten and tortured in solitary confinement.

I wrote to the Bophuthatswana Ministry of Justice and asked for a transfer. The answer I received was short and curt. I was informed that a transfer would not be possible, that Marwane had been tried and convicted according to Bophuthatswana's

Constitution and that meant he would have to serve his sentence there.

Our anti-apartheid movement was strongly opposed to the setting-up of the ten homelands and believed it was pernicious social engineering. The ideology of the Bantustans was totally repulsive to me and against everything I stood and fought for. Black people had been dumped in barren rural areas and told they were now independent, that they were no longer citizens of South Africa. In this way the apartheid government claimed that its people were in a democracy. It was nothing but a cynical exercise in the politics of divide and rule.

The tone of the letter from the Commissioner of Police had infuriated me. I decided to look at Bophuthatswana's (Bop's) Constitution to see if there was any loophole we could use. To my surprise I found that this constitution, no doubt drawn up with the help of Western lawyers, contained a Bill of Rights. This, by definition, meant that detention in isolation, whereby a prisoner was held in solitary confinement and had no access to a lawyer or his family, could not be lawful. I sensed an opportunity.

I pleaded with advocate Ismail Mahomed to help, and, as always, he agreed to at least study the case. He came to the same conclusion as I had. The Bill of Rights was a human-rights charter protecting the fundamental freedom of individuals, and it was embodied in Bop's Constitution. Mahomed believed we could win an appeal against Marwane's detention, conviction and sentence.

He applied to the Appellate Division of the Supreme Court. We wanted to have the 1967 Terrorism Act declared invalid in Bophuthatswana. This was the first time that a South African court had been required to test the validity of an Act

135

of Parliament against a Bill of Rights. It was a constitutional issue and was taken so seriously that for only the third time in its history, the Supreme Court appointed eleven judges for the hearing. Ordinarily a case would be heard by three or five judges.

I longed to be there for the hearing but my banning order forbade it: the Supreme Court sat in the city of Bloemfontein, an Afrikaans stronghold. Advocate Mahomed personally approached magistrates in Johannesburg and gave all kinds of undertakings that I would abide by my banning order and that he would be personally responsible for me. Permission was granted and, much as I would never normally delight in a trip to Bloemfontein, I was actually excited to be able to leave Johannesburg for the first time in several years.

It was a great joy to see Mahomed at work. He was certainly the only lawyer with the courage to contest the might of the judiciary. Unlike many others he was willing to take on controversial matters and argue them ferociously while knowing there was little prospect of success. He was unafraid of being humiliated in court; he had suffered the brickbats of court procedure many times.

Like me he would also have to apply for a special permit to even stay in the Orange Free State for the duration of the hearing. People of Indian descent were not allowed to be there, even in transit, without permission. Normally, lawyers would have to leave before dark, making the return journey day after day.

Mahomed and I took advantage of our special dispensation by travelling around a little during the adjournments. I had no particular interest in Bloemfontein, but it was special to drive up Signal Hill and look down on the city lights after dark. Just being away from the security police and their harassment was a relief.

On the day of our hearing, there was an electric atmosphere in the courtroom, a solemn and overpowering hush. Mahomed had never looked so alone as he launched his arguments in front of the panel of eleven be-robed senior judges. Chief Justice Rumpff tried to rattle him from the start but Mahomed used every ounce of his considerable intellectual tenacity, and answered a barrage of questions with dignity and passion. After his lengthy sojourn in court our counterpart attorneys in Bloemfontein approached him and congratulated him on a brilliant performance.

The decision took months to come through. I was at the Supreme Court in Johannesburg when it was announced, working on a treason case alongside George Bizos, Mandela's advocate. He had gone to his office opposite the courts during an adjournment and came back to tell colleagues with great excitement: 'We've won the Marwane case!'

I reminded him that, actually, it was my Marwane case. I raced over the road to Ismail Mahomed's chambers and took the lift to the sixth floor. I walked straight into his office and found him with a fellow lawyer, Martin Brassey. All three of us were overwhelmed with the significance of the decision. We had won our case. In the face of fierce opposition from all the forces the apartheid state and judiciary could muster, our logic had stood firm.

We needed to get hold of the actual judgement. Meanwhile, lawyer colleagues kept coming in to congratulate us. There was a feeling of tremendous jubilation, along with shock and surprise. South Africa itself did not even have a constitution and here was a team of State judges upholding a Bill of Rights.

It was incredible, almost absurd. We had discredited the Terrorism Act itself, the major instrument of oppression. The judgement felt to us like the possible dawn of something brighter for the future when we might have a Constitutional State and a proper judiciary to uphold it. It was a great victory, and all the sweeter for having come about during the period of my banning order, the most restricted years of my life.

The three of us celebrated at dinner that night. We were all lawyers and my banning order allowed for it.

Our next thought was for Marwane himself and his parents. We sent a clerk to their home and they were so happy and relieved that they set off for Mafeking, where he was being held, at once. A couple of days later they brought him to my office. He seemed shell-shocked, dumbfounded, and at a loss to understand his release from conviction and from his fifteen-year prison sentence. 'Mum Jana,' he kept repeating. 'Thank you, thank you.'

Soon afterwards I had the great pleasure of seeing an announcement on State television by Bophuthatswana's self-styled president Lucas Mangope to the effect that I was permanently banned from his 'country'.

I merely laughed. I had hardly been dying to go there.

It was no surprise to me to hear that Marwane had set off again for the MK camps. He was a trained cadre and would not want to waste time. I had seen this many, many times. In my experience, young men whom one might expect to sigh with relief and turn to a quiet life always did the opposite. The fight was far from over and they were needed to play their part.

Fighting for freedom demands a special kind of dedication.

It comes from the certainty that one is on the right side in a war of cruel injustice. I have seen youths facing the gallows who have neither wept nor expressed regret. Each of them told me he would do the same again if he possibly could.

So, just for a brief time, Marwane's parents had their son back. They had never expected this, their joy was wonderful to see. They thanked me, Clifford and Mahomed many times over, realising what a great step forward we had made together.

Years later, in the new democratic South Africa, Ismail Mahomed became the first black judge to be appointed, and in 1996 he was made Chief Justice, an honour greatly deserved.

# CHAPTER SIX

# A WINNING
# TEAM

Paralysed as I was by the devastating effect of my banning order, the ability to carry on my law practice was a lifesaver.

I found myself in a formidable team with two brilliant advocates and our camaraderie was all the greater because of the police state we were living in. Clifford Mailer and Ismail Mahomed were both mentors and brothers to me, sometimes even trying to protect me from myself when they thought I was being reckless.

They knew my activism came from a deeply-rooted sense of justice and that I was prepared to take risks. But there were things they didn't know, for example that I belonged to an underground ANC cell. They would have found that difficult to deal with.

They were fighting the system in their own ways, as dedicated lawyers prepared to confront the State at every step and turn. My mindset was simply to go further than that, to go as far as I could.

The first time I'd briefed Clifford – who today is a senior judge in England – I had actually been hostile towards him because he was white. I was fiercely pro-Black Consciousness at the time and found it distasteful to have to team up with someone like him. But we became great friends. Like other white activists at the University of the Witwatersrand he was taking part in student protests and taking risks. That was all he could possibly do.

Clifford was a first cousin to the brilliant American novelist Norman Mailer. He was interesting, sympathetic and in his own way as determined as I was to achieve justice and freedom in South Africa. I had met him through Ismail Mahomed, the senior advocate who worked with me to defend Michael Tsagae and his Soweto Revolutionary Council after the 1976 uprising and whom I'd worked with on many cases since then.

Ismail was related to Ismail Ayob, the attorney who took me on as an articled clerk. Ayob encouraged me to bring him in on some important cases and once he in turn had brought in Clifford we formed a natural trio. We had the fire and enthusiasm between us to do almost anything.

Mahomed was our natural leader, the senior figure. He was impressive, totally committed, but he would not have been seen dead at an ANC meeting. He was a lawyer, he said, that was his challenge and there was no room for anything else. 'I'm not a gun-runner,' he used to say. 'I wouldn't be any good at it. I'll just be a good lawyer instead.'

We had formed a winning combination over the years but Mahomed made it tough work at times. He was an absolute workaholic who would not hear of stopping for tea or lunch. He had an enormous capacity for hard work without needing the bio-breaks which we mere mortals had to have. He would work from morning till night without tea, coffee or food. When Clifford and I said we were faint with hunger he would throw us out of his office in contempt.

In December 1979, I heard that we needed to make an urgent application in the case of Zinjiva Nkondo, the brilliant young ANC firebrand who was the movement's Director of Propaganda. He had been on his way to Lesotho with a supply of ANC publicity pamphlets when his plane was diverted in bad weather and landed in Bloemfontein. Nkondo was detained, illegally we felt sure, and charged under the Terrorism Act.

Mahomed, always ready to argue a non-arguable case through the labyrinth of prejudice and bigotry in the South African courts, decided to make it a case of international law. We worked together for hours until Clifford and I said we had to have something to eat. Everything was closed by that time of night, so I offered to call my husband and ask him to bring us some food.

Mahomed erupted. He told us to get out of his office – 'Get out! Get out!' – and actually threw some of his leather-bound law books at Clifford's head. We escaped to the corridor and sat there guiltily eating until Mahomed relented and allowed us back in.

He could be grumpy, and sexist with it. We had a meeting scheduled in his office once with some senior colleagues, one of them now working with the Secretary-General of the United Nations Ban Ki-moon, and I turned up fifteen minutes late. I had driven in from Lenasia in heavy traffic and had problems finding a parking space.

'Why didn't you just stay at home and make samosas?' he yelled at me.

He was sometimes in despair at my close involvement with the grass roots of the anti-apartheid movement and once I'd been banned, he felt instinctively the sense of danger all around me.

While my husband and I endured our second fire-bombing at the hands of the security police, he and Clifford could not contemplate such a thing happening at their homes. Once again the attack had come in the middle of the night. Mercifully, neither of the two Molotov cocktails thrown at our house, and at our neighbour Dr Momoniat's surgery, ignited. But they smashed the windows and brought us all into the street in our nightclothes again, stunned and fearful of what might have been.

Mahomed and Clifford looked on me as something of a loose cannon and wanted to protect me, and possibly thought I had brought problems on my own head. I was at the coalface of activism and had direct contact with clients and their families, along with an open contempt for the authorities.

It wasn't just brotherly love that caused them to become exasperated with me and protective of me. They needed me to avoid detention so that we could work together. Clifford has told me openly that he and Mahomed were often totally exasperated at my 'recklessness'. Recently he said: 'I had no idea about the ANC cell. That could have landed you in jail for a long time. We needed you to work with us, although I knew all along that you didn't give a damn when it came to supporting the anti-apartheid cause. It was hopeless trying to rein you in.'

But I know I sometimes pushed him too far. In 1981, when I was still under my banning order, the South African government was sending military gunships to attack anti-apartheid targets in Angola and Mozambique.

In Matola, Mozambique, they killed sixteen black South Africans and a Portuguese national in one shocking raid on a building they knew to be an MK headquarters. Several operatives were kidnapped and their relatives were desperate for me to help find them.

I had to call Clifford at 5 a.m. to plead with him to go. He was always very courageous about these difficult assignments and agreed. He set off by road for the Swazi border accompanied by the activist Penuell Maduna.

They got to the Mozambique border and found it closed for the night. There was no option but to sleep in a nearby shack, sharing a bed. Clifford was furious, though in fairness I did not know what time border offices closed at night. He filed a report the next day and flew home. I turned up to meet him at the airport but he just strode right past me, his face livid with anger.

But these were years when events were forcing us to be spontaneous, to tolerate personal inconveniences.

In 1982 we were defending the brave and unstoppable Robert Adam, one of our few white defendants who had studied in London and who had come home to South Africa to join the anti-apartheid movement. He worked underground but was caught in September 1981 and was detained for a long period before his trial. I became close to his parents who were totally supportive of him.

When Rob was sentenced to ten years' imprisonment he told me he wanted to get properly drunk before going off to Pretoria Central. I bought some fruit juice and injected a lot of vodka into it. I left it for him in my consulting room downstairs from the courtroom. My advocate colleague David Soggot, who defended Rob, walked in, knocked back some of the juice, and was surprised at how it affected him.

Later he and Rob both said the vodka helped their mood. Rob then found himself doing eight months in solitary confinement. He served eight years until all political prisoners were released in February 1990. Academically brilliant, he achieved his degree as a doctor of nuclear physics while still in prison and today he is head of South Africa's Nuclear Energy Corporation.

Soon after working on his case, the banning order, which had for several years severely restricted me, was suddenly and unexpectedly lifted when the South African Government, without warning, brought in its Internal Security Act, implemented in 1983. It repealed and replaced the Terrorism Act, the Suppression of Communism Act and other restrictive legislation.

The cynicism and hypocrisy of the State knew no bounds. Its greatest fear was further crippling sanctions from the West, and it wanted to put on a show of fairness, particularly through the judiciary.

I heard the news on the radio in the early morning. I realised that my ban, brought under the Suppression of Communism Act, was now null and void after only four years instead of five. I was cautiously jubilant, elated. Winnie Mandela, Beyers Naudé and all our comrades would be free. But was it because the State planned something worse?

I called my mother and told her the great news. Winnie and Beyers called me in excitement. Whatever the next move, our personal freedom meant we could become more involved again.

Later, when the first of a series of States of Emergency was declared, we realised that a worse menace was on the agenda – detention without trial and virtual disappearances. The new Internal Security Act brought in preventive detentions by which suspects could be held incommunicado, a pernicious concept.

But at least I was now free to see clients wherever they were being held in the country. My colleagues and I had come to realise that the judges in Natal were more liberal than those in the Johannesburg area, so we began a strategy of bringing applications there.

I turned over in my mind the possibility of taking up my role in the underground cell again, but it had fallen dormant due to my comrades' various arrests and detention. Then there was a major setback: Cedric Mayson, the clergyman who had brought us together for our covert meetings, was arrested and detained. Jackie Selebi – who later became South Africa's Police Commissioner – and Enoch Duma, also both brave members of our underground cell, had already decided to flee the country. I was also sent instructions to leave but I hardly even considered it. I had a role to play and I had no intention of turning my back on it.

I was in the Supreme Court in Johannesburg one day during this time with advocate George Bizos who had represented Nelson Mandela at the Rivonia trial. A security police officer called Dietleef, who I knew from several previous confrontations, strolled up to me and slapped a subpoena in my hand. Under Section 205 of the Criminal Procedures Act I was being forced to come to court and testify as a State witness against Cedric Mayson.

Beyers Naudé also received a subpoena. We talked long and hard about the matter, the impossibility of giving evidence against Cedric, and the inevitable consequences – a prison sentence.

Ismail Mahomed stepped in to do everything he could to protect us. He applied his genius and combined it with tactful charm. He approached the authorities, appealing to them to allow a respectable lawyer like myself to stay free. In response they showed him my security file. Mahomed was absolutely horrified to see that I had been part of a cell collaborating with the MK in its sabotage operations and reporting regularly to Lusaka.

Once he had calmed down, his advice was for me and Beyers to agree 'innocuous' statements. We adamantly refused, and that would mean a jail sentence of five years for us both.

I talked to my mother and she accepted the situation with courage and understanding. Family members, friends, comrades and neighbours came to the house that evening to advise, admonish and commiserate.

After a sleepless night I got up and prepared myself for the court hearing. I turned on the news and heard to my utter astonishment that Cedric had obtained bail and had skipped the country overnight. He was in London and had already given a statement to the press, saying that he had felt compelled to jump bail in order to save me and Beyers from a prison sentence. His actions made worldwide headlines and for Beyers and me unexpected relief.

We did not appear in court, we did not testify and we did not go to jail. And for all his raging disapproval of my risk-taking, Mahomed was gracious about it. He even expressed envy at my courage.

In this way we continued our mostly amiable, sometimes fractious, relationship, which turned out, in many court matters, to be a good formula. When there was time to relax, we would have lunch together, taking over the restaurant until 6 p.m.; there was so much to talk about, so many legal manoeuvres we needed to discuss. I think we all treasured those times. Many seemingly unwinnable cases were debated and dissected during those lengthy meetings, and when we won, the victory was all the sweeter.

When we were occasionally stranded out of town it was no punishment to spend time together. We travelled as a team to Namibia, still South-West Africa at the time, to bring an application against an order preventing the Reverend Frank Chikane, the courageous head of South Africa's Council of Churches who dedicated himself to the movement, from entering the country. The authorities had been told he was a terrorist.

To our surprise we won the case after a five-minute hearing, but there was no flight home for several days. Stuck there from Monday to Friday we went on a sightseeing jaunt to the massive sand dunes on the Skeleton Coast, walking along the beach together still in our formal court clothes. Mahomed, Clifford and Sean Naidoo – a brilliant junior counsel and recent addition to our team – were in white shirts and pinstripe suits and I wore a silk sari. We probably looked a comical sight, but for us it was memorable, relaxing in our comradeship and celebrating our triumph in Chikane's case.

We saw a pack of African wild dogs on the beach, an incredible – though terrifying – encounter. They stared at us and we stared back, frozen with fear. We drove over to Swakopmund where I visited my friend Horst Kleinschmidt's mother at her pottery shop and bought souvenirs home, later presenting some handmade pots to Govan Mbeki on his release from prison.

Extraordinary to think where we were and what we were

doing, while Horst was running the ANC's fundraising operation in London and Govan was locked up on Robben Island. In everything we did during those days there was a circular link through the anti-apartheid movement to comrades elsewhere, a good and comforting feeling during hard times.

I often found it desperately sad to be around poverty-stricken clients whose husbands, sons or daughters were locked up or had been detained incommunicado. My friendship with my fellow lawyers was the antidote. Mahomed could be a star when he wasn't being anxious and grumpy. He entertained us hugely with his sharp wit and enormous sense of humour, ingredients which helped to get us through those dark days.

During my banning period there were times when Mahomed and Clifford attended courts without me. The Nkondo case, which had seen us working till midnight in Mahomed's office, turned into a cause célèbre and my only regret was that I could not accompany my colleagues to Bloemfontein when the Supreme Court dealt with it.

Mahomed had decided to tackle the case using international law. Nkondo had been travelling from Maputo in Mozambique to Maseru, the capital of Lesotho, when his plane was diverted. He had tried to continue his journey by car but was arrested at Ladybrand on the border. In the boot were hundreds of incendiary pamphlets, indisputable proof of his links to the ANC, an illegal organisation.

Nkondo was a very bright orator and poet and he had become the voice of Radio Freedom, the movement's method of communicating with the masses. He also put together the propaganda pamphlets.

Mahomed was determined that we could get the charges dropped because they contravened the sovereign integrity of

Lesotho. The case was listed for Christmas Eve. Clifford and Mahomed travelled without me, and although there was a powerful argument in terms of violation of international law, they lost the case.

This set off a chain reaction from the United Nations and the Organisation of African Unity. Nkondo's brother also brought an action against the Minister of Police to protest his detention. In a cynical move we had become familiar with, the charges were quietly dropped two months later and Nkondo was escorted to the Lesotho border and released.

His case was cited by the UN Special Committee Against Apartheid and later came to be applied in incidents involving all of South Africa's neighbouring states – Angola, Botswana, Mozambique, Lesotho, Swaziland, Zambia, and Zimbabwe, at that time called Rhodesia. Its significance was that it set a precedence by which South African courts could never again uphold the legality of abductions.

But while my work with Mahomed, Clifford and Sean was providing us with encouraging successes I had my own personal mission to pursue – I was now finally free to travel to Robben Island again.

Ilona Kleinschmidt Tip had meanwhile been making the ferry journeys and working with an increasing number of the political prisoners there. By the time I visited the island again, we had literally hundreds of clients needing help. I stationed myself in the consulting room and the clients came to see me in batches of ten or fifteen. I could give them only a few minutes each. I was seeing prisoners whose cases I had worked on years earlier. Some of them I had never actually met before. Now it was exciting, emotional and often sad to be seeing them in these circumstances.

My determination to bring them chocolate bars as a treat was stronger than ever since the warder had confiscated those I'd brought for Nelson Mandela. Now I filled my over-sized briefcase with snack bars and Cadbury's chocolates. There was hardly room for the legal files!

Robben Island was a bleak and difficult place and I hated the ferry journey. One time, on a stormy day, I endured the trip over but refused to take the ferry back to the mainland. A military helicopter was rustled up for me. Another time I stayed overnight in the hope of a calmer sea the next morning. One of the senior warders gave me a room in his house but the atmosphere was tense all evening. We had a fish barbecue and the prison officers attempted some camaraderie with me, but I loathed them and did not hesitate to show it.

One person I was to visit was Govan Mbeki, a giant of the struggle. Throughout my banning period I had never lost sight of a precious piece of paper that had come to me through a network of comrades on which he had written: 'Dear Attorney Priscilla Jana. Please come and see me urgently'.

I was full of apprehension, pacing the floor of the consulting room, now that I was actually about to meet him. He and Mandela and Walter Sisulu, all the Rivonia trialists, had spent many gruelling years hacking lime in the island's quarry day after day. I presumed that this vicious form of hard labour might have reduced a seventy-three-year-old life prisoner to a cowed demeanour and broken spirit. Instead I found myself dwarfed by the towering presence of a very athletic, sprightly man. He had a gentle disarming smile and twinkling eyes. He overpowered me with a fierce embrace, then wasted no time with trivialities: he had instructions for me to follow.

I came to treasure our meetings. Each visit was a celebration.

Mbeki had been secretly writing throughout his imprisonment and had great literary skills. He had been one of the
primary architects of the ANC's manifesto outlining its
demands for a just society. This became the blueprint for the
Freedom Charter, adopted in 1955 and the bedrock of our
beliefs to this day.

I began to smuggle his essays out of prison for him. The
theme of each was freedom. He believed in freedom from
hunger, freedom from inequality, from degradation and from
ignorance.

Mbeki was a born organiser and played a fundamental role
in positioning the ANC's social democratic programme in
alignment with labour movements, which holds to this day.
Ahead of his time in terms of ANC politics, in the early days
of his imprisonment, he argued strongly for the inclusion
of Coloured, Indian and white people in the movement's
hierarchy. This resulted in serious clashes with his comrades
and he often found himself alienated and alone. He was
undaunted, one of the strongest men I have ever met.

Away from the island, I was putting out fires all over
the place. Albertina Sisulu, MaSisulu as we all called her,
whose entire life had been dogged by house arrest and
banning orders, was prosecuted for furthering the aims of
the ANC. She was sentenced to a devastating four years'
imprisonment. I wanted to do everything possible to rescue
her from this. I immediately applied for leave to appeal, and
asked for bail.

The application was heard by the court that evening and bail
was granted at around 9 p.m., set in the amount of R10,000,
an enormous sum of money at that time. I approached all
my friends and relatives, and collected as much as I possibly

could. It was very late at night by the time we'd collected and counted the full amount, and rushed with it to the prison.

The prison officers were as rude and obstreperous as always. They refused to listen and I had to be extremely assertive and threaten to remain there until the bail bond was dealt with.

At around 2 a.m. they woke MaSisulu from a deep sleep, telling her abruptly to pack and leave. She was utterly confused when she emerged from her cell and allowed me to lead her to my car and drive her to my home.

My husband had dinner ready for us when we arrived, so there we were, in the early hours of the morning, sitting at the dining table enjoying mutton curry and rice. Unforgettable times, and when her appeal finally came to court we won, giving her at least some relief during a period when she was under intense surveillance.

I was in the unique position of having access to her husband Walter, who had been imprisoned on Robben Island until 1982 and then in Pollsmoor Prison. It was a heavy burden for me, as I often had to impart bad news about arrests, detention or prosecution of his wife, sons or daughters.

Physically diminutive, Walter had a huge personality and was inspirational to talk to. He exuded warmth and concern and it was traumatic for me to have to give him unpleasant news. During all the time I knew him he never once complained about his own condition or focused on petty, irrelevant issues. He used his limited time with me for the benefit of his comrades and the struggle. And he had a formidable skill when it came to encrypting messages to be sent to the leadership elsewhere.

Later in 1984, I had to tell him about the imprisonment of members of the newly formed United Democratic Front (UDF), among them his beloved wife. With fifteen others she had been arrested during protests against the government's plans to set up a Tricameral Parliament.

I was against this hypocritical move with all my heart. It was an insult to the black majority of South Africa. President Botha had announced there would be elections by which Indian people and Coloureds could vote for representation on a new body to 'share' power with the State. Blacks, who had been banished to their so-called homelands and could therefore be said to have independence, would have no rights.

There was a witty slogan, which I embraced completely. It said that like the washing-powder Omo, the new body would make whites whiter, make Coloureds brighter, and remove all black spots. It was an accurate assessment.

At a time when the ANC and Black Consciousness were both banned and thus dormant, there was a need for organisational resurgence. Many activists from the community and the labour force came together to form the United Democratic Front (UDF) as an effective opposition to the Tricameral Parliament.

I was totally against the notion of a sham election and encouraged a boycott of the elections in every way I could. I clashed with many senior members of the Indian community in Natal and elsewhere, disagreeing violently with leaders who said this could be a way forward.

That was what the State wanted the world to believe: that they had softened and become reasonable towards non-whites and were offering them democracy. They slated it as white people having full voting rights over whites, Indians having voting rights over Indian affairs, and also Coloureds. The blacks had been stripped of their South African citizenship and marginalised in their wretched 'homelands'.

Two years earlier, in 1982, Nelson Mandela had been moved from Robben Island to Pollsmoor Prison on the mainland and he now sent for me to advise that 'groupism' was not necessarily a bad thing if it turned out to be a means to an end.

I argued that South African Indians were not Indians; they were citizens of this country, part and parcel of South Africa. I was totally against us being placed into another sort of limbo. I told him I felt there should be no tampering with the national identity. The ANC had opened its doors to everyone. We should not now turn to using ethnicity as any sort of answer.

The Black Consciousness Movement agreed with me that the government was looking to divide and rule. Non-whites would be playing into their hands if they voted. It would be a step backwards.

I began to be labelled BCM rather than ANC, but I didn't give a damn. I knew all about being Indian in South Africa and I distrusted this phoney offer of 'democracy'.

The Tricameral Parliament was set up, only being dismantled when Mandela was released in 1990. As far as I am concerned it achieved one thing only – allowing fireworks during Diwali, which had previously been banned. Nothing else. It was a sham which underlined the disenfranchisement of black people.

Under this new authority there were social grants introduced for Coloureds and Indian people; blacks were excluded. It was all an insulting mess and I became despondent. But I am a Hindu and we believe there must be a dawn. No matter how bad conditions were, the evil could not be sustained.

I had to wait a further ten years for that dawn.

Meantime, there were UDF clients of mine, including MaSisulu, who were arrested and accused of treason for their protests against the Tricameral Parliament. Their crime? They had sung liberation songs and made anti-government speeches, or been present when others had made such speeches.

I was representing several of the arrested. Five of them, including my client Archibald Gumede, went underground after being given bail and decided to take refuge in the British Consulate in Durban. This was embarrassing for the British government, which had never supported our stand against the apartheid government and had, shamefully in my view, stood firm against the notion of sanctions.

Consulate staff did not want to expel the UDF members into the hands of the police, but also did not want to be associated with our fight. By October, three of the men left the consulate voluntarily, and were immediately arrested. Gumede and two others remained.

In mid-December these three decided to leave, and were also arrested and charged with treason. They appeared in a packed courtroom with crowds singing liberation songs outside.

Ismail Mahomed applied for bail for them, claiming that the State's documents were inaccurate; adjournment after adjournment took place while this was debated. It was becoming clear that the State wished to draw out the trial in an attempt to break the UDF, but it had the opposite effect. Mass rallies and meetings were organised nationwide in support of the sixteen now accused.

Mahomed was repeatedly refused bail at a number of hearings and in April 1985 the prosecution presented indictments against all of the prisoners. There was chaos in court, with Mahomed continuing to submit objections and applications for bail.

When it was announced that Pietermaritzburg Supreme

Court would be the trial venue Mahomed realised he might be successful there, and he was right.

In May the Supreme Court set bail at R170,000. It was a vast sum of money but was quickly collected by their families and supporters. The ensuing trial was a travesty, with the prosecution relying solely on the content of speeches and songs to prove that violence was intended. Lengthy arguments that dissected the meaning of the word revolution, and attempts to show that the accused and the UDF intended to overthrow the government, prolonged the case.

After a full year of arguments, the production of inaudible tape-recordings, more than thirty of which Clifford in particular had spent long arduous hours transcribing, and the wearing down of the prosecution by Ismail Mahomed in full flow, the entire trial collapsed.

The State had achieved something though. It had kept leaders of a key activist movement out of action for a very long time.

MaSisulu had been the only woman in the trial. Before bail was granted she was held alone in the women's section of a prison where she had no comrades or friends to even talk to. The men by contrast could play chess and other board games, and had their camaraderie to keep them going. Food that I managed to have brought to MaSisulu was shared with others. She helped in every way possible with preparation of our case for the trial, never once complaining about the heartbreak of separation from her family.

The Sisulus, every one of them, were a family of colossal courage. Years later, in the early 1990s, their vital role in achieving freedom for South Africa was recognised by a Kennedy award from the United States. It included a grant of around US$2m, an enormous sum. I was invited to meetings as a member of the family trust they had set up. Each and every one of them was facing dire straits financially at this time.

But before we could even discuss the needs of each person, their son Zwelakhe, who had become my dear friend and brother, declared that the award should rightfully go to all the people of South Africa. He insisted that it should be used to set up institutions to benefit all those in need. The Sisulu family was incomparable. In truly African terms they were like the baobob tree, which so beautifully protects all who shelter under it from the harsh elements of nature.

Writer Elinor Batezat, who edited the family's life story for publication – a book called *Walter and Albertina Sisulu, In Our Lifetime* – and married their son Max, has written of how MaSisulu introduced me to her as 'more like our daughter than our lawyer'.

I treasured my friendship with them and we remained close until they both died. Walter died at home in 2003, aged ninety. His wife, who had cradled him in her arms till the end, asked afterwards: 'Walter, what do I do without you?' She lived another eight years, dying in 2011 at the age of ninety-two. Throughout the 1980s, we had shared the joys and sorrows of innumerable clashes with the apartheid authorities – many culminating in important victories, others cruelly defeated.

Soon after the UDF trial ended in 1986, I felt very honoured to receive an invitation from the American Bar Association and the Lawyers' Committee for Civil Rights and the Law to deliver their keynote address at an important conference in Washington DC.

It was beyond exciting for me, a validation of my work over

the years as a human rights lawyer. I had not been able to travel for four years due to my banning order and of course had no passport. It did not surprise me in the least when my request for a passport was declined; I felt that a great opportunity to share my experience and knowledge was now lost.

But quite unexpectedly, two days before the conference was scheduled to start, I had a call from the security police telling me I had been granted permission to travel to America, for seven days only and for the sole purpose of attending the conference.

It was tremendously good news but it also put me under pressure because of the time constraints. My biggest concern was the preparation of a substantive speech. Naturally, I turned to Mahomed, whose friendship continued to burden him as I tested it to the full. He was extremely glad for me, and unhesitatingly came to my rescue, putting aside all his own commitments and promising to assist me with the speech.

Clifford Mailer, the vital third member of our close team, joined in. There was one night left before my departure. We met at Mahomed's house in Laudium, Pretoria, at about 7 p.m., setting to work and agreeing we might have to carry on through the night.

As I've already said, working with Mahomed under normal circumstances was a challenge. Under pressure it was a complete nightmare. His adrenalin was flowing, his impatience was rising and his temper was flaring. At every small mistake we made, his mighty wrath descended on us. He screamed, hurled abuse and had all kinds of tantrums. But he was a genius and all he wanted was the best. We knew that and appreciated his help.

When the script was ready Mahomed read it into a Dictaphone with Clifford in charge of the technology. At one point the tape ran out without us realising. So most of the dictation had not been recorded and it was already 3 a.m. Mahomed was virtually jumping up and down with anger. Clifford was a nervous wreck and I was paralysed with fear and exhaustion.

We had had nothing to eat, and time was running out.

We began again in a very tense atmosphere. By 5 a.m. we had completed a formidable paper for me to present, but of course it still needed typing up and checking.

Mahomed offered to have it typed by his secretary and delivered to me at the airport. He pressed me to drive his Mercedes to my house to pack for the journey. It was a kind offer, but I'd never driven the huge vehicle before and didn't know the roads well.

Somehow I got to my office to brief the staff on cases to be dealt with in my absence. While I was talking to Ilona, one of our activist clients from the Eastern Transvaal arrived in an obvious panic. He was carrying a parcel and said that he and some comrades had been caught up in a violent incident in which a police informer had tricked them into handling several grenades which were primed to explode. Two of his comrades had been killed and others badly injured. I had no time to pursue the matter, or to examine the package. I took it from him and put it in the office safe.

At the airport I waited anxiously for my speech to arrive. My name was being called, I needed to board the plane. At the final announcement I headed for the departure gate. Then I heard someone calling out and there was Mahomed, his hair dishevelled, calling out and running frantically towards me, waving an envelope. Here was one of South Africa's greatest jurists, putting on an almost comical display.

I was so relieved and touched that I wept as he reached me. Now I had a speech of 150 meaningful pages, not checked or corrected, but brilliant.

After a twenty-hour journey I arrived in Washington and just had time to shower at my hotel and rush off to the conference. Then Ilona was on the phone, hysterically informing me that my office was swamped with security police with bomb squads and sniffer dogs.

They were looking for the parcel – it contained a hand grenade. I told Ilona to hand it over to them and consult advocate Mahomed. His love and loyalty to me was being called on once again. It turned out that our activist client had been arrested, detained and interrogated until he gave up the fact that the hand grenade was in my office.

I managed to put this to the back of my mind and concentrate on the conference. There were many judges from South Africa present, and that pleased me. I was the first speaker in the programme and was allotted twenty minutes. I had no idea how I was going to summarise my 150 pages into a twenty-minute presentation but I did it and was congratulated. The speech was published by the American Bar Association.

That evening I had hoped to relax at the banquet laid on by our hosts, but I received a surprise visit from a government delegation. Apparently President Ronald Reagan had requested a meeting with me. I spontaneously declined, although my comrades Bill Frankel and Horst Kleinschmidt, both with me, pressed me to accept.

I saw no purpose whatever in talking to an American president who was refusing to acknowledge the ANC and the anti-apartheid movement in general, and who was not prepared to bring sanctions against South Africa.

I enjoyed snubbing him.

Horst, who was running the ANC's fundraising organisation in London – International Defence and Aid Fund (IDAF) – had been instructed to somehow get me to visit London for a meeting with the ANC executive. Naturally, I agreed to that.

I was enjoying my first taste of freedom very much. Horst had hired a limousine and we set off on a fabulous road trip from Washington to New York, such luxury. In New York, the authoress Betsy Landers hosted a party for me and I met some prominent members of the city's literary circle. I was inundated with questions and found there was a great deal of interest in South Africa. It was comforting to know there were others genuinely concerned for our plight and pledging support.

The next morning I was amazed to hear that there were many South Africans living in exile in America who had heard I was there and were desperate to meet me, including representatives from several political and humanitarian organisations, as well as journalists wanting interviews.

Among them was a delegation from the UN Security Council inviting me to address the Council on the impact of apartheid legislation on human and civil rights. I felt extremely honoured and wanted to accept. But advocate David Soggot, a close friend and colleague, advised me against it. He was concerned that I might not be able to return to South Africa. I have always regretted that I turned down the invitation but also accept that he was probably right.

The ANC had supported my visit to America and planned a busy programme for me in New York. They assigned their representative David Ndaba to take care of me. His real name was Sam Gulube, now Director-General in the Department of Defence and Veterans in South Africa.

During my whistle-stop tour there was time for a fabulous highlight – an open-air jazz concert in Harlem. It was a stunning experience for me. As we joined the thronging crowds I heard my name being shouted from across the huge park. It actually sounded like an echo.

Then I saw a young man running towards me, stumbling through the crowds of artistes, instruments and patrons. He almost knocked me over with his hug. He had been a client I had successfully defended and who had then gone into exile. We shared some wonderful moments.

The next day Horst was leaving for London and although my passport was specifically restricted to America, for just seven days, the ANC had sought sympathy with the British authorities and I was being allowed to go with him. Labour MP and anti-apartheid supporter Bob Hughes – now Lord Hughes – came on to the plane and escorted me through the airport.

We had a very tight schedule with meetings, consultations and interviews. I had to convey messages and instructions and take many messages of response back home. I met with Thabo Mbeki, the ANC revolutionary living and studying in exile in the UK, later to succeed Nelson Mandela as president of the new South Africa, and with other members of the ANC's Executive Council. Every minute of the day was accounted for. It was exhausting, but I was totally energised and inspired by the experience.

As I prepared to leave London, I heard a State of Emergency had been declared in South Africa. Dozens of friends and comrades, including Thabo Mbeki, tried desperately to dissuade me from returning. I would not listen: I had to get back. Staying in exile was not an option. My family, my friends, my clients and my country meant too much to me.

I was met at the airport by my husband Reg and Espree. We dropped Reg at his workplace in Fordsburg and drove on to Lenasia. I was glad to be back home, keen to relate my experiences to everyone, although it already seemed like a dream.

I was chatting animatedly to Espree when we both realised our car was being surrounded by a huge contingent of police vehicles and we were being pushed off the road. At the back of my mind I had suspected some sort of 'welcome' home, but this shocked me. I was terrified and panicky. The police escorted us to my house in Lenasia where I was told I was under arrest and I should pack a bag.

The phone was ringing. It was Reg. I spoke briefly to him in Gujarati. I said: 'Kuthra anhenya che' – 'The dogs are here.'

That incensed the police; they had understood and now became more aggressive. My friends and neighbours were arriving in the commotion and Espree was trying to get me to eat some chicken biryani she had prepared. But I could not eat, I could not even think. My friend and neighbour Hajira Momoniat came over to comfort me. Everyone was in distress as the police drove off with me.

They took me to a cell in the Kliptown police station in Soweto and left me there for a day and night with no contact with the outside world. I could not sleep or rest, or think. My mind was racing, and all the time there were murmured conversations taking place outside my cell. I was under constant observation by the police, checking on me and reporting back. Some sort of fuss was going on and I was not being told anything.

In the early hours of the next morning a group of security police came in and ordered me to take my belongings; I was leaving. I was gripped by fear. I thought of the cruel end to the lives of Steve Biko, Babla Saloojee, Ernest Dipale and many others who died in detention.

I felt numb, as if my senses had died. I could not feel or hear or see or smell. I don't know how long this went on. I had been bundled into the back of an unmarked police vehicle and had no idea where we were going. Then I heard a shrill command: 'Get out! Get out!' and I was dragged out of the car. There was Reg standing at the door of our house. We just stared at each other, then hugged and he brought me into the house.

I had not been dreaming. My friends and family, journalists and comrades crowded around me. I was told that the American Bar Association, together with the Lawyers' Committee for Civil Rights, had put immense pressure on President Ronald Reagan to intervene with the South African government and petition for my release. Due to his action I was now free. A supreme irony.

This trip I had taken, and this detention, spurred me on to continue my life of activism. There was no turning back. The whole world was behind us and we would one day win our freedom.

The eighties was a decade burdened with confrontations with the State and the judiciary. For me and my comrades and colleagues it was a fight all the way, often beaten back by the intransigence of the government, and sometimes gaining victories, small and large, over the system.

There was one major victory that took place during this decade. The result of eight years of battling for justice for Steve Biko, a struggle hero whose death in police custody had shocked our supporters all over the world, was a great breakthrough.

My friend and co-activist Professor Joe Veriava, in his capacity as Vice-President of the Transvaal Medical Society, a group of black medical professionals opposed to the imposition of apartheid policies in health, never gave up the pursuit of justice for Biko. Against almost impossible odds, he and four medical colleagues brought the entire matter to the Supreme Court, with my support. To achieve this he came up against the most formidable authorities in the country.

Biko had died of wounds inflicted by the security police during his interrogation in 1977. A post-mortem showed he died from a head injury with cerebral contusions, disseminated intravascular coagulation and renal failure. Yet the presiding magistrate at the inquest concluded it had not been proven that death had been brought about by an act of omission amounting to an offence on the part of any person.

Medical details of the hearing were sent, as required by law, to the South African Medical and Dental Council (SAMDC) – now called the Health Professional Council of South Africa. They contained details of the evidence of Dr Ivor Lang and Dr Benjamin Tucker.

Joe and his colleagues believed unlawful and criminal actions had been carried out by the security police, and in addition unprofessional conduct by those doctors who were involved in Biko's care. Biko was said to have died at his own hand by going on hunger strike. Yet the evidence showed he had been chained to a metal grille in a crucifix position and left to hang there for several hours while semi-conscious.

Joe said he was convinced the police and doctors should be held responsible. Lang and Tucker had failed to recognise or act on the seriousness of the brain injury, and therefore contributed to Biko's death.

The SAMDC held a preliminary enquiry to investigate our complaints and those of the South African Council of Churches, and ruled there was no prima facie evidence of misconduct. The full Council confirmed this ruling. The Medical Association of South Africa also supported the ruling and passed resolutions defending the integrity and bone fides of members of the SAMDC, at the same time attacking Joe and his colleagues for being critical.

Joe was up against one refusal after another from professional bodies denying any wrongdoing. He found the *South African Medical Journal* was complicit by declining to publish letters of protest from leading doctors critical of these decisions. He decided to pursue claims of unprofessional and disgraceful conduct by the doctors who had treated Biko.

Joe came to me to lodge a new complaint against the SAMDC based on the inquest records. I did not hesitate to go to Ismail Mahomed, and we discovered that another group, headed by three professors, were also laying complaints.

In March 1983 the SAMDC rejected all of these complaints and it looked as though the matter was back at square one. The authorities had circled their wagons; there was no way through for the blinding truth.

We decided to go to the highest authority, the Supreme Court, and I helped get funding for the application on behalf of Joe's group and the group comprising the three professors.

The court agreed we could bring a single petition. I turned to the American Association of Black Lawyers and they helpfully set up a meeting between Joe and their counterpart lawyer in Botswana.

The Supreme Court ruled in our favour, holding that there was indeed prima facie evidence of improper or disgraceful conduct on the part of Lang and Tucker. It ordered the SAMDC to set up a disciplinary committee to investigate their conduct.

In July 1985, nearly eight years after the death of one of South Africa's greatest heroes, a four-day hearing found Lang guilty on five counts and Tucker on three. Tucker was struck off the medical roll and Lang was cautioned and reprimanded.

At a hearing where Tucker applied to be reinstated to the medical register he said: 'I came to realise that during more than thirty years as a district surgeon I had gradually lost the fearless independence required of a medical practitioner when the interests of his patient are threatened.

'I had become too closely identified with the interests of the organs of state, especially the police force, with which I dealt practically on a daily basis.'

In the mid-1980s there was beginning to be a perceptible change in the relationship between the State and the anti-apartheid movements. The Supreme Court's decision towards Steve Biko's death seemed to herald a new, healthier era in which real progress could be made.

This was not due to any softening on the part of the apartheid government, however. More a measure of its reluctant acceptance that it had made South Africa ungovernable and repugnant to the world outside, and that righting such appalling wrongs as the cover-up over Biko was a reasonable way to improve its reputation and its future.

This change in attitude was never more obvious than in the case I helped to bring to court for my client Ebrahim Ismail Ebrahim. I had taken him on under extraordinary circumstances which, at the time, seemed almost normal.

An anonymous caller at my office had turned up with a handwritten message scrawled on toilet paper. He had retrieved it from the street below the police headquarters in John Vorster Square. Prisoners with no other means of getting messages out would often drop these scraps of paper from the tenth floor window where their cells overlooked the street.

In many cases, as with Ebrahim, it was the only way that their families or lawyers would know they had been detained. These notes would sometimes actually tell us police were using torture: stark messages for a stark time in our lives. Many of the passers-by on the street were black workers and would be sympathetic to anyone being detained. They would take the note to a lawyer, often to me.

Ebrahim's note had simply given his name and circumstances and asked me by name to represent him. I phoned Clifford Mailer and together we rushed off to court with an affidavit saying a client of mine was being detained. We put in an urgent application for his release, but the judge, colluding with the State, said police were denying he was in custody.

All we had was a piece of toilet paper and a scrawl.

We applied for habeas corpus to force the police to produce our client.

Ebrahim, who had already served fifteen years on Robben Island and subsequently been banned, had been living incognito in Swaziland, occasionally venturing in and out of Durban.

In December 1986 he was abducted at night by two security police who raided his home in Swaziland. A colleague with him was shot dead. Ebrahim was brought to Johannesburg, and later held in Pretoria prison.

He was being charged with high treason as a known MK operative, and an important part of our case was that allegiance to MK did not classify him as a murderer. We contended that he had been abducted illegally from a foreign country. We also submitted that the ANC and its armed wing MK were revolutionary movements, not organisations which sanctioned assassinations.

Ismail Mahomed, on brilliant form, somehow persuaded the court that the State's actions breached the sovereign rights of a foreign country and that the ANC was not a murderous organisation. He pressed the judge to take evidence from ANC leaders themselves.

The State, surprisingly, agreed to take evidence on commission in a neutral place, in this case London. This unique move was an extraordinary concession, which illustrated the mood of that moment – conciliation.

I travelled to London with Kessie Naidoo, an advocate who often joined our team and who is today a senior judge in Durban. A courtroom was made available to us for a week and I had the extraordinary experience of watching the South African State's legal team face the High Command of the ANC in England.

I felt immeasurably proud when Oliver Tambo, Thabo Mbeki, Jacob Zuma and others filed in, wearing dark tailored suits with collars and ties and looking every inch the sophisticated politicians they were. It was impossible not to be impressed. I am not sure what I was expecting, but I think the

State team was ready for a bunch of rough guerrilla fighters straight out of the bush.

We had several days of civilised hearings overseen by a British judge during which the ANC cleverly distinguished itself from other liberation organisations with reputations as murderers. They produced policy documents showing that they would never use soft targets, that their sabotage attacks were directed only at government installations, apartheid monuments and the system. There were to be no assassinations.

Both sides were civil to each other. The South African regime was witnessing the ANC's stature, one of cordiality and respect, for the first time. It was an eye-opener for them, a shock even. For me and my team there was also time to enjoy reunions with family members and friends living in London. We all stayed at the Cumberland Hotel and had plenty of free time outside of the court hearings.

And there was something else close to my heart that I was determined to somehow fit it in. My niece Mala, her husband Pritiraj, and their two small children Simi and Surekha were living in exile in Denmark. When I called them on the phone they were extremely excited. Mala sobbed and pleaded with me to somehow fly over to see them. I wanted to do that very much but did not believe it was possible. Somehow, Pritiraj began lobbying the Danish government to assist.

She and her husband were courageous members of the Black Consciousness Movement and had faced surveillance, police harassment and intimidation, culminating in two assassination attempts in 1978. They had fled to Denmark with their two daughters aged two and four to build a new life in a new country. But they never stopped fighting apartheid and set about developing international solidarity. They managed to build Denmark's fledgling anti-apartheid movement into the largest of Europe's solidarity organisations, and influenced the government to impose economic sanctions against South Africa. Nevertheless, while working tirelessly, they suffered a drought of news from home, and Mala has told me how she longed to know what was happening in the extended family – the marriages, births and deaths, and the family's political engagements.

She said to me recently: 'The quest to keep our identity, especially for our daughters Simi and Surekha, was a vital part of maintaining links with home.' She remembered me calling from London to say I was there. 'The magnetic urge to meet and share information was mutual,' she told me.

Her husband set about using all his contacts among Danish political sympathisers who knew and admired the work we were doing in South Africa. He wanted to get me into Denmark without the South African authorities knowing, then back safely to London. And all this was to be done in two days.

An MP from the Danish Socialist People's Party was his best hope. He pulled all possible strings and I then heard I was to go to the Danish Embassy in London and apply for special permission to visit. I was turned down by the bemused embassy staff who had never heard of anyone entering Denmark without proper documentation.

Mala was, I heard later, fully confident that I would come. She was baking special cakes and biscuits in a whirlwind of planning and preparing. Her much-celebrated aunt was coming and she was going to be welcomed with a feast.

Pritiraj, undaunted by the setback in London, persuaded the Danish Foreign Minister to meet him and give his approval. The embassy staff in London was instructed to grant permission for a visit of no more than twenty-four hours. It was worth every second – a full day of hugs, sharing news, eating a feast together and visiting the city sights.

Mala and Pritiraj told me they were totally fascinated to hear my first-hand account of how the struggle was shaping, the cracks emerging in the State structure and the waves of mass resistance. None of us had much sleep and it really didn't matter.

As instructed, I left when my time was up. We had been warned that the MP who had pulled out all stops to get me there would be in serious trouble if I stayed.

On our return to South Africa we learned that our application for Ebrahim's release had been turned down. His trial would proceed. It had been set down for hearing in the most inconvenient location, a tactic intended to undermine all of us, Ebrahim, his family and supporters, and us his lawyers. The trial was to be held in Piet Retief, a rural town in Mpumalanga, close to the Swazi border. Our legal team would have to drive for more than two hours every day to get there, and a further two hours to return.

Ebrahim told us that he had been detained for six months and tortured. His main interrogator, Dietleef again, had told him: 'I am not going to touch you now, but if you do not give us the information we want I am going to do something to you. If you survive it will make me think you are not human.' He was put into a sealed cell into which noise was piped day and night and the light never switched off. 'I was completely cut off for days on end and never allowed to sleep,' he said. 'I almost went mad, I really did.'

At the courtroom in Piet Retief there was no canteen or

nearby café. We located some people in the Indian community and they were kind enough to send food to the court for us. In addition there were no washroom facilities for me as a non-white woman.

Clifford was concerned and took up the matter in open court. But I was so furious I did not partake in that discussion. I simply pushed past white people and went into the whites-only ladies cloakroom.

One of my abiding memories of the tedious journeys to and from court was Ismail Mahomed singing throughout. He had a truly awful singing voice and chose melancholy philosophical laments. We were all tired and found it excruciating. Clifford and Sean Naidoo remember us all corpsing with laughter in the back of the car. I got the sense that Mahomed enjoyed that in his quirky way.

Ebrahim was sentenced to a further twenty years on Robben Island, the judge remarking that 'your first fifteen years don't seem to have done you any good'.

Two years later we won his release on appeal, citing the lack of jurisdiction in his abduction from Swaziland, a foreign country. It was a landmark case, acknowledged internationally. As recently as the 1990s I was asked to send Ebrahim's court records to America where lawyers for the ousted leader of Panama, Manuel Noriega, hoped to use it as a precedent in their claim that he could not be tried in America for alleged offences committed in his own country. I was not at all sympathetic to Noriega and his alleged drug-trafficking crimes, but it was good to know that we had made it into the annals of international law. His case had been, for us, a total validation of our victory in the Nkondo case, a measure of the genius of Ismail Mahomed.

Today, Ebrahim Ismail Ebrahim is in President Jacob Zuma's cabinet.

I savoured the victories we achieved, especially as they were earned despite opposition from our own professional bodies, the Law Society and the Bar Council. And many of our successes resonated down the years, assisting millions of black people by setting important precedents.

Clifford Mailer was no longer part of our team. In 1988, he had sensibly taken his wife and young sons to England, determined that neither of them would be called up for military service with the South African Defence Force. Mahomed encouraged him – it was the only option during apartheid – and I wished him well while all the time mourning his loss to our small team.

Sean Naidoo also decided to continue his career in England. I felt bereft at having to bid goodbye to both him and Clifford. I had had difficulties with both of them on our first meeting – Sean was Indian by birth but seemed to me to have adopted a very English manner and we clashed initially but later formed an enduring friendship. His aloofness, I learnt, was misleading. He was actually warm and witty, and a great lawyer.

Mahomed and I needed all our inner resources to carry on the fight with our diminished team. I will always be immensely proud of the battle we won for township residents continually dogged by the threat of eviction. They could not afford high rents and were constantly subjected to the experience of being ejected from their homes and abandoned on a city pavement surrounded by their belongings. But when Ismail Mahomed caught sight of a loophole in the system that calculated the rents, he went for the kill.

In a test case heard in August 1988 he argued that three

families evicted from their homes in the Jabulani district of Soweto had been treated unfairly and unlawfully. The judge agreed that they could return to their homes pending his judgement. They were all six months in arrears of rent. During lengthy and complicated legal arguments the court was persuaded that rentals had not been lawfully fixed and determined in the prescribed manner, and that the evictions were unlawful and there was no proper legal obligation to pay the set rent.

In previous clashes with police during evictions, twenty-two people had been killed. Now the actions of the masses were being vindicated. Our case led to a general rent boycott, which lasted four years and cost the municipality millions of rand. It spread beyond Soweto to fifty other black townships. People living in the brick bungalows and corrugated iron shacks in Sebokeng, Sharpeville and dozens of other deprived trouble spots found the courage to stand their ground, emboldened by our test case.

Every success we enjoyed over the years happened despite the aggressive opposition of the judicial system in general, a shameful truth. I relished the opportunity to spell this out in public to the world at large, as soon as I could.

My moment came in 1999 when the Truth and Reconciliation Commission at last threw some light on some of our country's most shocking secrets. Giving evidence at the TRC legal hearing, I straightaway posited that the legal system of South Africa had enforced and reinforced the social structures imposed in the interest of a small section of our society: the white population. I told the hearing that, although currently a member of the National Assembly, I had been an attorney for nineteen years in the field of civil liberties and human rights, acting in some of the most celebrated political cases in the country. I represented youth, students, activists and leaders from a wide spectrum of political and labour organisations.

I listed my arrests and detentions and of the three petrol bomb attacks on my home. I told them of random incidents from a list of hundreds: how friends and colleagues were instructed to inform on me during my banning order; how police slashed all four tyres on my car while I was consulting with a client in Magoebaskloof in the Northern Transvaal; how police locked me in a cell, leaving my mother in my car in suffocating heat, when I visited a client banished to a village near Pietersburg; how a judge's daughter, acting as his registrar during a court case, audibly called me a bitch in court, and my complaint about this was ignored.

I asked the hearing: 'The question here arises, "What did the Law Society do for me and others in my position?" I would like to boldly state – absolutely nothing.

'I felt on the contrary persecuted by the Society because complaints of a frivolous nature were often pursued vigorously against me, often without the source being disclosed to me.'

I related occasions when I should have been able to consult with my clients in confidence. Instead the police had been visibly hovering nearby and reporting back. Once I had been fined by magistrates for alleged 'contempt' when I protested at this. Clifford Mailer represented me and remembers how I sat in court openly turning the pages of a newspaper. I was certainly in contempt, and didn't care who knew it.

I told the hearing about iniquitous sentencing patterns, including the case where my client had inscribed the words 'Viva Mandela' on his coffee mug and was handed a four-year prison sentence as a result.

And I related how we won permission to inspect a cell at John Vorster Square where our client claimed he was given electric-shock torture treatment. By the time we were allowed the inspection there were no sockets or plugs visible in the walls. Counsel insisted that some shelves were removed and there were the sockets and plugs concealed underneath.

I wanted the hearing to see the pattern of neglect by the judiciary over the years, telling them that I did not know of a single magistrate who carried out visits to detainees, as required by law, to witness the conditions they were being held in, or who made reports of the torture, maltreatment and assaults that were being perpetrated. I described the use of parents, husbands, wives and children as State witnesses, compromising the accused and weighing heavily on their morale.

I called for members of the judiciary, magistrates and judges, to come forward and take honest responsibility for the behaviour I had listed.

It is to the eternal shame of South Africa's judiciary that not one of them responded.

A semi-apologetic letter from a Law Society representative was read to the hearing. That was all the accountability we were going to get.

# CHAPTER SEVEN

# A NEW LIGHT
# IN MY LIFE

Somehow it had never been the right time for me and my husband to start a family.

We both adored small children. I was always the first to want to hold my friends' babies and the last to hand them back. But we did not have a child of our own. So we were both as astonished as each other when we unexpectedly found ourselves with a tiny five-month-old girl to bring up.

I had returned to my office after a gruelling day in court and there discovered a noisy little bundle squirming on the emerald green sofa next to my desk overloaded with clients' files. Stunned into silence, I stared at my staff in disbelief and confusion; they stared back. Eventually they told me that the young wife of one of my clients in prison had left the baby there for me, and disappeared: no note, no bottle of milk, no change of clothes, nothing.

This child had been left for me in despair. She had been born into a family riven by apartheid's cruelty and her mother was responding to a chance remark I had made out of compassion and concern. I had taken Phinda Molefe, a country girl in her early twenties, to Pretoria Prison the previous day to visit her activist husband. He had never seen their baby and since he was my client I had offered to make it possible.

Phinda was moving from house to house, sleeping on the floors and sofas of ANC sympathisers. She had no family in the Johannesburg area and was penniless and bereft. Her own family was hundreds of miles away in the Eastern Cape and had many troubles of their own. She was struggling for survival and panic-stricken about bringing up a child in her life of turmoil.

On the long drive to prison I realised her overwhelming hopelessness. Glancing over to the sleeping baby in her arms I offered help: 'Let me look after your little girl until things improve.' It was spontaneous and came from my heart. And when we reached the prison and I picked up the child to put her in her father's arms in the lawyer's consulting room, I looked into that innocent face and felt an instinctive maternal love for her.

I knew that things were not likely to improve for Phinda and her husband. They were victims of this vicious struggle which could last for many more years. I admired their courage and their resilience but their baby needed a shelter from the chaos and perhaps I was the right person to provide it. Phinda was in distress and I knew even better than she did that her situation was very bad and about to get worse.

Her husband, Popo Molefe, a brave man who helped to set up the United Democratic Front as an umbrella organisation for all anti-apartheid groups, was on remand for treason and expected to be sent to Robben Island. I had represented him many times and knew he was facing a serious custodial sentence.

Phinda, ten years younger, was the daughter of a much-revered ANC leader in the Eastern Cape. He had worked tirelessly underground for the movement until he was arrested, convicted and sent to Robben Island in the 1960s. On his release after fourteen years Sipho Charles Hashe was immediately banned and subjected to house arrest.

Phinda's young life had been hellish. Her mother and her older sister were both involved in the movement and their home was used for political recruitment. There were police raids and firebombs which destroyed the house, then evictions during her father's imprisonment.

Her father had been targeted for years but continued to politically educate the youth and inspire students with the comradeship of Phinda's sister Mandisa, who was a student leader. Together they organised school boycotts, and eventually Hashe's daughter, nephew and others were forced into exile; he organised places for them in MK camps. This was a politically hard-core family with deep-rooted beliefs. Phinda was the youngest of nine children, caught up in political activity from birth.

Her father, Hashe, had revived the Port Elizabeth Black Civics Organisation (PEBCO) and with comrades he launched the three-day stayaway in November 1984 that came to be called The Black Weekend. It was a mass revolt against poor housing and extortionate rents, against low wages and inadequate transport, schools and medical care for black people. In the immediate aftermath, the family home was petrol-bombed by police while a helicopter hovered overhead.

A few weeks later Hashe and two comrades, Qaqawuli

Godolozi and Champion Galela, received a call from a man who said he was a British diplomat who wanted to help them. He could not come to their township, he said. They should come to Port Elizabeth airport to meet him. The three men were never seen again. A baggage porter said he had observed them bundled into police vehicles and driven away.

I knew the family well and had represented Hashe many times in court. His wife Elizabeth, Phinda's mother and herself a formidable activist, begged me to take her to police stations and prisons all over the country to find him. There were rumours that the men were being held incommunicado in different prisons in the country.

We travelled the length and breadth of South Africa together, looking for them. Elizabeth never accepted that her husband might be dead. She would hear from other imprisoned activists that they had seen him, that they had spoken to him through the wall of a prison cell. We went to remote prisons but no one had any record of him. On one occasion we went to a mortuary and she walked from shrouded body to shrouded body looking for her husband. I could not bear what she was going through. Long before she came to the last of them, none of them the man she hoped to find, I had fled outside sobbing.

I brought at least three applications to court and the Minister of Law and Order himself, Adriaan Vlok, in a sworn affidavit declared they had not been arrested and were not in custody. Elizabeth never gave up hope, but it was to be twelve more years until she heard for herself the appalling truth about her husband's disappearance.

Several security police, including two black 'askaris' – men who had been politically turned and who now worked undercover against their own people – asked the Truth and Reconciliation Commission for amnesty for the shooting and killing of Hashe and the others. Their lies and excuses were shocking to listen to. They said they had been told to eliminate the men as troublemakers in the community and had abducted them at the airport, then driven them to a disused police station near the remote town of Cradock.

Their stories varied. Several of them said the men had been shot, their bodies thrown onto a makeshift pyre and burnt, then their ashes tipped into the nearby Fish River. One notorious askari, Joe Mamasela, claimed instead that they had been interrogated and brutally tortured, beaten and choked to death.

A further ten years on, the National Prosecuting Authority's missing persons researchers discovered bone fragments at Post Chalmers Farm in Cradock, and matched them to the three men. All of the police witnesses had lied. The men's remains together weighed 26kg. There had been no ashes, and there would be no truth to give their widows closure. All they could do was hold decent burials after twenty-two years of waiting and hoping.

The TRC hearings were a torture in themselves for Elizabeth Hashe. She had all my sympathy as she listened to the police trying to save themselves, and she opposed amnesty for any of them. A strong though distraught figure, speaking to the Commissioners through an interpreter, Elizabeth told how she had brought up nine children – five of her own, including Phinda, and four of her sister's – and how she and Sipho willingly gave their hearts to everyone who needed help.

She told of police raids on their home when the one precious thing she owned, a sewing-machine bought for her when she was still at school, was kicked and broken by the white men disrupting her household and terrifying her children. She sold vegetables from a stall on the street and the police constantly harassed her claiming she had no licence, confiscating her goods.

When Sipho was arrested and detained, as he was frequently, Elizabeth would be threatened with eviction as the police said the house was in his name and his wife had no rights. 'One day I came home and all my belongings and my children were on the street outside,' she said. 'They refused to take my rent, saying I had to leave. Then they decided to take my money and my house, giving me a smaller, two-room house instead, where I had to live with all nine children.'

A Commissioner wanted to know if Elizabeth had reported the petrol-bombing incident to the police. 'How could we report the police to the police?' she asked.

She told the TRC that when Sipho had returned from Robben Island he asked her: 'Do you still accept me for your husband, because you know I will never stop fighting for the freedom of our people?' The last word she heard from him was that he had to go to the airport for a meeting. 'I'm coming back,' he said. And he told her where to find money he kept for the family, and money he kept for PEBCO.

As she spoke, I thought of the years I had accompanied Elizabeth to many hospitals, police cells and mortuaries in the long fruitless search for her husband. Once she was detained herself and left in a cell for a month before I could persuade a court to release her.

She told Archbishop Desmond Tutu, chairing the TRC: ' I want the Commission to empathise with me and understand what I feel. I don't want to cry, really I don't, but I would like some help.' Tutu promised her that her husband's ashes would be properly buried.

Joe Mamasela crossed the court to take her hand and ask for her forgiveness. She embraced him and I found that hard to accept. I asked her: 'How could you do that? I can't believe it.' She said we had to forgive in the interests of our country's future. She had a level of forgiveness which matched Mandela's, and which was beyond my level.

I had watched the TRC hearing on television and heard police describing how they crushed the brains of Elizabeth's husband and his comrades with their boots and threw the broken bodies in a lake. I could hardly bear to watch and listen. But closure is central to black South Africans' culture, and Elizabeth found value in it after all those years. Impossible though it was for me to share, I commend her for her forgiveness.

Phinda's father has been commemorated in a way he would have approved of. A school in Kwazakhele in the Eastern Cape has been named after him. Popo Molefe had visited the Hashe home during his work in setting up the UDF. Popo was extremely bright, a great organiser, and had all the potential of an exceptional leader. His speech to the South African Council of Churches conference in 1981 suggested the creation of a united democratic opposition to apartheid, and he later became the general secretary of the UDF.

It was natural for him to call at the Hashe household on a visit to Port Elizabeth. It was a focal point for student activism and Popo had come to know the family well. He fell in love with Phinda at first sight, despite their age difference. She was a political sympathiser who regularly attended meetings and rallies. Popo, a Tswana from Rustenberg in the Northern Cape, had been married before.

He and Phinda started their life together in Johannesburg. But Popo was forced by police harassment to work undercover for the ANC, often leaving her with only his comrades for support. Phinda's father had been absent for most of her life. Now her husband had all but disappeared, too.

She was supported by the UDF and gave birth to her baby at Johannesburg's Chris Hani Baragwanath Hospital, staying there for a month. She told me how she and the baby had no stable home or income and I was terribly moved by her plight. In the broader picture of the struggle this is what happened, families slipping through the net into despair.

I felt a strong and powerful love for this baby. I was connected to her whole family and I knew many households where children were being brought up by friends and relatives while their parents were in prison or had been killed.

Phinda was a warm-hearted girl, softly-spoken and respectful. She had said nothing in response when I made my spontaneous offer. She must have spent that night heart-searching before making her decision. And now I had a baby to care for, without the slightest idea how to go about it. Ilona, my assistant, went out to buy some sweetened yoghurt to feed her. That's all we could think of.

I called my husband with the startling message: 'I'm coming home early and I'm bringing a baby with me. It's going to be our baby, and she needs lots of things – clothes and nappies and food, whatever you can find.'

He asked me: 'Who is it, how old is it?' I told him we could talk about all that later. So Reg went out shopping and by the time I arrived with the tiny girl we had the essentials ready for her, plus literally dozens of dresses of the same size, colour and style. He had been on a panic buying spree and he had alerted our friends and neighbours, who all pledged support and advice.

Meanwhile, I struggled to even bring the baby home. I tried to strap her into the passenger seat of my car but she just flopped over. I had to keep stopping to pick her up again and settle her. I was totally confused, terrified actually with no idea to handle the situation.

Our baby had been named Albertina after the great heroine of the struggle, Albertina Sisulu. We shortened it to Tina and as she grew older she preferred that. But for now there were more immediate issues. How to bath a baby, how to wash that African hair which sprung up in uncontrollable curls, what to feed her? 'How are we going to bath her?' I asked Reggie. He was as clueless as I was. 'I've no idea,' he said. 'Let's put her in the washbasin.'

I had felt an immediate connection when I took Tina into prison to see her father, and that feeling remained. Reggie felt it too, and between us we discovered an overwhelming desire to love and care for this child who had come to us in such extraordinary circumstances, and tried to give her everything of the best.

I asked my neighbour Saras for help. She had children of her own and imparted all her motherly knowledge to me with bewildering speed. Within hours I had received valuable clues as to how to bath the baby and care for her hair, her appetite, all of her sleeping and waking needs.

Saras kindly offered to look after her while my husband and I were at work, our immediate concern. Later, Reg's sister-in-law stepped into the breach. She was home-based, bringing up small children of her own. She generously offered to care for one more, and that gave us valuable breathing space for several months.

What worried me most, and continually, is that Phinda would come back to claim her baby. The child's father was in prison, it was a chaotic arrangement, in fact no proper arrangement at all.

Reg and I found ourselves longing to get home in the evenings just to be with this child who was already bringing us so much joy. On her second day with us Tina greeted me with the tiniest of smiles when I came home from work and stretched out her arms. That was it for me: I adored her. She quickly gained a very special place in our home and our hearts. We were a big extended Indian family. Tina's mother was Xhosa, her father Tswana. But we did not see or anticipate any differences. All I really cared about was that we could keep her, that she would not be taken away as randomly as she had been given to us. I found that feeling unbearable and Tina seemed to share it. She didn't want to be separated from me even for short periods.

One day her mother called to ask if she could 'borrow' Tina because a diplomat from the German Embassy wanted to take her to lunch and discuss her situation. Foreign embassies were often sympathetic to activists in need and helped them financially. I understood why Phinda needed to go, and why she needed to take the baby with her. She promised to take good care of Tina and return her to me at my office after lunch.

I firmly believe it was the worst day of my life. As the hours ticked by, Ilona stayed with me, equally worried. By six o'clock, when we should have been closing the office, Phinda had not returned and we could not track her down anywhere. I was out of my mind with anxiety.

I will never forget the moment she reappeared and put Tina into my arms again. The apprehension remained with me though, through all the years until Tina was in her teens. Her father had not agreed to me formally adopting her, so my overriding fear was always that her parents, who had the right, would take her away from me at any time.

One night, Tina literally saved our lives, when the house was petrol-bombed. A few months after coming to us, we heard her crying loudly during the night. She usually slept well after a feed but on this occasion she was almost screaming. We tried to comfort her with a feed but nothing would stop her. Suddenly there was a loud blast and a huge fire started in the dining-room downstairs. If we had been asleep during the early hours we would have burnt to death in our beds. Instead, thanks to Tina, we were all downstairs trying to pacify her. As Reg battled to put out the flames, Tina fell fast asleep.

She was a child of the struggle, born at the height of apartheid into a heroic family of activists. She had been put into our care but nowhere was safe. We desperately wanted to save her, and ourselves, from life-threatening hostility from the State. Despite everything we did the danger was all around us, all the time. Reg and I, as would any parents, worried that we might one day lose our child.

Popo Molefe had been sentenced to ten years on Robben Island but was released after four. I was fearful that he would demand Tina's return, but by then he and his wife had parted and there was no settled home for her to go to. I asked him if I could formally adopt her, but he said he didn't want his child 'Indianised'. But I never imposed our Hindu culture on Tina, and by the age of four or five I had told her in simple terms about her parents and her own African culture.

Her mother came again to take the child to Port Elizabeth to introduce her to her grandmother and I heard back from Elizabeth Hashe that she was happy and grateful to know Tina had a stable home and family life. She had been flourishing with us. Bright as a button, curious about everything, she was a totally endearing child. Tina was loved at her nursery school and cherished at home. Reg insisted on sharing his food at the table with her; they had an extraordinary bond. For me this was a dream I had never dared to hope for: a child to love and care for.

She was naturally happy and optimistic, always singing. But there was still that nagging feeling inside me that this could end as quickly as it had begun. When Popo refused adoption I was heartbroken. He was unhappy himself; he had wanted a reunion with Phinda and their baby but she had met someone else and was living in Hillbrow, in central Johannesburg, with him. She had earlier come to terms with life without her husband, and now she had fallen in love. There was no going back for her and Popo was angry and upset.

Ironically, when he visited Phinda he met her best friend Tumi Plaatjie and was attracted to her. Later they married and had children of their own. When his new daughter was christened he wanted Tina to be christened too, so we had a joint ceremony.

Phinda herself was never anything but respectful and grateful to us for taking care of Tina when she had been unable to. But she had no idea of my anxieties. She once asked to have Tina for a weekend, and after she had taken her, Reg and I drove to her house and sat outside in the car, beside ourselves with worry. I could hear Tina crying. We sat there for hours; it was terrible.

The next day Phinda called to ask us to fetch her. Tina had been crying all night. She wanted to be with us, and we longed to have her back.

Another time Tina's father, newly married and prosperous with a very fancy house, wanted her to come to him for a holiday. It was 1990, the dawn of the new South Africa. Mandela was out of prison and heroes of the anti-apartheid movement like Popo Malefe had been rewarded. He was now Premier of North-West Province.

Tina was just five years old. She was too frightened to tell her father that she didn't eat pork or beef, that she was Hindu and a vegetarian. She had assumed Indian ways all by herself, without any pressure from us. She had been shocked at her grandmother's house in Port Elizabeth when chicken's feet were cooked. Now her father and his new wife were finding her difficult to cope with, and she was homesick. Tumi phoned to ask me to please come and fetch her. I could not get there fast enough to bring my lovely little girl home.

Our life with Tina was about reading stories together, long walks in the park, singing to her, and marvelling at her progress at school. She went to Auckland Park Primary, the best private school we could find, with a racial mix of pupils.

These were happy times, except that Reg and I had stayed together much too long. We had outlived our marriage and my sad lonely years during the banning order stayed in my memory. Reg had not stood by me; he had been unfaithful and our love was worn out.

We both adored Tina. He would spend hours on a Sunday morning washing her hair, brushing it and putting pretty ribbons in it. It was heartbreaking for both of us, on her behalf, when I finally left in 1989.

Now I bought a house in Mayfair, a nice suburb of Johannesburg, and took Tina there with me. Like so many others, I had bought the house in a mainly white area through a white nominee, the easiest and quickest way to do it. These houses had belonged to old-school Afrikaans people who built them beautifully, with Oregon pine floors and ceilings. Tina and I had a good solid home in which to start our new life.

I had known about Reg's affairs for years and should have left sooner. We were both heading reluctantly for divorce but it was not until 1989 that it actually came through, twenty-four hours before I married for the second time.

I had met Reagan through a professor friend and we got to know each other over a four-month period during which I invited him to Tina's fourth birthday party and introduced him to my family. My mother, astute but always accepting of my decisions, said she wanted me to be happy but that she had misgivings. She was right of course.

Meantime, we had a very grand wedding in Durban with Cyril Ramaphosa, now South Africa's Deputy President, and other anti-apartheid heroes like Jay Naidoo and lawyer Edwin Cameron among the guests. Tina was an important part of the celebrations, and she stayed close to Reg that day. He was still a very important person in her life. He and I were always Dad and Mum to her, and her biological parents were Daddy Popo and Mummy Phinda.

We had left the question of religion and culture completely open to her. She had been baptised with her half-sister and at one point she asked to go to madrasa classes for Islamic teaching. I allowed her do that, but she decided to opt out quite soon because the teacher was too strict.

We often went as a family to Jewish friends on Friday nights for the Sabbath celebration and Tina became familiar with the Torah and was able to recite from it. So from an early age she was exposed to many religious beliefs and persuasions and developed a good grounding and understanding of them and their cultures.

She could also sing in any one of the Indian languages with the correct pronunciation and rhythm, to the amazement of our friends and family.

Tina, not surprisingly, had been politically aware from a very young age. She was barely two when I first took her to a rally. It was a trade union event in Lenasia where we lived, and I naturally carried her there in my arms. As I arrived, the casspirs – the huge government armoured vehicles we all feared – began driving towards the crowd. I found myself in front of one and instinctively raised my fist, daring them to proceed. Tina, without any prompting, raised her tiny fist too.

When she was about seven I heard her talking to her cousin Nerissa, aged four. They were watching a dance competition on television. Nerissa said she liked the white dancers best and was immediately brought up sharply by Tina. 'Why do you like them?' she asked. 'You know white people are bad.' She told Nerissa how her father had been put in jail and that black children were not allowed to swim at the Durban beaches.

It was fascinating to me to hear the racism of apartheid from a child's perspective.

Nerissa quickly fell into line: 'Tina I didn't know that. But now I hate the white ones and like the black ones best.'

Tina was pragmatic: 'No, not all white people are bad. There are good ones like Uncle George (George Bizos, the lawyer who represented Mandela at the Rivonia trial) and Auntie Ilona (my legal assistant and friend).'

Nerissa, totally confused now, said she had decided to hate them all. Tina was exasperated. Her vision and perspective, at the tender age of seven, had developed way beyond her years.

Many times in her life she has had to patiently explain to others that her looks, so different from mine and Reg, bore no relation to our love as a family. At school, taunted by other children about her African hair and complexion while her mother was a sari-wearing Indian woman, she would quietly and rationally explain her background. She would patiently explain the relationship between her and my nephew Shivas to anyone who wanted to listen; she loved him like a brother and they are still inseparable today.

I am truly proud of the way she has grown to epitomise universalism and the rich power of diversity. What is important, she demonstrates to me continually, is love, understanding and respect across all divides – more relevant in South Africa than almost anywhere in the world.

Tina showed such maturity as a child that I took her to Robben Island with me when she was nine years old, to enter my old consulting room and talk about those terrible days when brave men, including her own father, were locked up for their rightful beliefs.

We have a video film of that visit, much treasured in my family, where Tina asks me poignant, unavoidable questions. 'But what did you do to make their lives better?' she enquired, looking fully into my eyes. She wanted to know about Nelson Mandela and about her own father. 'How did you help Tata and my Daddy Popo?'

The answer is that I did what I could, and that it was in fact a lot more than many other people were able to do. So I came out of Tina's questioning feeling reasonably OK. She is not a girl to accept any evasion.

Years later, when she was fifteen, I was appointed Ambassador to the Netherlands and her father finally agreed that I could formally adopt her in order for her to come with me and take advantage of the higher-education opportunities in Europe.

Tina was a natural for higher education. She was articulate from a young age, and very serious in many ways. She would challenge anyone in a political debate. Her pedigree is unassailable.

She attended the British School in The Hague and did well.

Recently, we talked about her upbringing, as we talk openly about many things.

She had quite a lot to say:

I knew from early on how I came to be left on a lawyer's sofa as a tiny baby. I know that my mother had needed to work out somewhere safe to leave me. She had to find a compassionate human being who would really care, with a knowledge of the struggle people were going through.

So she left me on your sofa. It must have been terrible for her to decide to leave a child like that, but she put me in a safe place. I always knew who my biological parents were. They were invited to all the birthdays and family events and treated the same as everyone else. In that way they were able to share in my childhood.

I was so lucky to have a loving home. And I never felt boxed-in by religion. It was my choice to be Hindu. I had been to the synagogue with Auntie Ilona and the madrasa with neighbours. I went to church with some Christians and at home we had Christmas trees and turkey. So I had a piece of everything.

At school I know I was very independent, that's how I like to describe it. There was a principal who was very bossy and dogmatic and I wouldn't listen to her. She reprimanded me, then told me not to tell my mother. As if I wouldn't tell you every single thing happening in my life.

I know I have a rebellious streak. How could I not, coming from a struggle family. I've always been so proud of my grandfather and my Auntie Mandisa who was in MK, and my grandmother.

I remember when you and I went to a function at Leiden University and we both stopped dead when we saw a big television screen showing the TRC on a continual loop, and there was my grandmother agreeing to forgive the man who murdered my grandfather. We both left the room in a hurry, we couldn't stand that.

Later I wrote my thesis on the contrast between the TRC in South Africa and the International Criminal Court in The Hague. I felt the TRC offered more humanity, allowing ordinary people to relate their stories. But many perpetrators got away with everything and were never made to pay for their crimes.

I felt they should have been made to get involved in black communities, perhaps bringing up an African child. If they really believed in peace and reconciliation they would have wanted to school and home a black child. They would have built schools, acted out their remorse properly.

To me there was a huge gap in the possibilities the

TRC offered. There was no true remorse. Even today research shows many white South Africans actually have no knowledge of the reality of life for blacks under apartheid.

Victims put themselves through the TRC sessions at the cost of great personal emotion. I'm proud that my own family members made so many sacrifices to achieve the freedom young people like me have today. They helped to dictate history, and they made me who I am.

I know I have an immensely rich history and because of that I believe deeply in human rights. When we went to live in Ireland for four years I chose to do my honours in political science, and I wanted to declare myself African, even at Trinity College, Dublin.

I've had to deal with a lot of anger, learning in detail about my grandfather's murder and my grandmother's pain and suffering. I have had anger and pride. I only heard recently that during raids on my grandmother's house when I was a newborn baby they had to hide me in a drawer. A drawer, pushed into a piece of furniture, out of sight for my own safety only days into this world.

And I remember anger when I was small, crying about wanting to go on the beach and the rides where the white children were playing.

Despite that, I had a very happy childhood with great parents. I remember my dad Reg was lovely to me. I was in Grade 7, in the car on the way home from school, when I heard he had died suddenly from a heart attack. It felt like the end of my world. I was hysterical with sorrow.

I have been so lucky to have you and my dad. I have

two sets of parents and it feels good. I admire Mummy Phinda for the decision she took to give me up. It took a lot of strength and courage and trust and I know now that many families suffered in the same way. Mummy Phinda is proud of me and tells me how much she loves you for mothering me, she's so appreciative.

I heard that my father was against me being Indianised and becoming Hindu. In his African culture there is an important link to the ancestors. But that is my choice to make.

It was hard for me at first at school. Other kids were nosey about why I looked different to my parents. They asked about my hair and my colouring, why was it different to theirs? I told them it was because my parents were Indian, simple as that.

One of my closest friends was Siphwe who was also brought up away from his biological parents. He had been abandoned, and that is scary in African culture. It was a white doctor, Lisa Sacks, who took him and cared for him. So his mother was white, and we were both different from the other kids.

I chose myself to be Hindu. It was familiar to me and I like the temples and the celebrations, the saris and the Bollywood movies and the bindi dot. And Hinduism gives you a choice to belong as you see fit.

Remember when we went to Zwelakhe Sisulu's funeral? I arrived as the cow was being slaughtered and I found that difficult to watch, but I understood it was important in my African birth culture.

I can speak Xhosa, and some Afrikaans, and I've had enriching experiences abroad. Arriving in the Netherlands on my sixteenth birthday I was soon fighting with Brits over colonialism. I could be very confrontational. Why not, with my background?

I studied international relations at Leiden University, then politics at Trinity, and my masters at University College, Dublin. I've been lucky, learning a lot.

But South Africa is my home. Now I work in the Department of International Relations and Co-operation and nothing is more important to me than humanitarian affairs where we deal with migration, refugees, internally displaced persons and asylum-seeker issues.

South Africa is very protective about this community, always in the forefront of international legislation. The country has made huge strides and I hope to be part of doing even more.

Tina is thirty now, on the threshold of a great international career in diplomacy and human rights. I could not be more proud of her. Our relationship is a total joy to me.

And she makes me smile. I heard a mixed-race South African man say to her: 'Why do you talk like a white person while you are just a bushy like me?'

She good-humouredly told him that she was neither a 'bushy' nor a white person. She was just a human being with a good English accent.

Once she was called a 'coconut', a disparaging term for black people who are white on the inside. Instead of getting angry she went into a philosophical explanation about how offensive that description was.

I've never had to rescue her during these incidents. She handles them herself, brilliantly.

We've shared a wild ride for thirty years and I continue to cherish every moment from the time that squally bundle was left on my emerald-green sofa.

On one of the most emotional days of my life Tina married her boyfriend Frank Chikane – nephew of one of South Africa's great anti-apartheid heroes – in a Hindu ceremony in Cape Town, in August 2015. Just the sight of her, absolutely beautiful in her pink-and-gold garara Indian outfit, brought tears to my eyes.

Frank, tall and handsome, smiled at her throughout. His African family sat close by giving all their support and love. The ceremony was perfect. There were tears and laughter and solemn moments as Tina and Frank took their vows, surrounded by our good friends and family.

Her biological mother Phinda was there and greeted me with her lifelong thanks for caring so well for Tina since babyhood.

I felt that everything came together that day. My dear friend Lindiwe Sisulu, Minister of Human Settlements and daughter of our heroes Walter and Albertina Sisulu, gave a touching speech in which she told the now-married couple not to teach fairy tales and nursery rhymes to their children but to tell them the story of our country.

For any parent following the Indian culture it was a sublime experience to see my daughter getting married. It is always a parent's dream to see her daughter marry the man she loves. The experience, the feelings, the emotions and the sense of accomplishment is unmatched. This was clearly visible in the radiance of both their faces throughout the ceremony.

My emotions were totally mixed – tears of joy dominating the sadness of what could seem like a separation. Tina has been a perfect daughter to me and has played an incredible role with love, affection, care and dedication to members of the entire family who love her deeply.

It was also an unusually historic moment, for both Frank and Tina are strictly speaking from a non-Indian culture and chose to get married the Indian way, for whatever reason. It brings together the whole essence of the true meaning of diversity in our country.

# CHAPTER EIGHT

# FALSE STARTS ON THE PATH TO DEMOCRACY

My happiest memory of the 1980s is, of course, the arrival of a new light in my life, the totally unexpected 'delivery' of baby Tina, gurgling her way through the chaos of apartheid at its most repressive and cruel.

But outside the four walls of our home, where our lives were enriched beyond any expectation by this addition to the family, the black community was being subjected to increasingly desperate measures from a government under siege.

The ANC leadership was largely imprisoned or in exile. But now the State had to deal with the UDF, just as determined and with as much fighting spirit.

A partial State of Emergency was declared in November 1985 with the intention of cracking down on political dissent. The State had given itself the power to literally kill its opponents without any accountability.

In the first six months of the State of Emergency, 575 people were killed, more than half of them by police. They were arrested and detained wholesale, held in undisclosed locations, and a curfew was declared to keep black people off the streets throughout the hours of darkness.

Political gatherings were strictly monitored and large gatherings were not permitted, particularly if they related to funeral or commemoration services for those murdered by the authorities.

Tina's own father Popo Molefe was enduring one of the most tortuous trials in the history of South Africa. Along with Mosiuoa Lekota and Moses Chikane he was accused of plotting to overthrow the government, and appearing daily in court at Delmas, outside Johannesburg.

The State's case was that the UDF intended to oust the government by violence and had incited the black community to rise up against the Group Areas Act, the woefully inadequate education system, the introduction of homelands and the political detentions.

The prosecution claimed that the UDF was the ANC by another name. Its members sang the same freedom songs, declaimed the same poems of liberation and used identical language at its meetings.

The defence argued that all of the UDF's complaints against the government were long-standing grievances within the black community that predated the creation of the party.

The judge ruled that the UDF leadership – Molefe, Lekota and Chikane – had been acting as an internal wing of the ANC, and gave them long-term sentences on Robben Island. By then Popo Molefe had already been detained for three years in Pretoria without a bail hearing. Now he faced a further ten on the island.

During his three-year trial, shortly before the tenth

anniversary of the Soweto uprising in 1986, the State of Emergency was extended to cover the whole nation. Huge numbers of activists, many of them my clients, were being detained without trial.

I was continually shuttling between cases. The dogged resistance of ordinary people made a mockery of the State of Emergency. They were not being beaten down; they were being joined by comrades from every walk of life. The apartheid system, despised throughout the civilised world, had been forced on to the back foot at last.

Our economy depended heavily on overseas investments but the West in particular had become wary of the very real possibility of civil war. In 1985 the Chase Manhattan Bank in New York sensationally changed its attitude to the apartheid government and began foreclosing on multimillion-dollar loans it had previously made.

The rand fell dramatically and President Botha, blaming 'communist agitators', was forced to go cap-in-hand to the governments of Germany and Switzerland.

Increasingly there was talk of Mandela's release being the only possible peaceful solution.

At this extraordinary time there appeared to be something of a breakthrough when Winnie, on a flight to Cape Town, boldly approached the Minister of Justice, Kobie Coetsee, who was travelling in first class, and spoke passionately to him about her husband's incarceration and an operation he was undergoing for prostate cancer.

Within days Coetsee himself visited Mandela in hospital. Then I received an urgent call from one of the warders at Pollsmoor Prison: Walter Sisulu needed to see me. He and his fellow Rivonians were distressed to find that on his return from hospital Mandela had been put in solitary confinement.

It was a night-time visit to the prison and I had never seen Walter so upset. The usual twinkle in his eye had gone. I thought he looked ill and I remembered his wife MaSisulu telling me that she felt all of the comrades were ageing fast and falling into ill-health. Govan Mbeki, still on Robben Island, was suffering from arthritis and had stopped playing his guitar.

Walter, usually so good-humoured, believed that Mandela might be really ill. Like him I was extremely worried. These were our leaders; they must not get sick.

Walter took the separation from his old friend very badly. He told me this was deliberate demoralisation, that the authorities were again trying to break them: 'The system is at it again. We don't know what they're doing but we can't take it any more. They have sprung this on us without any warning. We must fight it on every level.'

I left Pollsmoor feeling downhearted. This was a further step to try to break the ANC just when our movement was stronger than ever and ready for a battle to the end.

I briefed Ismail Mahomed and he agreed we should take court action, and that it was critical to act fast. Mahomed, Clifford and myself prepared an application against the prison department for separating the Rivonians, demanding they be put back together.

Walter wanted Mandela to join the application; it was an important component of the case. But when we met and informed Mandela of our court action he refused to discuss it. He was ill-disposed towards us, looking away from us and saying firmly: 'I do not want you to go to court on this matter. I am instructing you not to proceed.' He added that he could not tell us more 'at this stage'. Alarm bells were ringing. He was tough and we knew he was capable of harbouring secret plans, but we believed that whatever the plan he should include his lieutenants. We believed he should be petitioning the court to return him to his comrades but he was refusing.

Why? We pressed him but he would not answer. We realised that he must be complicit in something we had no knowledge of.

Mahomed and I had a private consultation afterwards and sent a message to say that we had dropped the case, he had given us no choice.

I sent a message to Oliver Tambo in Lusaka to say that Mandela had been separated from the others and that Sisulu was upset and wanted action. We had met with Mandela but he'd been angry and we concluded that he was in agreement about the separation.

I was very concerned. The ANC was totally committed to collective decisions, yet Walter Sisulu knew nothing, and if Mandela was making some sort of arbitrary decision – perhaps involving approaches by or to the government – this was of grave concern.

Tambo replied that he had no knowledge of these developments and was greatly disturbed. He instructed me to return to Mandela and get to the bottom of it.

Mandela meanwhile had sent me a message saying he wanted to see the UDF leaders. He wanted to see Cyril Ramaphosa, Valli Moosa, Allan Boesak and others.

On a return visit to Mandela at this time, Mahomed and I probably showed our suspicion. There was something resembling hostility in the room, then Mandela abruptly got up and left. We had asked him directly if he was planning some action without consulting Lusaka, and he had been evasive. When we told him Oliver Tambo must be consulted, he walked out.

We were shocked, and talked openly about Mandela's possible betrayal of ANC policy. Of course our conversation was bugged and I have since heard my own words coming back to me. I said: 'What am I going to tell the ANC abroad? He is avoiding us, he might even be betraying us. There is no ANC agenda to talk to the enemy. Far from it, there is a laid-down rule never to talk to the enemy.'

Much later during these troubled times, I was told that Mandela was suffering from food-poisoning and had collapsed in the corridor when he left us that day. I believe and understand that now, but at the time felt nothing but suspicion and desperate concern.

It was impossible to know what Mandela was planning and it was equally vital to show no weakness at this crucial time.

In hindsight, he had decided to act in a chief-like manner. He knew the mood of the country, of the young warriors who had emerged from the 1976 Soweto uprising, and knew full well that we were at war and the youth in particular would never agree to a negotiated settlement.

In retrospect, I do not hesitate to say that we were wrong to think there should be no talks. Mandela himself has said there is a time when a leader must be just that: he must lead, taking his own counsel with or without the support of his comrades.

He was acting calmly, rationally, but with utmost deter-mination. He disagreed with the ANC majority who said the government should come to them if there were ever to be talks. He has said since that talks were essential and that it made no difference who initiated those talks.

He asked to see Walter Sisulu and tell him something of his plans, and he met one-to-one with other Rivonians. We know now that Mandela had sent messages to Minister of Justice Kobie Coetsee, Foreign Minister Pik Botha and to President P.W. Botha and made it clear he wanted to meet and talk. Isolated and alone in a cell, which exacerbated the onset of the tuberculosis that would stay with him till the end of his life, Mandela was yet able to keep up his guard.

This was a low point in my relationship with him. Other comrades were clamouring for answers, knowing that I had access to him. I could not answer their questions, I could not give them a plausible explanation.

And now there was serious concern over the government's overtures to Govan Mbeki, a leader of the ANC on Robben Island, who was being singled out for attention with the offer of release dangled in front of him.

It was extraordinary that Mbeki, a declared and dedicated hard-line communist, should be the first of the leadership to be offered a way back to normal life, albeit with conditions.

Mbeki sent me a telegram and I travelled to Robben Island where I found him troubled and upset. The prison commander had conveyed to him the possibility of a conditional release. He would have to renounce violence.

A man of honour with cast-iron integrity and resolve, he would not even consider it. He was totally committed to the ANC and its ideals. I had drawn up his Will and in it he left everything to the movement, saying that his children were perfectly well-provided for and needed nothing.

It was my task to tell the Prison Department that Mbeki would not consider a conditional release. I had been shuttling messages to and from Lusaka and my assistant Ilona had travelled to London to consult with leaders in exile there. My main duty as I saw it was to be a comfort and support to Mbeki, who was agitated and concerned that he was being singled out. Of course we both suspected a government agenda which might be used against him. But eventually there emerged the possibility of unconditional release.

In Lusaka it was considered right that he should accept. I was able to see him and tell him that Lusaka agreed and the government agreed: he would be the first Rivonian to get out of prison.

We both suspected a trap and he insisted that I should be right there with him at the moment of the release. But we had not been told the date. When it happened I was at Cape Town's Mount Nelson hotel having tea with the parents of a client. Their son had been sentenced to ten years in Pretoria Central for sabotage as a member of MK.

Rob Adam's parents had become close friends of mine. They had become politicised through their son and we went to rallies together. His father learnt the words of our freedom songs in Xhosa.

While we talked I received a call from Ilona to say that Robben Island authorities had sent a message to say Mbeki had been released and was already in a helicopter heading to Port Elizabeth, his home town.

Journalists were mad for this story and desperately wanted to meet Mbeki. They offered me a seat on their chartered flight to Port Elizabeth and after we landed I drove with them to the Holiday Inn hotel to find him. He was being bombarded with a thousand questions from the press. Was he still a Communist? When would Mandela be released?

I felt bad about turning the journalists away. They had

actually brought me here to his side, and now I was escorting him inside the hotel where they could not reach him. It was just not the right time; he and I needed to talk.

Mbeki had spent twenty-four years on Robben Island, he was seventy-seven years old. He felt exhausted and bamboozled. He told me the old police officer who had first arrested him at Liliesleaf Farm had sat beside him on the plane and asked him: 'Now you can tell me where the M-plan is?'

This was the important blueprint of the ANC's strategy to overthrow the apartheid government. The 'M' stood for Mandela. It had never been found, despite its existence forming the basis of the Rivonia trial.

Mbeki had replied: 'Yes, I'll tell you that if you tell me who tipped off the police to arrest us at Liliesleaf Farm.'

We organised a suite for him in the hotel and sent someone to fetch his wife Epainette from her home in Idutywa in the Transkei so-called homeland.

She arrived the next day, tiny in a huge fur coat.

The authorities had provided Mbeki with some clothes for his release. There was a suit, shoes, socks and a pair of very chic Pierre Cardin turquoise pyjamas. We had to virtually dress him in these things, all of us laughing.

Once Epainette had arrived there was serious talk about where they were going to live.

It had all happened so quickly, and was still going so fast. Mbeki had no intention of giving up his ANC activities and he was fixing up meetings with the UDF leaders and the Transvaal and Natal Indian Congresses and youth leaders. He had no intention of going to live in a rural village in the Transkei homeland, a concept he had reviled since its inception. But

Epainette had a whole life there, running a shop, and she refused to consider a permanent move to the city.

I was acting as go-between, trying to find a solution, and in the meantime some wealthy white business leaders, blatant in their intentions, were coming to me offering to buy Mbeki a grand house in Port Elizabeth. He was appalled and refused. He would live in an apartment funded only by the ANC, and only in the city itself where he had access to his people, his supporters and his comrades.

Mbeki had been astonished to find the streets lined with people. They were five deep, singing and dancing in celebration and desperate to hear him speak. We went on a 'victory' drive around the African locations in Port Elizabeth and witnessed the intense jubilation. Mbeki waved, beaming, from the car and we stopped off to meet with community leaders.

He very much wanted to talk to them. He had much to say. I had suggested a restful holiday before he engaged in political activity and he had cut me off mid-sentence. 'There is no time for that,' he said. 'I have work to do.'

In truth he had never stopped working. His deep belief in freedom – from hunger, from inequality, from degradation and from ignorance – had carried him through his long ordeal on the island.

Years later, at the age of ninety-one and close to the end of his life, a clergyman asked him what had driven him all this time. 'My love for freedom!' was his answer. 'Freedom for all people.'

He was an economist and networked brilliantly with comrades on his various theories and strategies, playing a central role in the political training and education of inmates. He was their philosopher, mentor and guide. And he had written zealously in prison. I had been smuggling essays out for him and he wanted to publish them at last as *Learning from Robben Island*. Later, in 1996, he also published *Sunset at Midday*.

Mbeki's passion was positioning a social democratic programme in the ANC allied to the labour organisations, an important position still today. He was a hard revolutionary with a formidable personal history of guerrilla warfare and sabotage. Yet he was also a great romantic. He played his guitar and sang folk songs and love sonnets.

One day soon after his release we toured the Cape Peninsula together and as his driver navigated the mountain passes he sat in the back with me, held my hands and sang an old freedom song composed by a German Jew, Heinich Heine: 'The sea has its pearls, the sky has its stars but my heart, my heart, my heart has its love'. Mbeki was a romantic and he loved the company of women, but he was not a sentimentalist.

He remains an intellectual giant of our struggle, an exceptional man in stature and dignity, but also with an enormous sense of fun. He could be a light-hearted companion, an astute politician and a family man in complete control of his emotions. In sum, his whole being was dedicated to our cause.

On his release from prison I called his son Thabo in Lusaka for him. I witnessed an extraordinarily cool and composed conversation between a father and son who had not spoken for more than thirty years. It was a practical conversation about logistics without a hint of emotion.

When his son became President of South Africa in the aftermath of democracy, Mbeki said he felt 'fine, not because he is my son but because we have someone to carry on the work of the ANC and the people of South Africa'. On many visits to Robben Island I had been aware of his need for passionate hugs and kisses, and women friends of mine also commented on it, but he was an enigma and he did not betray deep feelings when talking to his son.

I admired him greatly. He was a thinker, a soldier and a gentleman.

He knew there was a need to reconnect with his people. He planned huge rallies in Port Elizabeth, in Johannesburg and in Cape Town.

Meantime, I was summoned to Victor Verster prison in the Western Cape where Mandela had been moved to a small house, although still very much subject to prison rules and regulations. Mandela asked me to tell Cyril Ramaphosa and other UDF leaders to play down the importance of Mbeki's release. He said all celebrations and rallies should be low-key so as not to offend the government which had made this conciliatory gesture to the ANC.

He was asking the impossible, then said to my amazement that he had personally assured government ministers that there would be no political upheavals upon Mbeki's release. He had been told that the release would 'test the waters' for the release of other Rivonians.

I realised that he did not want to rock the boat. He was having important meetings by then with Coetsee and the apartheid intelligence chiefs. He had confided in Winnie and other close comrades and by now we all knew there were negotiations in hand.

There was however no way to stop the tidal wave of joy and optimism as Mbeki became a free man. We had set up rallies and were now busy writing speeches with him. I had moved into the Holiday Inn so that we could work together.

But one morning we had a call from reception to say we had visitors. Two obnoxious senior officers from the police security branch were at Mbeki's door with a banning order in their hands.

Dullah Omar, one of Mandela's dedicated team of activist lawyers, was with me and he was outraged.

Mbeki asked us: 'What can I do about this?' We advised him that we should challenge it at Port Elizabeth's Supreme Court. The order, which would restrict him from any public appearances, and which he perceived to be another form of prison, was a betrayal of the government's pledges to release him 'unconditionally'.

They had perhaps been taken aback by the outpouring of celebration on his release, by the sheer exuberance of the crowds greeting him and the possible consequences of him firing up the ANC youth in particular with renewed hopes for a victory at the end of their fight. In the lead-up to their offer of release they had perhaps thought, 'Well, this is Mbeki, not Mandela, the main man'. Now the tumultuous reception shocked them. I believe this led to the cruel imposition of a banning order.

Mbeki had planned to immerse himself back in the fight. He would have had to go underground to do it, but it was clear to everyone that nothing was going to deter him.

The banning order stopped all that dead in its tracks. He had wanted to continue his life's work. All those years in prison and he was still prepared to go through it all again. He was untouched by fear. In those days his actions taught me the meaning of courage.

Now he would be virtually invisible. He considered it a restriction worse than prison.

Mbeki had been silenced and I was feeling strongly that things were going too fast and were not sufficiently focused.

While Mandela was having his private talks with government figures I felt, with many others, that Tambo and his Lusaka cabinet were being almost ignored and sidelined. Tambo was the leader of the ANC. He should have been key.

We worried that too many concessions were perhaps being made – a feeling many still feel today. We wanted more favourable conditions towards the people, with programmes to include blacks as leaders in the civil service departments and bridging programmes to move blacks from bantu education into normal schools. There seemed to be huge gaps that were not being addressed, and with no time to fix things.

I was an attorney paid by the ANC, a unique situation. I had never charged fees. If I had then thousands of my clients would never have been defended in court. My commitment to the struggle meant I accepted that. The ANC instead paid me a salary, and paid my assistants.

But they also undertook to pay counsel, and as negotiations flew their way to a settlement, these bills were never met. I had to personally intercede with the advocates to accept staged payments, or none at all, and it became a huge financial burden for me as well as a humiliating process.

I felt at the time that the ANC hadn't planned this thoroughly. We had all wanted apartheid to be extinguished; it had been a terrible demon in our lives and we all wanted and needed and expected it to end. But there should have been a blueprint to deal with the redistribution of wealth and the huge disparity between rich and poor, to give people a reasonable meaning to their lives.

Family life, destroyed in so many ways by the apartheid laws, needed to be restored.

Mandela was eager and many people thought he was giving

too much away. Many believed he was anxious to come to a settlement in order to be able to participate in his lifetime and also to secure his own freedom after so many years.

He was on a roller coaster to freedom for the sake of all of us but still keeping his own counsel and there was disquiet among many organisations such as AZAPO, PAC, the Black Consciousness Movement and others. They were desperate for Mandela not to give too much away.

The epicentre of the whole struggle was being discussed, the planning and plotting and debating, all gearing up to Mandela's release.

I was in a unique position because politically I was very much part of the UDF but not really an office-bearer. I was the lawyer representing all the factions and I believe I had good insight. There was a lot of confusion. When I found that Mandela was having separate meetings with Indian, Coloured and black African leaders, I found this totally unacceptable.

I had lunch with him at Victor Verster and it was really very tense. I wanted to know why he was seeing different groups. He called it groupism and said there was much merit in it, citing Russia and the Soviet Union as an example. I was disappointed, telling him that he was leader of all South Africans whether Indian, Coloured or whatever, and he should address all of us as a people.

I understood of course that it was easier to manoeuvre group by group. In the current political climate as it was then it would have been difficult to hold meetings where different groups came together, and would arouse suspicion among the authorities at an already sensitive time.

But I did not subscribe to Mandela's views and felt disturbed. I felt he had been in prison for a very long time and was perhaps unable to fully realise the need for solidarity. I had had my own struggle with identity, and found my home with the BCM, who taught me to belong. Because of that positive experience I was against any divisiveness.

Mandela listened to me but his chieftainship would always take priority at these times. He had natural stature and great authority. Nothing I said was going to change him. So I left that lunch feeling unhappy. I did not think any less of him, but I was unhappy. I turned his words over in detail in my mind.

We all had an expectation at that time that Mandela was almost infallible. In the minds of his people he had been elevated to saint-like status and now I was being reminded that in fact he was as fallible as any other ordinary human being. Strong-minded myself, and someone who had suffered considerably at the hands of the apartheid State, I could see all too clearly the areas where I felt he could have been stronger.

Civil unrest in the country had spawned some appalling practices, among them the so-called 'necklacing' of informers. A lynch-mob would attack such people in their communities, placing a rubber tyre around their necks, soak it in petrol and set it on fire. Mandela, I felt, should have come out in condemnation of this practice, not least because it was bringing the ANC into disrepute internationally at a time when we needed all the support we could get.

It was no secret that his wife Winnie had singled out informers as the worst kind of traitor to the cause, and she had made an inflammatory speech at a rally in April 1985 in which she declared: 'We have no guns. We have only stones, boxes of matches and petrol. Together, hand in hand, with our boxes of matches and our necklaces we shall liberate this country.'

Mandela did not openly condemn this incitement and I

found that deeply disappointing. It pains me to say this in relation to him but I feel strongly to this day that when a leader is faced with choosing the best outcome for a personal event or the best outcome for his people, he should give himself over to the bigger commitment. It is possible that he talked to Winnie and tried to calm her. But there came a time, soon after his own release, when Mandela needed to take a stand about her speech and about a horrific murder associated with it.

The ANC in exile was appalled at Winnie's pronouncements. Oliver Tambo, in an attempt to appease all sides, said publicly at a summit meeting of non-aligned nations in Harare: 'We are not happy with the necklace. But we will not condemn people who have been driven to adopt such extremes.' Privately he asked Dr Nthato Motlana, a comrade of Winnie's and a fellow member of the Black Parents' Association – set up to guide and protect youths on the frontline of State aggression – to find a way to temper her extreme public statements.

I had myself had to think through the issue of informants and how to deal with them. In the underground cell I belonged to, run by Thabo Mbeki, we had been instructed to draw up a detailed report on this very issue.

MK members coming back into the country were being arrested due to informers infiltrating rallies and meetings. It was clear there was a network, paid handsomely by the authorities, to undermine and betray us. And these informants were our own people. It was one of the most emotionally fraught aspects of the struggle. They were openly driving big cars, moving into nice houses, displaying sudden opulence in township terms. They needed to be dealt with.

There were many collaborators too among the black

members of local councils in the townships cooperating with the State. I knew of a young man who joined a mob to necklace an informer and found it was his own uncle. He tried to get out of the crowd and was seriously assaulted. Feelings were running so high, the volatility was open to detonation at every moment.

Necklacing had become the signature treatment for informants. At a funeral gathering in East Rand where Archbishop Desmond Tutu was speaking, someone claimed they saw a girl smiling or talking to a police officer. She was attacked at the funeral, right there and then, and accused of working with the police. Mob behaviour had got entirely out of hand.

In my cell, we had been debating these issues. Our deliberations came to a sudden end when Cedric was arrested and the cell disbanded, and to this day I cannot say what could have been a fair method of punishment and dissuasion for informers. I believe punishment was due, but I would never have condoned necklacing. It was barbaric.

By 1989, with Mandela's certain release pending, Winnie had gathered together a group of so-called bodyguards. Nicknamed the Mandela United Football Club, they wore tracksuits as a uniform though no football was being played, and we became aware that they were tough youths who had begun terrorising township neighbourhoods.

By the time this gang's activities were properly investigated, the accepted fact was that it included several agents of the State, set up to foment violent divisions in the community. It emerged that they were linked to twenty human rights abuses including eight murders and incidents of kidnap and assault.

My own strong feeling is that Winnie had been driven to

a point of almost no return by the intense persecution of the State. She had been imprisoned and tortured, reviled, torn from her children in dawn raids on her home, and banished to a remote part of rural South Africa where she was forced to live under continual hostile surveillance.

She had recently, defiantly, returned to Soweto an enraged person.

The husband she loved deeply had been incarcerated for life and might never be released.

She had proved to be too fiery and independent for the ANC, UDF or any other organisation, and was acting independently with all the considerable strength and conviction she possessed. She took to wearing combat uniform and a military-style beret and she was a force in the land.

I had remained reasonably close to Winnie through the years but our paths were not crossing so often now, and both of us were caught up in intensely busy lives. Those lives collided in the aftermath of the killing of teenager Stompie Moeketsi, who Winnie's gang stated was an informer.

With hindsight I see clearly now that Winnie had been set up, in so many ways. She was hosting a gang of roughnecks in her own home, not realising that they were State agents paid to disrupt the struggle at its grass roots. And they succeeded so well that Winnie was completely drawn in, only to have them turn against her when matters finally came to the Johannesburg Supreme Court.

It was an extraordinary situation for me to be in: I was lawyer to Mandela and being consulted by him regularly in prison while his wife was caught up in a hideous situation where a young boy was killed.

And I was close to that hideous situation in other ways too.

I had known Stompie for several years, and had actually met his family. He was one of many young people who lived in the Parys area of the Orange Free State and who had come to Johannesburg to fight the good fight in whatever way they could. Stompie was the youngest ever political detainee in our country, spending his twelfth birthday in jail. He was expelled from school at the age of thirteen.

He and other teenage boys were essentially street kids. They had no permanent home. They had found their place in the struggle and that meant they had to be in the city. They ran pretty wild, throwing rocks and petrol bombs at police vehicles, acting as runners for ANC comrades needing crucial messages passed, and doing errands for legal practices like mine.

These boys often came into our office. We trusted them. In their own way they were a useful and dedicated faction. When a client of mine, Terror Lekota, was released from Robben Island, he and I agreed it would be good and supportive to go to meet some of their families.

I had represented Stompie in court several times over a period of more than three years. Like many others he had been radicalised at school and was dedicated to doing what he could to change the status quo for poor blacks.

He was eleven when I first met him, an endearing and loveable boy, chubby with a beautiful smile. He would insist on carrying my briefcase and walking with me from my office to the car.

The first time I represented him in court for public disturbance offences and taking part in the burning of police vehicles he was too short to see over the rail of the dock. But although physically small, he was feisty and totally motivated.

Stompie had nowhere to live; he just slept on someone's

porch or in an old car. Like many others he had no stable home in Johannesburg. He was a product of the 1976 riots, inheriting a deep-seated anger and awareness of the inequalities and doing what he could to disrupt the status quo. As he became a teenager more and more of his friends would be convicted and sent to Robben Island or to Pretoria Central or Kimberley.

When I met Stompie's parents I was welcomed with open arms. They lived in a poor location in a sub-economic home, brick-built with just one room. It had no electricity or running water, but it was hospitable.

I remember his mother being distracted by concern and worry about her child. He had been detained previously and I wanted to comfort her. She was a mother trying to make ends meet, unable to help her son find a job or a worthwhile life.

The household was teeming with people. Stompie had brothers and sisters. All I could do was to tell his mother that we were doing our best for him. She never saw him again. It was too expensive for him to ever get home, there was no money for that.

Stompie was a great favourite with my staff. A girl student who came to my office part-time was especially fond of him. She showed him how the computer worked and got him to photocopy legal documents. He enjoyed being a useful member of our team. Despite being illiterate, he was bright and sharp enough to actually be able to help with the admin.

My staff and I bought him food and occasionally he slept in the office. This is the depth of the trust we had in him. I don't think we favoured him. We took care of all the street-kid clients we represented, but Stompie particularly endeared himself.

Looking back it seems extraordinary that their unsurpassable leader and hero, Mandela himself, was also a client and that these two facts collided unhappily when Stompie became a victim.

Mandela had recently told me that Winnie was having problems with her lawyer, my former employer Ismail Ayob, and he wanted me to take her on as my client instead. My staff and I knew that she could be very demanding. She often turned up in our office, despite not being a client, without an appointment and wanting to use the phone and other facilities, at the same time ordering my staff to run errands for her. Sometimes Winnie would send her daughter Zindzi with demands, and the staff, already run off their feet, told me they were tired of it.

I asked them to consider us taking Winnie on and every one of them said they would resign rather than work with her. It was hard for me. I had to tell Mandela, facing him in the prison waiting-room at Pollsmoor: 'I'm really sorry. My staff say it would be impossible to deal with Winnie.'

He seemed surprised that employees could dictate terms to me like that. But I was running a democracy and it was a collective decision.

Mandela had seen many press cuttings about Winnie's behaviour with her 'football club', and although he was clearly worried he nevertheless could not understand how anyone could turn down a Mandela brief.

He had asked me many times to tell Winnie not to be so confrontational, never alluding directly to the necklacing practices but speaking quietly, almost in a code. He knew what was going on.

Neither he nor I was prepared for what happened next.

Early in the morning of 31 December 1989, I was telephoned at home by the mother of one of Winnie's football club gang. MaSisulu also called me and both of them said something bad was going on at Winnie's home in Diepkloof, and that I should go there.

It was six in the morning when I arrived; Aubrey Mokoena's van was parked outside. It was often there all night and there was a good deal of talk about his relationship with Winnie. Years later Mokoena, a student resistance leader, became a distinguished member of Parliament.

He came out looking flustered when I knocked on the door. I said I'd had a call and was worried. 'It's OK,' he said. 'It's just a meeting of the football club.' He didn't want to let me into the house, saying it was 'not a good time'.

It has since been established that, as I was being sent on my way by Mokoena, poor Stompie was being brutally assaulted in an outbuilding of Winnie's house. Six days later his badly-beaten body was found on wasteland nearby. His throat had been cut. He was fourteen years old.

I cannot describe the horror and grief among all of us at my office. We had been anxious for days about Stompie's disappearance during the holiday period and had sent messages around the township for news of him.

We recalled how there had recently been an impromptu meeting of the so-called football club members in my office where all the talk had been of Stompie being an informer. It was an outrageous accusation. He had been seen with a disposable camera, an unusual item for a street kid, but my student assistant had given it to him.

She had given 'evidence' to what looked increasingly like a kangaroo court and told the meeting how she had attended a party with her parents on the previous evening and each table had been given a disposable camera in a 'goodie bag'. She knew that Stompie would love it and gave it to him as a special present. She was terribly upset that the youths believed it was some sort of prize for Stompie from the police, a means of taking photographs for them.

But her 'evidence', we all now knew, had failed to persuade the football club gang.

Stompie had been brought to Winnie's house, it emerged, with three other boys, all accused of being informants, all beaten. Stompie was the only one who died.

A complication was that Winnie and others later claimed the four boys had been sexually abused at the Methodist minister's home where they had been sleeping intermittently, and were 'rescued' from that place, rather than being kidnapped.

In addition, Winnie herself had left her Diepkloof home for Brandfort on 29 December to attend a funeral and could produce witnesses who were there with her. She returned to Diepkloof on 31 December and claimed she had seen Stompie using an outside tap to wash himself.

It was the evidence of football club members which put Winnie's version of events in doubt, even though each one of them was described as an evasive, contradictory liar by the prosecution and the judge.

To this day, this shocking incident taints Winnie and the ANC. The brutality, the damage done to everything we believed in – our comradeship, our solidarity, our nobility and dignity as counterpoint to the State's cruelty – were all dealt a massive blow.

For me, so close to every strand, it was heart-breaking. The ripple effect of this cold-blooded murder took its toll on all of us, and forced some of us into unthinkable compromises.

Stompie's family, devastated by grief, was unable to comprehend how their boy's life could end at the hands of his own comrades.

It seemed to me that this was one of the lowest points in our history. All peoples' revolutions throw up terrible episodes but this was shockingly close to me and my work, everything that mattered in the struggle.

However, there was more heartache to come, as this evil spawned further evil.

My good friend and neighbour in Lenasia, the brave and gentle Dr Abubaker Asvat who dedicated his entire life to the care of others, was shot dead in his clinic on 27 January, just weeks after Stompie's death and as a direct result of it.

He had come to my house early that same morning. I was in a hurry to get to the airport as I had a client to represent in court in Durban. 'Hurley', as we all called him, looked ashen. He told me he had been at Winnie's house after her gang assaulted Stompie, and he had told them the boy was so badly hurt they must take him to hospital, he could do nothing for him.

Hurley told me he had been in anguish ever since. The boy's dead body had been found and his family believed that Dr Asvat, and perhaps I too, was keeping some facts from them. He was in turmoil and wanted to talk.

He was the kindest man, a doctor who selflessly treated patients throughout the black community often without pay, whatever the danger to himself. As well, he was a wonderful friend and great company. Each Friday evening he would host dinner at his home, and Winnie, myself and others would be there to talk over current events. Dr Asvat had helped and supported Winnie during her period of banishment, assisting her in setting up a mobile clinic in Brandfort and providing expert support and supplies.

I felt bad that I could not stay and talk to him that morning. I had to catch my flight.

But when I reached Durban and was on my way to court I received a message that he had been shot and killed. I was shocked beyond belief.

On my return that evening I went to his house with heartfelt condolences for his family. I think Winnie also came. I must say that maybe I was naïve at this time. I did not believe she had any part in what happened to Stompie or to my friend Hurley.

I had been astonished when I first heard that she had been in the house during the assault on Stompie – claims coming from the football gang, and therefore unreliable. Now there were rumblings that Dr Asvat had been killed because he had witnessed the scene of Stompie's assault and murder.

MaSisulu, who was Dr Asvat's nurse and receptionist, was to become a crucial part of the investigation into his death. She had seen the youths who entered the clinic, and had heard the shots. But she could not, would not, appear as a witness for the State at Dr Asvat's inquest. No subpoena on earth would force her to do that. I felt so much inner conflict about this. MaSisulu was a towering figure in our movement and in our lives. She held the key to solving my friend's murder, yet I knew that she was being coerced into staying silent.

It is not for me to judge any of the players caught up in this monumental tragedy. I can only say that I felt heartsore to the depth of my being as these events unfolded, and that feeling has never left me.

I also believe strongly that Winnie contributed more than almost any other individual to the anti-apartheid struggle which consumed our lives for so many years, and that at the worst of those times she found herself at the centre of 'horrible things', as she later conceded at a Truth and Reconciliation Commission hearing years later.

The ANC hierarchy itself, while reeling at the events unfolding, conceded that Winnie had been 'left open and vulnerable to committing mistakes which the enemy has exploited'.

And now she faced the ultimate humiliation: she was to be tried by the State judiciary, questioned by a white prosecutor with her fate in the hands of a white judge.

I had been staying close to Stompie's family at the time of his disappearance and death, and I had comforted them and agreed to be in court as a watching brief when Winnie Mandela herself and several members of her Mandela United Football Club eventually stood trial accused of kidnap and assault.

But I was called to Victor Verster to see Mandela who forbade this in stark terms. 'You represent the Mandela family,' he said. 'There can be no conflict of interest. You cannot represent Stompie's family.'

I left him feeling downcast. I had told him of my upset and he had said that in life you had to make choices. He said I had come to a crossroads where I had to make a choice, and that I must be directed by him as to that choice.

As a lawyer I knew he was right. There was indeed a conflict of interest. My disappointment came from the knowledge not that he was determined to support Winnie, but that he was prepared to compromise his own reputation, and the all-important reputation of the ANC, by physically accompanying her to court.

He had a blind love for Winnie, supporting her no matter what, and I admit that at that moment I looked at him and felt disappointed in his decision. I knew he was deeply in love with Winnie, I knew he felt guilt that she had brought up their family without him. But now I was disappointed in him.

He was my great leader, our great leader, and I was seeing someone who was capitulating.

On the very verge of his release from prison after twenty-seven years' incarceration, Mandela was being forced to wrestle with his own conscience over Stompie's death, and now he had made his choice.

On the day of his release from prison on 11 February 1990 I should have been there with him, despite my grave misgivings about his attitude to Stompie's killing. But I had been travelling by road from a court hearing in Durban back to my home in Johannesburg.

We had all known that the release was imminent but no exact date had been given, so it turned out that I watched the actual event on television when I stopped at my uncle's house in Pietermaritzburg to break my journey.

Mandela was a free man by the time Winnie and her football club came to trial in 1991. He had taken a stand and decided to accompany his wife to court in a very public display of support. I will never know how much it grieved and distressed him to hear the terrible heart-rending facts of the case.

Winnie spent five long days in the witness-box, stubbornly evading questions, failing to fully explain her involvement, and emerging as a convicted criminal.

She was sentenced to six years' imprisonment for being an accessory to kidnap and assault.

She had not fought convincingly to save herself and it was to her lawyers' credit that they later persuaded an Appeal Court judge to accept that she took no part in the assault on Stompie or the other boys. It was accepted, both at the trial and by the Appeal Court, that Winnie had been in Brandfort during the two crucial days of the boys' kidnap and assault.

The Appeal Court judge upheld her conviction for complicity in the kidnap, saying that she must have known there was an intention to use her vehicle to collect the four boys from the Methodist manse late at night and bring them to her home. But he was not convinced that she took part in the assaults. There was only the word of palpable liars to testify to that. He dismissed the conviction for assault, and reduced her sentence to two years' imprisonment, suspended, and a fine of R150,000.

Bishop Peter Storey, leader of the Methodist Church in the Transvaal, made a sad speech at that time, saying that Stompie's death, and the kidnap and assault on others, was 'an unspeakable crime which probed beneath the surface of South Africa's shame'.

He talked of 'deeper hidden wounds that these years have carved into the people's souls and these are the wounds of erosion of conscience, devaluing of human life, evasion of truth and a reckless resort to violence'.

He said he had hoped against hope that certain people who enjoyed respect and adulation would not be directly implicated. He meant Winnie, and it was clear that she had come out of the case very badly.

Her reputation was almost terminally damaged, and she did

not fare well when summoned to the Truth and Reconciliation Commission hearing years later.

I always felt there was a bigger picture to this terrible tragedy, a context which no one had the will or time to explore properly, and that Winnie, sadly, had not helped herself by throwing any further light on it. Whatever the truth, she had allowed herself and – more importantly – the anti-apartheid movement to be dragged in the dirt for all the world to see.

And I still considered the matter of Mandela's decisions to be unfinished business between us.

I took the opportunity to confront him one day when he came to my office to make some international phone calls. He wanted to do that in the privacy of my workplace, away from the staff at Shell House and his own office.

We had tea and talked and I raised the question with him of how he had forbidden me to support Stompie's family. I told him of my frustration and asked as tactfully as I could if he thought his appearance at Winnie's side in court had been appropriate. He said: 'Yes, it was. It was carefully thought out, taking all the factors into account. I believe I was right.'

That was his style, he was a chieftain.

I still felt the sting of disappointment but there was going to be no further closure.

And I was facing difficult struggles of my own. I had married Reagan, fifteen years younger than me, in 1989. I had been aware of our cultural differences and so was my family. He was from a mixed-race family, the 'coloured' population, and until then I had not realised how much displacement and insecurity was part of their make-up, in their DNA.

Many 'coloured' people are unable to trace their own

ancestry. The white forefather component is almost always missing. This is a scarring experience and I had not been aware of its likely impact in a mixed marriage like ours.

Reagan was a brilliant self-made lawyer. He had left home on the day he matriculated, won a bursary to the prestigious Rhodes University in Grahamstown, then a scholarship to do his masters at the London School of Economics and later in Los Angeles.

He was intellectually bright. I fell madly in love with him, he was young and understanding and handsome. There was no chauvinism, he shared in the running of our household.

But he was insanely insecure. I literally could not look at, talk to or even greet another man. One night we were at the theatre and Martin Brassey, the advocate who dealt with the landmark Marwane case with me, came over to give me a hug. He didn't talk to Reagan, who interrupted the conversation to tell Martin aggressively: 'Why have you ignored me?' Martin apologised profusely of course. There was a terrible scene on the way home.

I'd had no idea of his tendency to violence. His irrational jealousy led inevitably to screaming rows and domestic abuse. I could never be described as having a victim personality but I know now that there is an established pattern of even strong women like myself suffering continual abuse. We are embarrassed and humiliated, and frightened, and often fail to address it.

Reagan's temper was out of control. Once when Mandela himself called early in the morning I took the call while still in bed, and Reagan could hear Mandela telling me how he loved me for my support and caring.

He went mad, taking the phone out of my hand and banging

it down. I felt as though I was dying. I was being mortified in front of my clients, and I was being physically attacked.

He once threw the phone across the room because Govan Mbeki had called me.

When Walter Sisulu and other great activists were finally released from prison in 1991 it was an unforgettable occasion. Cyril Ramaphosa came to counsel's chamber in Johannesburg where they were due to arrive, looking for me.

I arrived with a black eye. Reagan had smashed the whole house up that morning, the television and pieces of furniture. And he had attacked me.

I felt shame and embarrassment, and finally I prepared to leave him. I'm sorry to say that my lovely daughter Tina witnessed Reagan's behaviour and was traumatised by it.

By then I had come to realise that Reagan was actually opposed to the ANC. He did not empathise with the movement, and I had given my entire working life to it. By then I had taken him to see Mandela in Victor Verster, and on his release Mandela had come to our home in Johannesburg.

I learnt also that he had had an unhappy violent childhood, being beaten by his mother for minor incidents, while standing naked in the cold in their backyard. Sympathetic, I had gone to therapy with him.

At last I saw what my own family, Ismail Mahomed and my close lawyer colleague Sean Naidoo had warned me about. There was a huge political and personal divide between me and Reagan.

The marriage was doomed. Reagan followed me everywhere, suspicious and disruptive.

In 1993 I saw in the newspapers that I had been nominated for parliament. I was disinclined and told Mandela that I still had many civil actions to deal with against the police. He told me: 'We need women and we need lawyers. You are going to parliament.'

Accepting a parliamentary role helped to end my marriage, as I would be spending most of my time away from home, in Cape Town. Reagan was refusing to leave my house, and I solved that by selling it from under him.

Our marriage had been a Hindu ceremony conducted by a priest who was not registered to do marriages, so, in law, there was no problem ending it.

Reagan died two years ago and I like to think my unhappy memories died with him.

Meanwhile, I was spending time with Mandela. He graciously came to my law practice and met every member of my staff, shaking their hands and talking to each of them. They were delighted to meet him, the client at the top of our list for so many long years.

We travelled together a little at that time. Mandela very much wanted to meet Tina's family. Her grandfather was still missing and his fate would not be known until years later during the Truth and Reconciliation Commission.

I flew to Port Elizabeth with Mandela and his fellow prisoner Ahmed Kathrada. We called at Elizabeth Hashe's house and it was such a huge experience. Everyone wanted to shake his hand, we were bombarded everywhere we went.

As we left a small boy on his way to school tapped on the car window. He said: 'Who are you? Are you someone really important?' Mandela replied: 'No, you must be thinking of someone else.'

We realised during that trip that things had not normalised at all, not for families like the Hashes. They were still living in abject poverty with no new hope for the future other than the chance to vote for the first time in their lives.

Yet Mandela was so conciliatory, so willing to forgive. The level of reconciliation he demonstrated was perhaps his greatest personality trait. It was genuine with him, unshakeable.

I sometimes felt that one could go too far with forgiveness. He took tea with Betsy Verwoerd, widow of Hendrik, the 'architect of apartheid' and one of the most abominable monsters the world has ever known. I was unable to see why it was necessary to appease his family. In addition, Betsy Verwoerd had made a limp comment afterwards, not seeing Mandela's gesture as anything out of the ordinary.

I felt the same when Mandela invited Percy Yutar to dinner at his house. He was the prosecutor at the Rivonia Trial, the unreconstructed apartheid racist who had called for the death sentence for Mandela and his comrades.

Ilona and I were at his house one day when this subject came up. We saw that Mandela was rather embarrassed and defensive in the face of our opposition. He tried to tell us a sorry story about Yutar's sad Jewish background and how his hand had been chopped off by robbers who had attacked his father's butcher's shop. 'You must understand he had a difficult life,' he said. We remained unimpressed.

And while there was occasionally an opportunity to touch on these matters of great sensitivity, a larger phenomenon was manifesting itself on the streets.

The apartheid government's last stand was to fund the opposition Inkatha Freedom Party to bring havoc, burnings and deaths into the townships in a shameful black-against-black war which threatened everything our struggle had achieved up till now.

# CHAPTER NINE

# PAIN AND SUFFERING ON THE ROAD TO CHANGE

It was devastating to know that township wars were destroying our country's reputation in the world at the exact moment in history when there had seemed to be cause for huge celebration.

Nelson Rolihlahla Mandela, aged seventy-one, had emerged from prison against all possible odds and was finally in place to claim his rightful status as president of a South Africa where all people could live in freedom and safety.

Instead of that transition, those of us who had fought alongside him were powerless to stop the flow of blood in internal violence that left 14,000 dead between his release from prison in 1990 and the country's first democratic elections in 1994.

It was a measure of the utter desperation of the National Party's ultra-right-wing elements that they teamed up with Zulus from the Inkatha Freedom Party (IFP) to together destroy peaceful negotiations.

There was nothing less than civil war in KwaZulu-Natal, in the east of South Africa, an area dominated by the Zulu. Under its chief, Mangosuthu Buthelezi, the IFP was hell-bent on a nation of its own, rejecting peace talks between its rivals in the ANC and the apartheid government.

Veterans of the struggle like myself looked on with horror and dismay as the IFP rampaged through townships and workers' hostels, armed by the South African Defence Force itself. They formed death squads and carried out assassinations, drive-by shootings, and military-style attacks on trains.

The so-called train squads formed up on railway station platforms, 300 men at a time wearing red headbands and carrying everything from automatic weapons to iron rods. They would fire from the platforms or get on board the trains.

A senior member of the South African Police Force, Wayne Hugh Swanepoel, was to tell the Truth and Reconciliation Commission later that his unit boarded trains, shooting at random and throwing people from the carriages, 'in order to cause the ANC and the IFP to blame each other'.

The unbanning of the ANC and other major parties in February 1990 had threatened the IFP's domination of KwaZulu-Natal and they were using everything they could – international monetary support, arms from South Africa's military, and the deliberate turning of a blind eye from the authorities – to maintain their status quo.

In a seven-day war in March 1990 more than a hundred people were shot dead, 3,000 homes burned down and 30,000 people forced to flee.

The police were giving logistical support, arms and ammunition, and even taking part in attacks. Buthelezi is known to have asked for hit squads to assist him at a time in late 1990 when he feared he was losing the fight.

In Johannesburg, where I was being consulted by labour organisations, I decided with lawyer colleagues that we should bring an urgent application for a restraining order against Buthelezi. We supplied many affidavits proving the IFP's involvement in attacks in the townships, and we were also concerned that migrant workers from Swaziland, Lesotho, Botswana and elsewhere were being sent home without jobs because they were being harassed.

We submitted the application under the banner of the Black Parents' Association. This was a powerful group of people which included Winnie Mandela and Dr Nthato Motlana, a highly-respected doctor giving his services for free in the townships. They worked with the headstrong youth and had achieved mutual respect among them.

We lost our application. Many things had changed with the release of Mandela and the unbanning of political parties, but many things had also stayed the same. A kind of hell existed in our country. Buthelezi had sold out and was working with the existing government, threatening the peace talks.

The much longed-for Convention for a Democratic South Africa – CODESA – had started its historic deliberations in October 1991 to find a middle way for opposing sides to move together towards freedom.

But the IFP walked out of the talks, intent on disruption, and aligned itself with the Bantustan governments, the collection of independent 'homelands' now trying to hang grimly on to power. White right-wing groups were only too happy to join in the destruction.

Everything we had fought for and stood for, and suffered for, was now at stake.

Mandela, who had sensed the coming disruptions while still in prison, had invited Buthelezi to visit him, hoping to achieve an understanding. That failed, and now I was going to Mandela at the ANC headquarters in Shell House to tell him: 'Your reconciliatory approach is all very well, but at what cost? Ordinary people are suffering and dying.'

He believed he could control it. He appealed to his people, but the Zulus – South Africa's most populous ethnic group, with warrior leanings – hardly acknowledged Mandela.

Buthelezi was their leader.

It was a crucial moment. My law firm had cut across all sectors at the heart of the conflict. We had always considered the IFP our people. They were black, like us. It was impossible to even think of a plan intended to work against blacks, our own people.

The trade unions were coming to me and I told them the way forward was to patch things up. But most of the IFP workers did not belong to our ANC-aligned unions. The rift widened.

For Mandela, this rivalry was a scourge. For twenty-seven years he had been outside these issues – the growing power of the youth, the emergence of strong women, and the labour movement that had evolved so fast were new elements to him. He needed to re-think.

So it came down to Jacob Zuma, a guerrilla fighter who had headed ANC intelligence in exile, to confront his own people and try to find peace. He was a Zulu and spoke their language. In London when we had taken evidence on commission from the ANC he had shone.

Since then we had become friends. I found him a bright and passionate leader and came to know him well. We went to jazz concerts together and my mother invited him to her house in Durban for curry.

Zuma was on top of what was happening among the Zulus, and he had no vested interest. Unlike Mandela, he could afford to try and to fail, if that was how it turned out, without losing face. I asked him bluntly: 'Can you possibly succeed?' He told me: 'I have to. These are my people.'

On the ground he had a great connection with people from all sectors. He met with elders, and he spoke at rallies. He negotiated behind closed doors.

In public, the IFP had by now formed the so-called Freedom Alliance with interested parties and threatened further violence.

In the winter of 1993 alone there were 1,577 deaths.

While Zuma talked to his people, behind-the-scenes talks took place with the Freedom Alliance. The country was sick of the ongoing township wars and in danger of losing its international allies and trading partners.

With six days to go before our first democratic elections in April 1994, and after four years of turmoil, the IFP and Buthelezi did an about-turn and agreed to participate.

Like all other South African citizens I had been watching with something like despair. I had taken no part in CODESA and was not actively involved in politics. And at that time, I still had a domineering and jealous husband who wanted me at home.

But the clouds were parting and we were making that incredible journey towards a unified government, a dream we had longed for for so many years.

I was acutely aware, though, that Mandela was suffering emotionally as never before at this time. There is no doubt that he was still very much in love with Winnie and had been able to put aside the stories he had heard about her affairs. But in reality they were finding it hard to bring that love back to life now that he, no longer the physically irresistible forty-four-year-old man he was when he was torn from her and sent to Robben Island, had come home. It was hard for him to compete with the younger, bolder men who had openly courted Winnie over the years.

I was concerned that Mandela was not happy, and aware that the ANC and the UDF wanted nothing more than to separate him from Winnie.

On the one hand I would visit the Mandelas at their house in Diepkloof – Winnie had built it when their modest home in Vilakazi Street was burnt down – and feel the strained atmosphere for myself. On the other, I felt strongly that this was actually one of the world's most profound love affairs and could surely be mended.

Even after I had visited for coffee one day, bringing little Tina and my husband with me, and found Winnie's handsome young lover Dali Mpofu sitting in the lounge with her and her husband, I felt things could be put right.

Certainly I thought it was bizarre, and brazen, particularly on Dali's part. Why would he, an ardent supporter of the anti-apartheid movement and an ambitious lawyer himself, want to undermine Mandela, the cuckolded husband, in such a public display? I took this badly, but I still thought the fundamental love between the Mandelas would come right.

It was clear that outside pressure was being brought to bear, to persuade Mandela that he should leave Winnie. I disapproved strongly of this and talked to senior people in the UDF.

I said to Valli Moosa: 'Why are you interfering? This is his personal life.' He told me: 'No. Mandela belongs to us. He belongs to the people. We have a right to get involved, to encourage him to leave her.'

The UDF and the ANC were terrified that Winnie was poisoning Mandela against them. I had heard her once on the phone to Oliver Tambo, screaming at him. They had learnt to fear and hate her. She was shouting at the top of her voice: 'Never mind crossing the Limpopo River full of crocodiles when you come back to South Africa. You will have to cross me too, and that will be even more dangerous.'

I'd had to ask her who she was talking to. When she said it was Tambo I was astonished. We were sitting in her lounge; she was absolutely raging, and I was shocked. But she was in no frame of mind to listen to me.

So I was well aware of the campaign to remove Mandela from Winnie and put him on that solitary plinth where he could be a lone, strong leader, single-mindedly at the heart of his people again.

I always felt that if Mandela had not been pressured externally he might have been able to work out the marriage problems. But instead I was watching the disintegration of the relationship. I had wanted Winnie to be up there on that plinth with him, she deserved it. Even the political leaders who loathed her – afraid of her power – were not beyond her charm and charisma.

When Oliver Tambo died I was sitting with other dignitaries in his home as many great men came in to pay their respects. Thabo Mbeki, Cyril Ramaphosa, all the big names from our revolution. Someone said: 'Isn't it wonderful that we live in the sort of equality of community where we don't have to stand up every time someone important enters the room?'

We all smiled. Then Winnie walked in and everyone instinctively stood up.

I had seen that before. People who said the nastiest things about her, who criticised her outright. When they met her they found her so charismatic they practically swooned over her.

After my difficult staff meeting at my law practice, where the staff said they would all leave if I took Winnie as a client, we had walked to the lift and Winnie emerged from it. They fell back in awe, every one of them. Winnie had that effect. Mandela himself has said he could not have got through his years of imprisonment without the thought of her.

And now his heart was breaking. He moved out of the house in Diepkloof and into an address in Houghton, a smart suburb of Johannesburg, provided for him by a wealthy supporter. He was lonelier than he'd ever been in his life.

All the freedoms he had fought for were now within reach and, yes, he did belong to the people and in many ways he was married to the ANC, but the red-blooded man in him was grieving and lost.

In April 1992, notwithstanding the historic events unfolding around him, he called a gathering of the press and announced that he had separated from Winnie. His dear old friends and comrades Walter Sisulu and Oliver Tambo sat either side of him.

I watched the sad, dignified announcement on television. Mandela took no questions. He called Winnie by her Xhosa name, Nomzamo, and said: 'Comrade Nomzamo has and can continue to rely on my unstinting support during these trying moments in her life...'

He was referring to the scandal surrounding the behaviour of Winnie's football club gang and the death of young Stompie, followed by the murder of Dr Asvat. But he was at pains to say this controversy had not influenced his decision to separate from her.

He said: 'I shall personally never regret the life Comrade Nomzamo and I tried to share together... I part from my wife with no recriminations. I embrace her with all the love and affection I have nursed for her inside and outside of prison from the moment I saw her.'

It was dignified, but pitiful.

And now, shortly afterwards, I was hearing that he wanted to come to my house. I received a call from Barbara Masekela, his assistant, to say that he wanted to visit. I said I would hurry home from my office, and I would arrange for my helper Anna to let them in.

When I came home I found Anna frying samosas and getting out the best crockery with a great fuss. She worshipped Mandela.

My cousin Shanti was also there. I hugged and kissed Mandela but I saw a face I had never seen before. I knew all of his expressions – I knew when he was angry and his face darkened, when he was joyful his smile lit up the world, and when he was tense he was a real chieftain, holding his head up firmly and looking straight ahead with authority.

I had never seen him like this. His face was contorted with anguish. He looked devastated, that is the only word I can use. Even his hug for me was not his usual all-enveloping bear hug.

I felt awkward, Barbara felt awkward; Mandela himself was awkward.

And what to say? 'Commiserations', or 'Congratulations', or even 'Perhaps it's a good thing. Even though it's the end of an era, maybe that's good'.

The truth is that I could not imagine the one without the other. In a historical or political or emotional context, he and Winnie could not be seen separately. To me it was a Greek tragedy, a colossal sorrow. I said I was so sorry, I was close to tears. And Mandela said it was 'inevitable'; he kept repeating that word.

Shanti at that moment came to serve tea to him, kneeling on the floor before him as she poured tea like a handmaiden. It was dreadful. She was showing her adoration and it was totally incongruous.

We sat together for about an hour, talking in monosyllables. He said, 'It's over.' And while he murmured these awful thoughts out loud he seemed to me to have actually shrunk physically and emotionally.

I had never seen him without him appearing to tower over us all. His height, his bearing, his enigmatic personality. All that was so imposing, so chieftain-like. But that day his enormous stature had gone.

He seemed to me more sombre than the day he was sentenced to life imprisonment. He had been defiant then. Now he was cowed, he had emotionally collapsed. Nothing in his life had affected him as much as this. I didn't expect him to break down; he had other ways of caving in and the evident misery enveloping him seemed worse than sobs.

I thought he must have come to me as a dear friend, to someone he had trusted for so many years, and a woman with a woman's understanding. We were fond of each other and he had often held my hand as though he would never let it go. That day his hands had no strength, he had no strength. I could have asked everyone to leave us so that we could talk alone, but he was perfectly capable of doing that himself, and he chose not to.

He was a proud man but he had seen Winnie's need for love and comfort over the years when he was not there, and he had dealt with that. Now, however, it was happening in front of him and I think the disrespect and recklessness of Dali Mpofu's presence was what he meant when he said it was all 'inevitable'.

Among his woman friends who were supportive in those dark days was Tambo's wife Adelaide. Mandela liked her and she did her best to introduce him back into society. She was rather an enigma to me. A great and indomitable freedom fighter in her own right but not very good to her own staff, speaking very harshly to them and being very demanding, I knew her well; she was my neighbour in Johannesburg. She adored Tina and we often went on excursions together.

At that time there were women lining up to be introduced to Mandela, with a light in their eyes. He was not interested, though he was regaining his strength and getting things done. He instructed me on various legal matters. I tracked people down for him, and I looked over a business contract which Zindzi's boyfriend was talking her into.

I was also nominated to lead the Independent Election Commission for our all-important voting day. The National Party said I was too much of an ANC activist and didn't want me, but I was glad. I wanted to be involved in the election on the ground; I wanted to savour this prize we had won.

And it was euphoric, unforgettable. We stopped leading normal lives. The excitement was unequalled, indescribable. It was 27 April 1994. I'm so glad I saw this in my lifetime. The feeling could never be replicated; it was the most wonderful day. People forgot their grievances and pressures and challenges. There was only one thing that mattered – the election.

We drove around Lenasia and Soweto, free to go out there and talk to the crowds standing all day in their hundreds of thousands. No water, no food and no complaints. They would not give up their place in the queue for anything. Everyone was happy and greeting each other, this upbeat feeling after 350 years of oppression. It was unbelievable to see black and white people queuing together, talking, laughing. And it was incident-free.

I felt so proud of everything we had done together. To live through this day, and then at night attend a rip-roaring party held by the ANC where we made speeches and gave interviews and celebrated the ultimate feeling of success.

And still the long lines of voters were there, so that the third day of voting had to be extended to mid-evening.

My mother, aged seventy-four, of course wanted to vote. So I took her to the polling booth and she was very excited. But she didn't read English and I was anxious that she might put her X in the wrong place. We went over and over it and I'm pretty sure she got it right.

The ANC had teamed up with the country's trade union congress COSATU along with the South African Communist Party and between them they took 62% of the vote. It was not the two-thirds majority required for outright government, so they agreed to rule as a Government of National Unity, with the National Party and the Inkatha Freedom Party.

I had been nominated for Parliament and Mandela would not take no for an answer. 'We need women and we need lawyers,' he told me. 'You're coming with us.'

In fact I was actually nominated for the post of South Africa's first Public Protector, but according to those who opposed my appointment I was 'too ANC'.

I was still running my law practice in Johannesburg and thought I would be able to keep it open. But it was not possible. I would be in Parliament in Cape Town from Monday to Friday, often sitting late.

So I had to make the decision to close the office. Locking it all up was immensely sad. I had had a great life there, many successes and some failures. I was sad for myself and my staff but we were in a different world now.

I had been so deeply involved, not just with politics. South Africa's Youth Revolutionary Council held its meetings there, entire trade union movements had been formed there, and I had been involved in every plot going, as well as socialising with comrades and planning marches and rallies.

My office had been an integral part of the community's life. It had been so powerful and exciting and totally meaningful to have done all that in a period of twenty years; it felt like breaking up a family. We had a farewell party with fellow lawyers and neighbours, and my staff Nana and Leslie and Ilona. We cried as we locked the doors. They had been unforgettable times and they had come to an end.

The ANC was not only unbanned but was running the country. I would be with them in Parliament, writing the laws instead of contesting them.

We moved everything out and found a warehouse for the many filing cabinets. A friend offered his storage facility in

Bree Street, Johannesburg. We packed and labelled everything and put it in the warehouse. But a few years later it was badly flooded and everything was destroyed. I was utterly bereft, priceless documents and treasured files and unique statements were lost. In its way it was the entire history of the apartheid legislation of my country, and it was ruined beyond repair.

I was allocated a house in Acacia Park, a suburb of Cape Town and the parliamentary 'village', but it was little more than a damp prefab and I refused to stay. I moved to the Cape Sun hotel for a short while then moved into a brick house next to my great friend MaSisulu. Tina had come down from Johannesburg with me and was happily attending a Cape Town school.

At my swearing-in as a Member of Parliament I was almost overwhelmed. For legislators like myself it was going to be amazing to be able to overturn the terrible laws of apartheid.

It was empowering just to stand there and take the oath. Mandela was seated in front of us as we were called into the chamber one by one. The house was full and the procedure was solemn. I could see the irony in having rejected all colonial matters only to now find ourselves part of a ceremony headed by a man in full regalia and robes, carrying a sceptre.

But I relished every moment. When I had been sworn in I could not resist breaking the rules yet again and running over to Mandela to take his hand, before going to my seat. Nothing could have been greater than to become an MP with Nelson Mandela as President. We had a leader who we revered and adored.

That night we had a huge party with cocktails and a dinner-dance at Spier wine farm outside Cape Town. We did this jig, the conga, where people joined hands. I found myself holding the hand of Tony Leon, leader of the Opposition, the Democratic Party, later changing its name to the Democratic Alliance. I pulled away, horrified, and I told him: 'I'd rather die than hold your hand.'

I couldn't believe that comrades who had been through the trenches, brutalised by the National Party, were now socialising with them. In one stroke they were all dancing together. But not me. I had seen intolerable depths of suffering. It was going to take more than one stroke of a pen on an agreement to get me to dance and hold hands with them.

Of course the world was full of admiration for these acts of reconciliation, and it was remarkable. But my own truth would not let me join in, not at that level.

Ahead for many of us was the process of revisiting the laws of apartheid and discovering how truly terrible they were en masse, and that was where my heart lay. I was deputy chair of the Justice Committee where we all willingly worked till 2 or 3 a.m., excited and energised, and ultimately exhausted. We were working on overturning the very laws that had made our lives hell.

And the entire system was founded on written statutes. Pik Botha, the menacing old Foreign Minister, had once boasted he had 'a very sound justice system'. What he meant was there was a sound statute for each and every cruelty.

One late Saturday evening we were plodding ahead when an old IFP member called Mziza got up and said he had to go home to do his washing. We had been focusing on a heavy subject. We all had a laugh and told him to shut up. If we stayed, he had to stay.

In those early days of Parliament I took the time to visit Solomon Mahlangu's tragic family out in Mamelodi. I saw that nothing had changed. 'Mum Jana,' they said, 'we are told we have this great freedom but look the streets are still poor, everyone is still in tatty clothing and broken-down old cars are still parked everywhere.'

It felt sad; nothing had changed for them.

And I was feeling the challenge of helping to set up the Truth and Reconciliation Commission. This issue had been central, crucial, to the settlement the ANC had agreed with the Boers. It was one of the first bits of legislation I was involved in. I found the terms of our settlement so difficult in this context. It had been agreed that no perpetrators would be put on trial. There was to be no Nuremberg. On the other hand, no blanket amnesty.

Perpetrators of some of apartheid's cruellest crimes would have to apply one by one for amnesty. The intention was to bring everyone to book, and that people known to be perpetrators would be prosecuted if they did not apply.

Adriaan Vlok, the former Minister of Law and Order, and Police Minister directly responsible for authorising so many atrocities, so many terrible crimes against humanity, did not come to the TRC. He was not pursued or prosecuted and is free to this day. In my view this is completely wrong. Wouter Basson, the notorious 'Doctor Death' who had run the government's secret biological warfare programmes intended to poison and kill blacks, did not apply for amnesty.

The arrogance and lack of remorse on the part of evil-doers like these is breathtaking.

In a bizarre episode, years later, Vlok approached my activist friend and comrade Frank Chikane, a minister of the church, and asked for forgiveness, sinking to his knees and washing his feet.

I remembered the many times Frank had called me from America where he was garnering support for the cause, complaining that a particular suit he wore made him feel weak and faint, and that it was making him sick. He sent it for dry-cleaning but it did not improve. I told him: 'Frank for heaven's sake. Clothes can't make you ill.' But I was wrong. His suit had been treated with a poisonous chemical and was intended to slowly kill him. Vlok's department was responsible for that.

The extent of the Boers' capacity to profess they were God-fearing and religious while committing gross crimes against humanity, has never failed to astonish me. Vlok himself had sworn on oath in front of me that Sipho Hashe – my little Tina's own grandfather, ambushed and tortured and burnt to death – had not been detained. Vlok was complicit, he was part of it, and there has to this day been no recompense, no closure.

The man who personally tortured my friend Joe Veriava actually came up to him in a Johannesburg supermarket to try and shake his hand. He didn't go to the TRC for amnesty; he lived a scot-free life in the community, unpunished.

I feel strongly that this cannot be right. But it was Mandela's personal vision. When I tried to talk to him about it, as the TRC was being set up, I told him: 'This is not like other countries where a regime has been toppled and has now disappeared. We have to live with these people from now on, every day of our lives. Our people need closure.' But he was adamant that we should not hamper the country's development. He was sure that amnesty would bring in the main perpetrators. But it did not. The foot-soldiers came forward but the generals didn't.

Mandela was an astute politician but could be naïve when it came to judging individuals. He thought all whites would come forward; he really believed that.

The biggest failing in my view is that the TRC did not see the process through beyond forgiveness. As a Hindu, even a devout believer, you cannot have forgiveness without remorse. Remorse is fundamental and needs to be acted out.

I appealed to Mandela once at a meeting in Shell House. I said this whole process is more complicated than you might think. It involves deep analysis and decisions. I was very preoccupied with this at that time. During the struggle in India there had been huge conflict between Muslims and Hindus, with many killings.

One of Gandhi's lieutenants went to him and said: 'Bapu, I have done a terrible thing today. In the rush of violence I shot and killed a Muslim child. I am sorry, the child was innocent.' And Gandhi told him that if he was truly sorry he should perform an act of remorse. 'Adopt a Muslim child and raise him in your own home as a Muslim,' he said. The man carried out this instruction and I see it as the perfect act of remorse.

We have seen no such acts of remorse in my country.

I also feel strongly that amnesty in South Africa should have led to reparations. We should have had a serious attempt to force whites to comply. They should have gone as teachers to give hours of their time to train uneducated people in their skills.

But Mandela was unshakeable on these matters. His centrality was reconciliation and forgiveness.

I have to concede that the way the TRC was set up exemplified *ubuntu* – that magical word in the Nguni Bantu language which means: 'I am because of you – a person is only a person through other people'. And I accept that, importantly, the world was full of admiration for South Africa's magnanimity.

Also in hindsight, if we had insisted, it might have caused the talks to collapse. It simply grieves me that there was no genuine reconciliation on the part of the Boers. It is greatly disappointing that more than twenty years on we still do not really have unity or equality. I think back to those snake-like queues on Election Day and I grieve.

In my position as deputy chair of the Justice Committee I fought as hard as I could for a stronger, tougher TRC. We finally voted on it at 3 a.m. and I had little support. There was euphoria, a new South Africa, and the world was smiling with us. No one wanted to put spokes in the wheel.

I still feel badly that the TRC removed the rights of victims to seek justice in the civil courts. The first hearings took testimonies from victims and people had a chance to tell their stories. More than 22,000 people came forward and it was cathartic for many.

The second set of hearings were for amnesty applications. There were 7,000 of them. Only crimes defined as 'gross' were dealt with, meaning maimings and killings. Excluded were the systemic violations of human rights, the forced removals to group areas, the expulsion of millions to the bogus 'homelands'. There were no provisions for them.

The third hearings were for reparation. It was intended that victims would be given bursaries for education, or jobs. But very little was achieved. The average compensation was R25,000. Elizabeth Hashe received R35,000 for the destruction of her family, the disappearance, death and torture of her husband, and the twenty-two years of agony she was forced to wait to discover what happened to him.

The basic problem, I realised, was that the ANC had no money. So we were making major concessions, maybe too many concessions, but once the wheels began to turn you just couldn't put the brakes on.

Our committee had looked at Truth Commissions elsewhere, in Chile for example. But they were different, small oppressed communities where regimes had been crushed and removed. As a result we were more conciliatory. Even the opening lines of our miraculous new Constitution spell it out: 'We, the people of South Africa, [...] believe South Africa belongs to all who live in it, united in our diversity'.

In my maiden speech in Parliament I chose a subject very dear to my heart. I spoke on the rights of the child, feeling very strongly about how they as a group had suffered as no other. Family life was anything but normal for them under apartheid and they had no decent education or career prospects. Many had been brutalised while fighting for freedom.

I was on the National Children's Rights Committee as a legal adviser and very much wanted acknowledgement that they were the future of the country and of the world. There needed to be a proper agenda for them in terms of transformation.

I spoke of the Soweto uprising in 1976 and said they had been victimised more woundingly than adults. I looked back to many years earlier when I had met Bishop Trevor Huddleston and Abdul Minty, indomitable pioneers of the anti-apartheid movement, and alerted them to the wholesale brutalisation of children under apartheid. They set up a conference to debate this, but it was held in Harare, Zimbabwe and since I was a banned person at the time I could not attend. But I had taken part in a British television documentary called *Suffer the Children*, drawing attention to the many arrests and detentions of youths without trial, and assaults on them while in detention.

I believe that was behind a bizarre invitation I had received at that time to meet with British Prime Minister Margaret Thatcher, sent to me through the British High Commissioner in South Africa. There was no question of me wanting to see her: I would have openly raged about her stance on our country – damning Mandela, lionising Buthelezi and refusing sanctions. I had no intention of helping her to appear compassionate towards children or anyone else. My fellow advocates and my staff urged me to go, but I wanted nothing to do with her.

Now, years later, I was able to travel and gladly accepted an invitation from Graça Machel – who was to become Mandela's third wife – to speak at a UN conference on The Impact of Armed Conflict on Children.

Tina, aged eleven, came with me, and when she agreed to speak to a packed conference in Addis Ababa, talking of her parents and her tragic family history without any notes, she of course stole the show and it made me incredibly proud.

We went on a tour to Australia too, where I chaired a conference on the controversial laws governing surrogate motherhood. I believed in surrogacy as a necessity for infertile couples but felt strongly that the laws needed to be tightened. I took part in similar conferences in Britain and in America.

I knew Mandela had a special place in his heart for children. He had even discussed allowing fourteen-year-olds to have a vote in our elections, something I determinedly persuaded him to withdraw. I knew better than him that many of our children had been deprived of education and lived in remote rural areas with no concept of the wider world. I wanted him rather to concentrate on setting up solid structures for education. I must confess to disappointment today that a proper structure has still not been established for higher standards of education.

I was continuing to see Mandela in these times, visiting his presidential residence as a friend and colleague.

Once he called me to ask if I would like a diplomatic post in Italy. It sounded like a sort of paradise but I had work to do in South Africa. And my mother, who was unwell, was staying with me and Tina. Soon afterwards I met MaSisulu in the corridor in Parliament. She said: 'Oh you know Tata (her husband Walter) and Nelson have gone to visit your mother to wish her better health.'

I felt the most terrible panic. My mother did not know either of them well and might not even open the door to them. Worse, she might think two black men on the doorstep were looking for work, and turn them away. I was hot with mortification, running to my office to call her. Before I spoke she said how lovely it was that Mandela had just visited her. I was so relieved, and also touched that he had so kindly thought of her.

My work on the Justice Committee was invigorating and challenging. It was empowering to pass legislation for the Human Rights Commission (HRC) of South Africa. I pressed for it to be more proactive than in other countries and to have legal status, taking perpetrators to court.

That was satisfying but I don't feel the HRC is today as active as it could be. The terrible killings of thirty-four workers by the police at a Marikana platinum mine in an area north-west of Johannesburg during wildcat strike action in 2013 were a blight on our new South Africa, and there was in my view a clear case for prosecution.

In my first term in Parliament I worked on nine committees. Occasionally there were difficulties.

I was chair of an ad hoc committee where Dr Essop Pahad, later to become Minister in the Presidency, had been accused of contempt of Parliament by insulting a member of the Democratic Party. Thabo Mbeki, then the Deputy President, had insisted that I should be the chair, despite my reluctance. I said I would make a fair decision that would not compromise my integrity.

I found him guilty. Pahad walked out of the meeting, intentionally snubbing me. Then I had to decide a sentence for him. I gave him the least possible: I sent him back to Parliament to apologise. He did that, though not with a good grace.

I had stayed close to the Mbekis, father and son. By now Govan was well into his eighties and a member of the Upper House, the National Council of Provinces.

I found myself in a ridiculous situation once when Govan's wife Epainette, also of a great age, came to stay with her son Thabo at the ministers' accommodation in Cape Town. She was unwell and asked me to buy her some things. She wanted a fully-fitted bra that came almost to the waist, a huge upholstered piece of clothing. I visited some stores and came back with three so that she could choose. Epainette liked two of them and gave the other, in a small bag, to the security guard at the house so that he could hand it to someone to return to me.

Lindiwe Ngwane, then the Deputy Minister of Trade and Industry, was going to be passing the Mbekis' residence so I asked her to collect it. Of course she looked inside the bag and reported back to all the women in Parliament that I had left my bra at Thabo's house – with all the attendant implications. All I could do was laugh it off.

At this time Tina and I were spending most of our weekends in Johannesburg or Durban. Travelling back on the plane once in 1996 we somehow got talking to South African tennis ace Amanda Coetzer who was with Martina Navratilova, both on their way to the Australian Open.

Amanda was fascinated by Tina's braided hair and wanted to know how she could get the same look. A little bemused at a white woman attempting African braids, we told her where to find Tina's hairdresser.

Soon afterwards I was working in my office in Parliament when Tina came looking for me after school. She said the BBC wanted to speak to me. It was about Amanda Coetzer's new look, on the tennis courts in Australia. She had told the news crews all about the lovely young girl she had met and how she wanted that look. It wasn't politics, but it was very sweet nonetheless and Tina was thrilled.

The 1990s were extraordinary days in so many ways. The exhilaration of witnessing the end of apartheid, the euphoria of a black-dominated Parliament, and the continuing comradeship between us, the veterans of a struggle which had enthralled our sympathisers all over the world.

But there were great personal sadnesses for me, too. In 1996 my dear mother passed away at her home in Durban after a sudden illness. My brother Raj, who had remained so close to both of us all through the years, found her on the floor of her apartment after suffering a heart attack.

We were devastated. Not only bereft but totally lost. I still miss her terribly. I miss her genuine warmth, comfort and caring and above all, I miss her love. She was truly a mother, and irreplaceable.

Her name was Hansrani, which means a female swan. My

father's name was Hansraj which means a male swan. There could not be a husband and wife so different from each other and so remote in their outlooks. My mother was the sweet, gentle, soft, God-fearing, simple, beautiful and petite lady who was not formally educated but highly intelligent. My father, on the other hand, was tall, robust, very confident, brilliant, highly educated and an extremely worldly man. My mother came from a very humble home; he came from an opulent background. Yet theirs was a marriage made in heaven. Were they happy? They appeared to be blissful and extremely content with each other.

My mother was totally devoted to her husband and loved her children unconditionally. A typical example would be that when she cooked something special, she made sure that we had the best and if there was any left, she would have it. Sometimes she would even say there was enough for her when she knew there was nothing left.

She was deeply committed to dignity, respect and strong values, and was uncompromising about it. I know she often had brushes with her mother-in-law who forbade her to be friendly with people thought to be 'unsavoury' or so-called 'low caste'. She would break her customary obedience then.

She was extremely hard-working and a cleanliness freak. She was excellent at home economics and never complained about the drudgery of housework. She was blatantly frank and open and often offended people but this did not deter her. She could be very stubborn. She believed in God and prayers and defied my father by visiting the temple. He was an atheist himself.

Also, she was petite but extremely strong and bore upheavals resolutely. When my father was shunted from his post as a school principal for his anti-apartheid beliefs she had to take us children and all the household goods at short notice to accompany him. She never expressed regret or disappointment, although I know we all disappointed her in some ways. For example, my older brother married without her consent, and I abandoned my studies in medicine. My younger brother also did not pursue his studies as she would have liked.

She was our pillar of strength and support. She was there for me throughout my life, through my divorces and my banning orders and when I married outside our racial group. She did not care what people said or did; she cared for us.

Tina and I were distraught at the news of her death. And a year later Tina's beloved Reg, my first husband, also died suddenly, a terrible blow.

We clung to each other through these difficult times. By 2001, when I was offered an overseas posting as Ambassador for South Africa, it seemed a good moment for us to embark together on a new era.

# CHAPTER TEN

# MY AMBASSADOR YEARS

My nine years as an ambassador for South Africa started unexpectedly, and came uninvited.

I was stunned when I received a call to my parliamentary office one day and was told I was going to the Netherlands.

I put the phone down and realised I had no idea who had called to give me this information, and no formal offer of an ambassadorship.

Maybe it was a prank. I spent two days in a state of bewilderment, then the letter of appointment arrived. I felt ready for a new challenge and at that time – before today's instant access to emails and conference calls – an ambassador literally represented the country's president abroad.

I was sent to Pretoria for an orientation programme, which I rather ridiculed. I was being taught how to formally lay a table and how to greet foreign dignitaries. I felt I was already capable of that, and I didn't intend to be setting tables for banquets without the help of trained staff.

Much more problematic was my legal relationship to Tina, who was only fifteen. She could not accompany me unless I adopted her, and her father had resisted this for many years.

Now, however, he agreed that it was important for her to travel with me. The education and cultural opportunities would be hugely beneficial. To me, we had already been mother and daughter for fifteen years.

So myself, Popo Molefe and Tina's biological mother Phinda, who travelled down from Port Elizabeth, had a rather tense meeting. I made lunch at my house and we all signed the papers, but it felt awkward. Inside, though, I was extremely happy that Tina was my daughter in the eyes of the law after all these years.

By then, she and my nephew Shivesh, four years younger than her, were as close as any brother and sister. He spent many days and nights at my house and was company for Tina when I was held up in Parliament till late at night. I asked him if he would like to accompany us to the Netherlands, a huge adventure. He said no, that he should stay with his parents.

But one week before we left, with everything packed and ready to go, Shivesh came to me and said he wanted to come with us. Now I had to also formally adopt him, and that was difficult with my brother and his wife, Shivesh's parents, looking on with mixed emotions. The adoption went through, and we set off as a family.

Those days felt hectic and even the flight to The Hague was fraught, with Tina walking up and down the aisle of the plane in front of me, agitated and upset.

I finally discovered that she thought I had forgotten her birthday. She had turned sixteen at midnight during the flight, and I was fast asleep.

As soon as we arrived I telephoned ahead to ask my secretary, who I had not yet met, to arrange a birthday cake and to gather some of the staff's children to help us celebrate.

A huge formal delegation was waiting for me. It felt enormously grand to be chauffeur-driven to the South African embassy, an awe-inspiring building furnished with heavy solid pieces in the old Dutch style.

Security outside was intense, since the embassy had been constantly under siege during apartheid with protestors keeping a daily vigil. The biggest scandal was when a mixed-race couple apparently simulated sex outside on the pavement in a protest at the Immorality Act, which forbade relationships between black and white.

My office was spacious, with a massive formal desk at its centre and a private reception lounge off to one side. I spotted a framed photograph of Hendrik Verwoerd, the devil himself – the Dutch-born architect of apartheid who presided over forced removals and the concept of 'homelands' – on my mantelpiece.

My staff looked on horrified as I threw it to the floor and stamped on it until the glass broke and Verwoerd's face was no longer recognisable. They were getting a taste of how it was going to be with me around.

I was asked to formally greet the thirty-five members of staff, all in suits or formal dresses, lined up with their backs to a mahogany-panelled wall. Their first sight of me was in a flamboyant brightly-coloured sari, horrified at the stiffness of all this. I told them to please relax and then chatted to them individually about their families.

A senior member, the accountant, who had been at the embassy for thirty-five years, had done some homework. He asked me to tell them the story about my French underwear, which was clever of him really because it broke the ice between us once and for all.

I related the story, telling them how I had argued with Thabo Mbeki at a conference on national identity, telling him that we Indians want to be known as South Africans. As I was leaving the conference some journalists came to talk to me and overheard a woman friend of mine asking me why I had been so hard on Mbeki, adding: 'I've only ever seen you wearing Indian saris. Why is it so important to be called South African?'

I told her that, well, I only buy French underwear but that doesn't make me French. My national identity is South African and that really matters to me and the next day my choice of underwear had made all the newspaper headlines.

So my new Dutch colleagues laughed at this and we all made friends.

I took the position seriously; my job was to represent South Africa abroad, and at that time it was a great responsibility. Today the role is rather diminished in ambit and scope, but there is still authority.

In The Hague it was particularly important because it was the seat of the International Criminal Court, and the Rwandan Tribunal, which examined the country's genocide, had been held there. I felt I was in familiar territory.

I was able to bring Nelson Mandela over to the Netherlands on four occasions and that was hugely significant in a country which allied itself so closely to South Africa.

It was fun for me to share a helicopter with Mandela and Queen Beatrix of the Netherlands. Later, in the official car, we drove through streets crowded with people loyal to the

Queen and desperate to see Mandela. I found I had to wave, so I copied the royal wave used by the Queen and chuckled to myself.

I had organised a banquet to celebrate Mandela's visit. He, of course, stayed at the royal palace, adored by the Netherlands aristocracy and by the Queen herself. He attended Prince Willem Alexander's wedding and very nearly outshone all the other attendees, despite his humility. The Dutch absolutely worshipped him and believed he was close to God.

On another occasion, I hosted a concert for him. I had no budget for it and our embassy really had little money. But I followed the royal family's example and booked the Carré Theatre where the Prince had held his wedding reception.

It was madly expensive. The invitations, embossed in gold-leaf and decorated with African beads, cost a fortune on their own. We agreed to a feast including crocodile steaks and other African delicacies. I brought in the top events organiser who said the final fee would be 500,000 euros. Of course I agreed to it, then the nightmare began. I simply had to find sponsors.

I personally called some obvious supporters like Philips, the electrical company, Royal Dutch Shell, Unilever and Makro, and to my enormous relief they offered very generous sums. Mandela was the magic word. They were paying for the glory of being in his company at dinner, and at the concert.

And I named the concert Faranani. It's a Venda word meaning 'togetherness'. It was a resounding success, with Mandela seated in the front row among the royals.

I was able to spend some time with him during his visit, though I was not always entirely happy with events. At his hotel in Amsterdam a group of anti-apartheid activists turned up without an appointment and wanted to see him. Mandela told me he was too tired, he simply wouldn't go down to the foyer to greet them.

But shortly afterwards a wealthy banker turned up and he wasn't tired any more. I didn't want to be judgemental; I just observed the reality of it – Mandela's life and dreams were joined to those of the ANC and the ANC's coffers were empty. He saw no problem with favouring the banker, and in fact openly encouraged anyone with funds to donate to the cause. He had spent twenty-seven years in prison for the Party, and he was still working tirelessly for it.

While in The Hague I wanted to be a political presence. I was fully behind South Africa's objection to Israel's building of a wall to segregate the Palestinians. Our own revolution had links to the PLO and we now made a case to contest the inhumanity and illegality of Israel's actions. I led the delegation to the International Court of Justice.

Meantime, I had been finding it difficult to become part of the Dutch community as a South African. My appearance was all about being Indian and it was hard for people to understand where I fitted in.

One time I attended a trade show where the Indian Ambassador, also a woman, was to be the guest of honour. I arrived before her and a gaggle of people rushed to greet me and put a garland around my neck. When she arrived, unannounced and unnoticed, I was terribly embarrassed. I went to her and took the garland off to give to her.

On another occasion I arrived to address an international women's organisation and there was obvious disappointment when an Indian woman wearing a sari appeared. I had to ingratiate myself and explain.

I had expected Holland to be one of Europe's most liberal

countries. They had lax laws towards drugs and prostitution, but somehow they found it hard to accept a woman as an ambassador. People often thought my driver was the ambassador when we arrived at events. On seven out of ten occasions, as we got out of the car at the same time, he would be formally welcomed and I would be ignored.

My normal choice of sari was brightly coloured – blues, fuchsias and golden yellows. I received instructions from the Queen's staff on more than one occasion telling me to wear black or brown for a formal event. I had to point out to her ADC that saris were not made in dark colours.

In terms of identity I found it difficult at first to place the Surinamese living in the country, who looked like Indians to me, although they wore traditional clothes differently and with crocheted scarves. I was curious about them, and learnt that they were Indians who had come to Guyana in the north of South America in the 1870s, to work in the sugar cane plantations, just as Indians had travelled earlier to South Africa. They were indentured labourers, but they had integrated very well.

I talked to them a great deal and discovered life had been very difficult for them. South African Indians had been more prominent because Mahatma Gandhi had spent years with them and championed them. Through him India was one of the first countries to ever condemn apartheid.

I connected well with the Surinam people, better than their own ambassador because we had more in common. They spoke Dutch, which impressed me, and I met them often at functions like the unveiling of a bust of Gandhi. I became very friendly with a Surinam journalist called Rabin Baldewsingh who made a TV documentary about me and Tina and Shivesh.

He was fascinated by our home and the fact that we had a prayer place there and were actively Hindu.

This was just one of many areas where I found I could become involved as ambassador. One of my functions was to promote trade, but I also very much wanted to connect the judiciary to our own new judiciary in South Africa.

I managed to set up some training courses for South Africa's new black judges. I also promoted youth programmes between our countries, with reconciliation as the theme. Tina was happy to take part, telling her own family history as an example of working through the past to a better future.

Whenever possible I promoted African culture and events. We celebrated Africa Day on 25 May with a huge display of food and dance. Thabo Mbeki visited for a performance of *The Lion King*, with the cast making a huge fuss of him. And we brought over the South African band Freshly Ground and the musical show *Gumboots*.

We also took part in the North Sea Jazz Festival every year and it was a joy to see that African singers and musicians were among the best in the world.

I was invited by local NGOs to accompany King Willem to the international climate conference in Kyoto, Japan. It was strange, really, since I would be representing the Netherlands rather than South Africa, but I could not turn it down.

Just being in Europe was widening our horizons. We could jump in the car and go to Brussels for weekends, and the Dutch arranged splendid family outings for us. We had boat rides and an amazing horse-drawn carriage drive through Amsterdam. Christmas, a novelty for us, was celebrated hugely in Holland. Everyone in the streets was offered cookies and chocolates, and Santa Claus greeted all the children.

Tina was happy, though she experienced a few bumps at the British School. On one occasion, a teacher explaining a poem to her class turned to Tina and spelt out a question slowly: 'Tina do you know what a so-lil-oquy is?'

Tina, irritated, asked her why she was being spoken to like that. She was one of only two black pupils there, along with a Nigerian girl. The girl gained 90 per cent in a geography exam and the teacher was totally dumbfounded. An African somehow knowing about the rest of the world!

Of course Tina was furious. From the moment we arrived in the Netherlands she had been making a point. When we were held up at the airport because they had a new visa system she told officials: 'When you colonised parts of Africa did you have to have a visa, or even permission to be there?' But generally she and Shivesh were happy in the city, living in our splendid official residence and travelling the whole of Europe.

We survived the anomalies with good grace. For example, I was invited to judge the Miss Netherlands beauty contest. Me, a known feminist! But I chose to approach it as an empowering process that could lead women to success in whatever area they chose. Even if they chose modelling or fashion, it would at least be their choice.

We did not do swimsuits. We had traditional dress and cocktail dresses, and 70 per cent of our marking was on their intelligence and their vision of the world. I had to spend fifteen minutes interviewing each contestant. I asked them about their role models. Most of them said Winnie Mandela, although some said Indira Gandhi or Margaret Thatcher. I had to smile.

I had more serious and onerous duties too. Mandela had

asked me to try to take care of a Libyan national, Abdelbaset al-Megrahi, the man at the centre of the Lockerbie bombing.

He had been tried and convicted of masterminding a bomb which blasted a Pan Am flight as it travelled over the town of Lockerbie in Scotland en route for New York in December 1988, killing all passengers and crew, and eleven civilians on the ground. There were 270 counts of murder against him.

Muammar Gaddafi, President of Libya, had refused to hand over al-Megrahi and his co-accused for several years. He relented only in the face of threatened UN sanctions and the personal intervention of Nelson Mandela.

An extraordinary construction, a Scottish court and attendant offices, had been built in the town of Zeist, and was staffed entirely by the Scottish military and judiciary. It was here, at Camp Zeist, that al-Megrahi had been convicted and his co-accused – who had a watertight alibi – had been acquitted.

Now al-Megrahi was awaiting an appeal. Many believed there were serious inconsistencies in the prosecution case, and that he was innocent. Mandela was among them. He wanted me to assist in the preparation of the Libyan's appeal, and bring him any comfort that I could.

I visited him often in the extraordinary Scottish surroundings of Camp Zeist and found him quiet, courteous and full of anxiety. Al-Megrahi had been the security chief of Libyan Arab Airlines and an officer in Libyan intelligence. He was educated and well-spoken. He had studied his case reports and transcripts minutely and marked out all the inconsistencies. He protested his innocence throughout. There was nothing he needed my legal expertise with: he had already done all the work.

All I could do was to sit and talk to him, occasionally bringing his wife and young son with me. The family was totally devastated. Al-Megrahi had been sentenced to twenty years in a trial led by three senior judges. I found my heart went out to him. He was lonely and desperate, and it was clear that he had been regarded as some sort of devil.

It had been agreed he should be tried in a neutral environment, albeit a totally Scottish environment but in a neutral country. In Scotland itself it would have been impossible to find an impartial jury.

He would be brought to see me in a reasonably comfortable consulting room. He wore a shirt and trousers, no prison uniform, and we had tea or coffee together. He was terribly distressed about his family. He wanted to go home and didn't want or need anything from me.

I had met and consulted with many terrorists in my time. I had not found them sentimental or obsessed with the welfare of their family. This man was different. He was very traumatised the whole time I knew him. He had expected, and been promised, help, which did not come.

I formed the opinion that Libya had had to put forward a scapegoat, and it was him. The case against him, with conflicting evidence and flawed forensics – as well as witnesses later found to have been bribed – would fail, he had been told. He had to go through it for his country, but he would not be convicted.

Now he faced twenty years in prison.

He had a good case to present on appeal and despite the national anguish over Lockerbie a survey had shown that 61 per cent of British people believed he had been wrongly convicted.

I was in court with him when the appeal judgement was given. Both of us were optimistic, thinking he would be freed. Arrangements had been for me to bring him to our embassy and return him to Libya. Mandela took a close interest in the case on behalf of African justice and his own instinctive compassion. I was keeping him informed of progress.

But on 14 March 2002 the appeal was dismissed. Al-Megrahi and his wife were totally and utterly crushed. Pitiably, he turned to me in court, still believing that Mandela could intervene to free him.

I had to make the phone call to tell Mandela it was over. He was disappointed and very distressed. He told me he would find a way to fight on.

Al-Megrahi was to serve his sentence in Scottish prisons. Soon afterwards Mandela called on Christian churches throughout the world to intervene in 'this clear miscarriage of justice' and this led to a report of the scientific and forensic evidence by leading scientists appointed by the Church of Scotland, pointing up many flaws and inconsistencies.

As Al-Megrahi's lawyers prepared a further appeal he was released on compassionate grounds by the Scottish Justice Secretary due to a diagnosis of terminal cancer, and this second appeal was dropped.

Al-Megrahi died in May 2012 at his family home in Libya.

I felt that, along with other work I had done to represent my country in the Netherlands, I had achieved everything except the impossible.

One final accomplishment, which still fills me with pride, was being able to add a bust of Mandela to the great Hall of Justice in The Hague alongside Mahatma Gandhi and other peace-makers.

I had applied to the International Criminal Court and after a long wait, they agreed. We commissioned a Russian sculptor and I organised a major ceremony. Mandela himself could not be there but his granddaughter represented him, and our Minister of Justice attended.

It was soon afterwards, towards the end of my tour of duty in 2006, that I received a call offering me the Ambassadorship in Ireland. I knew it would be very different, but our anti-apartheid movement had always had close links with the revolutionaries there, and I agreed.

Tina and Shivesh were to come with me.

Ireland was different from the outset. No delegation came to meet us at Dublin airport and there was no official residence ready for us. We spent a week in a horrible hotel and I began to have regrets.

This was not like the Netherlands at all, where Queen Beatrix herself had sent a gilded coach to fetch me on the day I presented my credentials. But I had come from a revolutionary background and I felt I would at some stage begin to feel familiar with Irish culture.

I wanted to meet Gerry Adams, the President of Sinn Fein, an organisation that had links to the MK, the armed wing of the ANC, but which had always scoffed at us for being 'too soft'. Their cause had been less severe than ours. They did not suffer the pass laws and the forced removals, the torture and murders. Their oppression, though stretching back through the years to enforced poverty and the potato famine, and more recently discrimination over jobs and career opportunities, did not match the cruelty of apartheid. Yet their deep-seated hatreds had led to wholesale bombings of civilians, something we in the MK had carefully avoided.

I had always been fascinated by their tenacity and their tactics, and their charismatic leaders. Adams was the real thing – charming, flamboyant, attractive, and absolutely devoted to the South African cause. He was a great fan of Mandela. But I came to realise that whereas South Africa had moved on from its retaliatory bitterness, the Irish had become stagnant in their issues. I found no forgiveness or reconciliation there.

It was perplexing to me, this white-on-white discrimination, something totally outside of my experience. I addressed meetings about the way forward after a peace process and I was struck by the absence of that South African ability to forgive. Ubuntu – the creed that ties our people together – is not in the Irish national psyche or culture.

Our Truth and Reconciliation Commission would almost certainly not have worked there. I worked with SPIRASI – the Spiritans Asylum Services Initiative – an organisation dedicated to helping refugees and migrants, and we held many discussions and meetings on reconciliation between the north and south of the country. It was much more difficult than I had ever imagined.

However I still felt that I could usefully engage. I addressed a multi-party forum in Belfast, where Tina and Shivesh held their own workshop with the youth, talking to them about their future. They worked with young people for three hours and were shattered when, at the end, a boy organising photographs said all the Catholics should stand on one side, and the Protestants on the other.

I had a natural sympathy for the IRA and Sinn Fein going

back many years. I simply had not realised the animosity in the south. When I talked to my Dublin staff about South Africa's connectivity with the IRA they advised me in hushed tones: 'Ambassador, you cannot say that.'

All the same, I went to Sinn Fein's annual party conference, the Ard Fheis, and I was happily befriended by Gerry Adams. We visited each other's homes often and had intense political discussions.

I had a poster of him in my official residence but was dissuaded from putting it up on the wall. I countered by hanging a poster of hunger strike martyr Bobby Sands in the entrance hall.

I was being typically defiant but at the same time struggling with the different mindsets in Ireland and in my country. To us apartheid was an evil doctrine which we dismantled. In Ireland the anger and the hatred goes so much deeper. My staff were horrified when I employed an English driver. Everything one did seemed to have a significance to it. But I kept my driver; he was brilliant.

He was very amused one day when he drove me to an arts festival to raise money for AIDS sufferers and some children watching me get out of the car asked if I was the Queen. He told them 'No, but she's still very important, she's the Ambassador.' They were thrilled and wanted to touch my sari.

But later that day I was going to tea at the home of a prominent local family. The driver dropped me outside but I went to the wrong door. The woman of the house looked at me in contempt, told me to go away, saying, 'I have nothing for you today' and slammed the door. She thought I was a beggar.

I had been both a Queen and a beggar in the same day, an identity crisis in Ireland.

In general, though, there was a lot of generosity towards South Africa because of what we had fought for and the freedom we had won. Our role as a country in the Good Friday Peace Agreement was always acknowledged. Cyril Ramaphosa, today our Deputy President, had been the facilitator. I never managed to bring Mandela over to Ireland. The mid-2000s was the period he began to decline. But Thabo Mbeki came on an official visit, signing a plaque at an event close to my heart.

I had been impressed with the strong women in Ireland's revolutionary history and I had managed to track down a true heroine Mary Manning, who had led an eight-year strike against a Dublin store selling South African fruit when she believed there should have been sanctions against our government. We honoured her with a special plaque and Mbeki's presence lent weight to its importance.

Ireland's former president, Mary Robinson, who campaigns worldwide for human rights, supported many of the functions I organised and we became friends.

Archbishop Desmond Tutu visited us too, and I managed to host many cultural events. We put on a performance of *The Magic Flute* at a Dublin theatre, bringing the lead singer Pauline Malefane from South Africa. She had achieved great success in the township opera *U-Carmen eKhayelitsha*. The British producer who put on our show, Mark Donford, later married her and they now live in South Africa.

We met singer Michael Jackson when he visited Ireland in 2006, and Tina has a much-treasured photograph of herself with him. My illustrious neighbours included singer Bono and his wife Ali, and Bob Geldof was an occasional visitor.

I managed to combine this political appointment of mine with some culture and a little fun. A highlight was the very moving Christmas Carol Service at the famous St Patrick's seminary in Maynooth, not far from Dublin. I took Tina and Shivesh with me and we still talk about it.

Living in Ireland was a fascinating learning experience. I had to remind myself continually that the Irish had not entirely won their fight. Britain still governs Northern Ireland, as part of the United Kingdom, and the fire of resentment still burns along with all its complicated threads.

I was nevertheless occasionally jolted by an unexpected public demonstration of this. I attended a formal banquet hosted in Belfast by Gerry Adams. It was intended to celebrate the fact that, in the aftermath of the Good Friday Agreement, the Sinn Fein leaders who had been refusing to take up their elected seats in the British Parliament would now do so.

The banqueting hall was packed. But then a cohort of Gerry Adams, a man generally believed to have been behind the bomb blast atrocity in Omagh, County Tyrone, ten years earlier, walked in. Dozens of guests rose up and left the hall in protest. Adams managed to say something about regretting that, and the evening continued with many empty chairs.

It was a spontaneous protest of the sort of which I am capable. I understood the politics. The Omagh bombing, which killed twenty-nine and injured 220 others, had crossed a line in the most appalling way. It was not be forgiven or forgotten.

Yet it was the southerners, the Catholics, who had walked out. Irish politics were to remain an enigma to me.

A great source of happiness while there was the educational opportunities available to Tina and Shivesh. She did well at Trinity College, Dublin, where she studied history and political science, undertaking projects very thoroughly and growing into an accomplished, confident young woman. Shivesh attended school, then Griffiths College. He was naturally brilliant and didn't have to make the same effort. Both of them did well and made me proud.

And we enjoyed a real family life with wonderful outings together, relishing the experience.

Tina began to see an Irish boy from a prominent medical family who I liked a lot. She seemed happy with Owen O'Higgins, the son of Niall O'Higgins, then President of the Royal College of Surgeons in Ireland, and his wife Roisin, a renowned paediatrician. They had met at a party in Dublin to celebrate Niall O'Higgins's retirement, when we sat as a family at the top table

All seemed to be going well between Tina and Owen, although I was completely taken aback when Tina caught me off-guard one night at a social event, taking me aside to show me her engagement ring.

But I knew there were problems. We had often invited Owen to join us, only to hear that his mother refused to let him come, citing some family task or other. I worried that he was dominated by her, and I knew that would not sit well with my strong-minded, independent Tina.

Things came to a head when we planned a trip to Prague, Budapest and Vienna. All of us were looking forward to it, and Owen was invited. The night before the trip his mother forbade it, and Owen caved in.

Tina was furious, and called off the whole relationship there and then. For weeks afterwards I had to comfort her rejected suitor. There were tears and pleas and distressing scenes which I found difficult to cope with. I told him the decision was Tina's, not mine.

Looking back, our lives were thoroughly enriched by our experiences in Europe, but ultimately, we belong in South Africa.

The three of us returned to our roots and that is where we live today.

# EPILOGUE

My entire adult life has been dedicated to dismantling the apartheid system and attempting to replace it with something wholesome and good for all South Africans. I cannot regret one minute of it.

There were times when I did not dare to dream that we would come this far. To experience freedom in my lifetime, to survive the banning orders and the cruel oppression that threatened to permanently beat us down – that has made it all worthwhile.

And to have met during my lifetime the great towering figures of Nelson Mandela, Govan Mbeki, Ireland's Mary Robinson and Queen Beatrix of the Netherlands – these are sublime memories.

Today we are twenty-one years into our freedom and I try to hold on to the notion of hope as it was personified by Mandela himself.

I asked him many times on Robben Island what could possibly keep him going. There was no talk of negotiations or freedom at the time, our families were suffering, our children dying, and there was no sign of an end to the ordeal.

Yet he was always well spirited, always hungry for news and planning for a future.

He told me: 'Hope. That is what keeps me going. I believe in it. I cling to it.'

I try to join in that spirit of hopefulness. Very positive things have happened to our country.

But I feel we should be seeing a distinct upward trend towards a better life, and I don't see it. I see the opposite – increasing poverty and more shacks springing up every day on the edges of our towns and cities. It breaks my heart to see people needing to beg, their children starving in squatter camps. It is more than sad: it is tragic.

I believe that our great visionaries, even Mandela, focused entirely on political freedom. It was an overwhelming obsession and I believe now that conditions at grass-roots level, the actual living standards of the great mass of ordinary people, were neglected as a result.

This is a huge minus point for our country today. We finally put apartheid, colonialism and slavery behind us after 350 years, but we are not yet reaping the rewards of that great fight. It is going to take much longer.

The government must of course take responsibility. Even the constitutional rights of our children are not being properly implemented, their educational rights and freedom from abuse are not being fully addressed.

We have criminality and fear, and xenophobia towards people from the very African countries who supported us in our long struggle.

Great leaders would address this, but I fear our great

leaders have gone. Mandela, Govan Mbeki and Walter Sisulu were political giants and visionaries, but they were all severely handicapped by their advanced age by the time they were able to govern.

Today there is a second tier, more interested in personal enrichment. Even those I know from Robben Island or other prisons have an attitude that says: 'We've done our bit, we've paid our dues. We have the right to enjoy the fruits of all our suffering.' They are heavily involved in investments and business, concepts alien to the High Command of the ANC when I knew and worked alongside them.

There are also some young men in politics who I admire and I hope they will come forward to lead this country and shine.

The hope that I have comes not only from Mandela but also from my faith in South Africans as a truly remarkable people. We endured a period of total oppression unknown anywhere else in the world and we have emerged relatively unscathed. As a nation we know no bitterness or resentment or hatred.

There is deep-seated damage of course, but our spirit of ubuntu, that uniquely African sense of togetherness in human worth, will see us through to yet become one of the greatest nations in the world.

We have accomplished much more than other African countries freed from colonisation many years ago. We have made visible strides in so many spheres, and we have produced incomparably strong women, which makes me proud.

My own daughter Tina, with her extraordinary family history, has an unshakeable faith in South Africa's future. She has hope and trust in the people and the country. She believes in South Africa's forward progress and her part in it.

I could not wish anything better for this country than its future in the safe hands of Tina and her colleagues and peers.

# ACKNOWLEDGEMENTS

Firstly I want to thank writer Barbara Jones who inspired me throughout the preparation of this book and who has become a good friend.

I also want to pay tribute to the great female activists of South Africa:

Frances Baard, trade unionist and organiser of the ANC Women's League, who helped draft our Freedom Charter; Thuli Madonsela, now South Africa's Public Protector, who worked closely with me on the Children's Rights Committee; Martha Mahlangu, mother of my young client Solomon, hanged for a murder he did not commit; Winnie Mandela, a fearless and formidable leader who kept her husband's name alive during his long years of imprisonment; Charlotte Maxeke, the 19th century religious leader and social worker in the forefront of anti-apartheid protests; Epainette Mbeki, staunch Communist activist and wife of the great Govan Mbeki; Fatima Meer, a powerful public figure and academic close to the Mandela family and Nelson's first biographer;

Mary Moodley, grassroots organiser of several trade unions; Phyllis Naidoo, teacher and lawyer who sacrificed her whole life for the anti-apartheid movement; Lilian Ngoyi, legendary president of the ANC Women's League who led the 1956 women's anti-pass protest to the Union Buildings in Pretoria; Albertina Sisulu, my dear friend, wife to Walter Sisulu, who was imprisoned with Mandela on Robben Island, and mother to an entire family of activists. My thanks also go to: Professor Saths Cooper, the great and inspirational leader of the Black Consciousness Movement; Lesley Hudson, my intern during the busiest days of my Johannesburg law practice and today a successful academic and close friend; Horst Kleinschmidt, the indispensable pillar of IDAF in London, the anti-apartheid fund which supported my penniless clients; Brigitte Mabandla, student leader of the Black Consciousness Movement who lived in exile in Tanzania and who later became South Africa's Minister of Justice and Constitutional Affairs; Clifford Mailer, the counsel who tolerated my excesses during many a difficult legal case, now a senior judge in the UK; Janaki McKenzie, a loyal family friend and there at every important event in our lives; Cedric Mayson, a giant of our freedom struggle who recruited me into an MK underground cell, the bravest of men; Popo Molefe, a long-term client of mine who served time on Robben Island, and whose baby daughter Tina came into my family as a result; Hajira Mamoniat, my dear friend and neighbour during the bad old days in Lenasia; Vuyisile Mdleleni, my close comrade in our MK underground cell; Nana Mogari, my assistant in the tumultuous days of my law practice; Sean Naidoo, counsel in some of my most difficult cases and still a great supporter and friend; Beyers Naude, who has sadly passed away but whose importance to our hard-won freedom lives on to this day; my dear friend Espree Pather with whom I share so many memories of our struggle; Jackie Selebi, who died in recent years and who had been at the centre of our underground MK cell; Lindiwe Sisulu, a life-long comrade and friend whose activist family look on me as one of their own; Ilona Tip, a treasured friend who was continually at my side during the worst years of apartheid and our fight against it; Hanif Valli, a fine lawyer whose work includes gruelling sessions as a prosecutor at the Truth and Reconciliation Commission, and who was once a trainee of mine; Moosa Vally, who worked with me as the vital go-between linking the United Democratic Front and Nelson Mandela at a crucial period in the freedom negotiations; Professor Joe Veriava, my great friend and comrade who suffered from police brutality while protecting me, and who has never complained; and his wife Philippa, a pillar of support to both of us.

My brother Raj, his wife Lavita and their son Shivesh are a mainstay of my life, and much loved.

| 1 | 2 | 3 | 4 | 5 | 6 | 7 | 8 | 9 | 10 |
|---|---|---|---|---|---|---|---|---|---|
| 11 | 12 | 13 | 14 | 15 | 16 | 17 | 18 | 19 | 20 |
| 21 | 22 | 23 | 24 | 25 | 26 | 27 | 28 | 29 | 30 |
| 31 | 32 | 33 | 34 | 35 | 36 | 37 | 38 | 39 | 40 |
| 41 | 42 | 43 | 44 | 45 | 46 | 47 | 48 | 49 | 50 |
| 51 | 52 | 53 | 54 | 55 | 56 | 57 | 58 | 59 | 60 |
| 61 | 62 | 63 | 64 | 65 | 66 | 67 | 68 | 69 | 70 |
| 71 | 72 | 73 | 74 | 75 | 76 | 77 | 78 | 79 | 80 |
| 81 | 82 | 83 | 84 | 85 | 86 | 87 | 88 | 89 | 90 |
| 91 | 92 | 93 | 94 | 95 | 96 | 97 | 98 | 99 | 100 |
| 101 | 102 | 103 | 104 | 105 | 106 | 107 | 108 | 109 | 110 |
| 111 | 112 | 113 | 114 | 115 | 116 | 117 | 118 | 119 | 120 |
| 121 | 122 | 123 | 124 | 125 | 126 | 127 | 128 | 129 | 130 |
| 131 | 132 | 133 | 134 | 135 | 136 | 137 | 138 | 139 | 140 |
| 141 | 142 | 143 | 144 | 145 | 146 | 147 | 148 | 149 | 150 |
| 151 | 152 | 153 | 154 | 155 | 156 | 157 | 158 | 159 | 160 |
| 161 | 162 | 163 | 164 | 165 | 166 | 167 | 168 | 169 | 170 |
| 171 | 172 | 173 | 174 | 175 | 176 | 177 | 178 | 179 | 180 |
| 181 | 182 | 183 | 184 | 185 | 186 | 187 | 188 | 189 | 190 |
| 191 | 192 | 193 | 194 | 195 | 196 | 197 | 198 | 199 | 200 |
| 201 | 202 | 203 | 204 | 205 | 206 | 207 | 208 | 209 | 210 |
| 211 | 212 | 213 | 214 | 215 | 216 | 217 | 218 | 219 | 220 |
| 221 | 222 | 223 | 224 | 225 | 226 | 227 | 228 | 229 | 230 |
| 231 | 232 | 233 | 234 | 235 | 236 | 237 | 238 | 239 | 240 |
| 241 | 242 | 243 | 244 | 245 | 246 | 247 | 248 | 249 | 250 |
| 251 | 252 | 253 | 254 | 255 | 256 | 257 | 258 | 259 | 260 |
| 261 | 262 | 263 | 264 | 265 | 266 | 267 | 268 | 269 | 270 |
| 271 | 272 | 273 | 274 | 275 | 276 | 277 | 278 | 279 | 280 |
| 281 | 282 | 283 | 284 | 285 | 286 | 287 | 288 | 289 | 290 |
| 291 | 292 | 293 | 294 | 295 | 296 | 297 | 298 | 299 | 300 |
| 301 | 302 | 303 | 304 | 305 | 306 | 307 | 308 | 309 | 310 |
| 311 | 312 | 313 | 314 | 315 | 316 | 317 | 318 | 319 | 320 |
| 321 | 322 | 323 | 324 | 325 | 326 | 327 | 328 | 329 | 330 |
| 331 | 332 | 333 | 334 | 335 | 336 | 337 | 338 | 339 | 340 |
| 341 | 342 | 343 | 344 | 345 | 346 | 347 | 348 | 349 | 350 |
| 351 | 352 | 353 | 354 | 355 | 356 | 357 | 358 | 359 | 360 |
| 361 | 362 | 363 | 364 | 365 | 366 | 367 | 368 | 369 | 370 |
| 371 | 372 | 373 | 374 | 375 | 376 | 377 | 378 | 379 | 380 |
| 381 | 382 | 383 | 384 | 385 | 386 | 387 | 388 | 389 | 390 |
| 391 | 392 | 393 | 394 | 395 | 396 | 397 | 398 | 399 | 400 |